Public Opinion

CBS NEWS REFERENCE BOOKS

CIVIL RIGHTS
A Current Guide to the People, Organizations, and Events
by A. John Adams and Joan Martin Burke

PUBLIC OPINION
Changing Attitudes on Contemporary Political and Social Issues
by Robert Chandler

A CBS NEWS REFERENCE BOOK

PUBLIC OPINION

*Changing attitudes
on contemporary political
and social issues*

ROBERT CHANDLER

R. R. BOWKER COMPANY, New York & London, 1972

Published by R. R. Bowker Co. (a Xerox company)
1180 Avenue of the Americas, New York, N.Y. 10036

Copyright © 1972 by Columbia Broadcasting System, Inc.

Printed and bound in the United States of America

Library of Congress Cataloging in Publication Data

Chandler, Robert.
  Public opinion.

  (A CBS news reference book)
  Bibliography: p.
  1. Public opinion—United States. I. Title.
II. Series.
HN90.P8C54   301.15'43'309173092   72-1739
ISBN 0-8352-0548-7

Contents

v

Preface

It takes no great gift of hindsight to conclude that the closing years of the 1960s marked the climax of a unique period in contemporary America. How lasting the changes, how permanent the scars left by the concentrated social, political, and cultural upheavals of those few years remains to be seen. But whether transitory or not, the conflicts of the period were nonetheless of the most penetrating kind, both emotionally and societally.

The catalog of crises and controversies seems inexhaustible: the Vietnam war, the racial conflicts, the ghetto riots, the drug culture, the campus riots, the feminist movement, the decay of the cities, the environmental movement, the counterculture, the law-and-order issue, consumerism, government credibility, political bombing, to name only a partial list. Each tended to feed on the rest; each escalated to crisis proportions, but as the decade ended, appeared (with some few exceptions) to subside.

This volume holds a mirror to some of them. The public opinion polls which follow were either commissioned or conducted by CBS News, designed primarily as a journalistic tool to give breadth and dimension to coverage of the major issues of the period. Although the surveys were conducted for specific broadcasts at specific points in time, they were fashioned and utilized to provide broad-based pictures of public attitudes toward the major issues.

Because some of the studies were one-time polls, conducted in periods of turbulence and flux, they give no indication of trends. Others, in particular the studies on the Vietnam war and on youth, cover several points in time and trace changes in attitudes. All of them, however, provide fascinating insights into the attitudes of a public in ferment.

They should be read (and the introduction to each of the chapters attempts to assist the reader in this respect) in the context of the events which surrounded them. In a sense, the data can be studied as one might view a family album; a snapshot is discussed in the context of a particular place and time and may recall specific events. So too, should these findings; they represent attitudes frozen in time, influenced by and influencing the events of the moment.

What we have, then, is a series of quantitative insights into a public in the process of change, often pulled and tugged by forces and events of which it had little understanding and less control. Although the period covered by the surveys consists of little more than two and a half years, from early 1968 to the end of 1970, the variety of elemental social and cultural conflicts covered is, in retrospect, rather startling.

While the studies constitute a historical perspective into the attitudes of those years, they provide insights into current issues as well. The recent findings on marijuana research, for example, and the continuing studies of attitudes of college students, reveal that while the political commitment of youth no longer appears as intense as it was in 1969 and 1970, the cultural disaffection appears to have been enhanced. None of the issues covered in this volume have sufficiently abated as to be relegated to the category of history; they are still high in the public consciousness, if not as intensively as two years ago.

In addition to its research and reference value for special, public, college, and university libraries for the insights it provides into contemporary problems, this volume will also serve as a guide to survey technique for the student and practitioner of survey research. Enough time, effort, and testing went into many of the specific questions and question sequences in sensitive areas to warrant their consideration in future surveys by others in the field. Some of the individual studies ventured far enough off the beaten track of social research approaches to difficult subjects to lend encouragement to those who would be unorthodox if they could but be convinced that they can also be effective.

The surveys undertaken by CBS News itself were a group effort, and the author would be remiss if he failed to credit the principal contributors to that effort. Gerald Hursh, the energetic and imaginative Director of Survey Research for CBS News, organized and ran the CBS News Poll and was principally responsible for the more imaginative of its undertakings and techniques. Warren Mitofsky, Associate Director of the CBS News Election Unit, in which the polling operations resided, brought to it the statistical insights and discipline that made it a thoroughly professional effort.

Acknowledgement is also due the management of CBS News, in particular Richard S. Salant and Bill Leonard, for their dedication to the idea that statistical data are a useful tool of broadcast journalism, and to the producers, writers, and correspondents who welcomed that tool. Finally, thanks go to the staff of the Election Unit, who as interviewers, supervisors, coders, and tabulators did most of the real work, and to Joe Bellon, whose imagination and persuasiveness were responsible for this publication.

Introduction

Survey research has found its users in the past several decades primarily among the academic and business communities. It has become a primary tool for social research, for obvious reasons, and in the form of market research has also become an indispensable part of the industrial/marketing process.

Only sporadically, however, had it been used as a journalistic tool. The occasional political polls that were reported by journalists, the newspaper and newsmagazine syndication of the Gallup and Harris polls, tended to constitute the limits of survey research as a journalistic vehicle.

Certainly there was little effort to integrate survey research into specific journalistic enterprises. Only an occasional "takeout" by one of the newsmagazines tended to utilize a public opinion study as an integral part of its report. The use of polls by newspapers and broadcasting journalism as part of an original reporting enterprise was rare, except in the case of political campaigns.

One reason was the time factor. The traditional personal interview poll utilizing nationwide samples is not only a costly project, but a time-consuming one. From inception to completion, it takes no less than three weeks, generally four or more. For a daily newspaper, or a radio or television news broadcast, the story could conceivably be "dead" by the time results were available. But just as magazines could prepare well in advance for certain large-scale treatments of broad subject areas, so the broadcast media had certain types of projects that utilized longer periods of preparation. Mostly, these were documentaries or "public affairs" broadcasts, requiring months of advance filming and editing before their actual presentation.

Many such documentaries dealt with subjects which virtually cried out for the answers that only survey research could provide: how many, who, where, why? It is, after all, people who make news, who form public opinion, who create social problems and solve them. So through the 1960s, television documentarians began to explore the uses of survey research for some of their broadcasts.

At CBS News, the interest was particularly high. Dr. Frank Stanton, President of CBS, Inc., had earned a national reputation in his early studies of audience measurement techniques and maintained a vital and continuing interest in all forms of social and marketing research. Early in the decade, CBS News had applied systematic survey research methods to election coverage in conjunction with Louis Harris and IBM. In 1965, Bill Leonard, who had supervised this breakthrough in election coverage, became vice-president of CBS News in charge of documentaries, and immediately began to explore the utilization of survey research in these broadcasts.

The first direct application was made in the case of the "national test" broadcasts, "The National Drivers Test," the "National Citizenship Test," and the "National Environment Test," the latter included in this volume. While survey research was utilized basically as a device to enable the home audience "taking" the tests on television to compare their scores with those of a national sample, there were residual benefits as well, in terms of a general measure of public knowledge and awareness of the subject matter, along with demographic analysis.

Soon, however, survey research was integrated into actual broadcasts in a more serious way. One example was the documentary, "16 in Webster Groves," an examination of the attitudes of teenagers in the affluent St. Louis suburb of Webster Groves. Another broadcast, produced by this author, was based totally on a survey, the 1967 study, "The People of Vietnam: How They Feel about the War." This was an independent attempt by CBS News, in association with Opinion Research Corporation and The Center for Vietnamese Studies, a Saigon survey research organization, to examine attitudes of the South Vietnamese themselves.

During this same period, the use of telephone surveys, as opposed to the more prevalent personal interview studies, was gaining greater acceptance thanks to two factors. One was the availability of WATS lines service from the telephone company, permitting a better economic base for telephone surveys. The other was experiments which indicated certain advantages, particularly in the interview and monitoring aspects of polling, over personal interviews.

Telephone polling opened new possibilities for survey research for "hard news" purposes. A well-organized, well-trained cadre of managers and interviewers could turn out complete studies in a matter of days, rather than weeks, and these findings could be available while a particular news story was still current. Indeed, when advance knowledge of an event was available, such as a major Presidential address, preparations could be made in advance and the study begun immediately after the event.

The idea of a CBS News survey research unit utilizing telephone interviewing was first broached in 1967, as an activity of the CBS News Election Unit, but preparations for the Presidential campaign of 1968 precluded a start until 1969. At that time, Gerald Hursh joined the author, who was director of the Election Unit, and Warren Mitofsky, the unit's statistical chief, as head of survey research.

Hursh, who had an extensive background in social research and polling, served as the organizational and "creative" force in the new Survey Research Unit, hiring and training interviewing personnel, setting up testing and monitoring techniques, and writing the questionnaires. Mitofsky, an expert in sampling, drew the telephone samples and also the computer tabulation procedures and participated in analysis. The author served as overall editor and liaison with management and producers of CBS News.

As a journalistic tool, the CBS News Poll proved successful from the outset. The first survey included questions on the space program for use in the coverage of the historic Apollo 11 moon flight, and on the ABM program, then at the height of Congressional debate. The studies on Vietnam, ordered up at specific occasions as the news demanded, provided both the regularly scheduled news broadcasts and the occasional Special Reports on the war with sharply etched details of American attitudes, extremely useful when timed to a Presidential policy speech. Other larger studies, such as the Bill of Rights survey, provided the basis for special broadcasts or features.

Included in this volume are two studies which predated the CBS News Poll. "Black and White Attitudes" was conducted in the spring of 1968 by Opinion Research Corporation for use in the "Of Black America" series. "The Generation Gap" was completed in early spring of 1969 by Daniel Yankelovich, Inc. for use in the documentary series of the same name. Neither survey, even had the CBS News Poll been in existence, was appropriate to a telephone study. The "Black and White" study utilized a large sample of blacks, with a relatively low incidence of telephone ownership, and in any case was probably too sensitive for the impersonality of a telephone survey. "The Generation Gap" required a large sample of college students, and this too would have been impossible to achieve by telephone.

The only measurable failure of the CBS News Poll was in the area of longevity. Economic circumstance occasioned its demise in November of 1970, to the extreme regret not only of its staff but of CBS management. Perhaps at some time in the future, it can be reinstated; it served a useful purpose in broadcast journalism.

The Bill of Rights

Individual rights are generally applauded in the abstract; approval tends to diminish in the concrete application of these rights as opposed to the rights of others or the collective rights or demands of society.

A CBS News correspondent recently painted his home in a series of colors which outraged some of his neighbors. Had he lived in the woods, his home out of daily sight, the chances are nobody would have challenged his right to self-expression. It so happens, however, that he lives in the middle of the fashionable Washington neighborhood of Georgetown, and his neighbors found his new facade not merely offensive to their esthetics, but violative of their property rights.

Much the same kind of conflict emerges with rights long hallowed in the American tradition. Most people will agree to the right of free speech or a free press, to the right of a fair and speedy trial, to the right against self-incrimination, to the right of petition for redress of grievances—to these and other provisions of the Bill of Rights—so long as there is no test or conflict involved. When the exercise of individual rights "costs" people something, when it collides with what other people believe to be their own rights or the rights of society, then the consensus of approval begins to disintegrate.

This disintegration reaches its height in times of stress and difficulty for society, simply because conflicts between individuals and society are greater and more various. Therein lies a paradox. Implicit in the granting of rights, as in any guarantee or warranty, is the understanding that they shall be equally operative in times of stress and turbulence and in "normal" times. Indeed, in the case of human rights, it is more important that the safeguards they warranty be preserved under stress than under calm, since they are generally left unchallenged in the absence of conflict. Yet it is precisely in times of turbulence, when rights are put to the test, that society tends most to waver in its support. The paradox is that at the moments of greatest danger to these rights, their foundations begin to give way.

The past several years have been such a time. Civil disorder, student unrest, a divisive war, changing values and life-styles, rising crime rates, all these and more have sharpened conflicts among individuals and between individuals and society at large.

More specifically, these conflicts have put to the test the basic provisions of the Bill of Rights. In the interests of "national security," of "law and order," of the "prevention of riots and civil disorder," many of the guarantees of the Bill of Rights are under assault. Freedom of the press, of speech and petition, the right to a fair and speedy trial, the protections against unreasonable search and seizure, protection against self-incrimination—these and more are under increasing pressure.

There is a tendency to dismiss this pressure, this antagonism toward fundamental rights in time of stress, as a manifestation of an "ignorant" public, of inadequacies in the teaching of American history and traditions, of a lack of appreciation for the dangers to individual freedom which the Founding Fathers experienced and anticipated. But there is more to it than that. The initiative for government actions and legislation which, if not in violation of Bill of Rights provisions, are at least in conflict with them, originates not with an "ignorant public," but with sophisticated government officials, learned in the law and the Constitution, acting not in ignorance but in the interests of some conflicting motivation.

Consider, for example, the new preventive detention laws, the "no-knock" search legislation, and the wiretapping laws. In each of these, there are Bill of Rights considerations at issue—the right to a speedy and public trial without excessive bail, the protection against unreasonable search and seizure. These laws were written by leaders conscious of the history and the rationale of the Bill of Rights. They were written under the belief that the dangers posed to individual liberty by criminal activity exceeded the possible dangers posed by a relaxation of Bill of Rights safeguards against government.

The conflicts surrounding the Bill of Rights are not limited simply to legislation. Recent U.S. Supreme Court appointments have tended to focus on the Bill of Rights perspectives of the respective appointees. The debate over former Assistant Attorney General William P. Rehnquist dwelt largely on his philosophy in the Justice Department on First Amendment rights, particularly with respect to the government handling of dissenters against the Vietnam War.

Rehnquist was universally acknowledged to be a brilliant and able Constitutional lawyer. What concerned many Senators, however, was whether his philosophical and ideological outlook was one which placed a greater emphasis on such societal values as national security and law and order than on the individual protections inscribed in the Bill of Rights.

Nor was this concern only an academic one. Consider one of the most dramatic Supreme Court cases in recent years, *The New York Times* v. *the U.S.*, dealing with the *Times'* right to publish the Pentagon Papers. The universally acknowledged right of freedom of the press was subjected to considerable pressure, not merely from elements of the public and from the government, but from members of the Supreme Court itself. The decision, in favor of the *Times,* was not unanimous; the vote was six to three. The conflict was sharp and unmistakable. The late Justice Hugo Black, in his concurring opinion, wrote:

> In the First Amendment, the Founding Fathers gave the free press the protection it must have to fulfill its essential role in our democracy. The press was to serve the governed, not the governors. The Government's power to censor the press was abolished so that the press would remain forever free to censure the Government. The press was protected so that it could bare the secrets of government and inform the people. Only a free and unrestrained press can effectively expose deception in government. And paramount among the responsibilities of a free press is the duty to prevent any part of the Government from deceiving the people and sending them off to distant lands to die of foreign fevers and foreign shot and shell.

Justice Harry A. Blackmun, on the other hand, concerned himself with the effect of publication on the national security, and in his dissent wrote that if publication causes "the death of soldiers, the destruction of alliances, the greatly increased difficulty of negotiation with our enemies, the inability of our diplomats to negotiate, to which list I might add the factors of prolongation of the war and of further delay in the freeing of United States prisoners, then the nation's people will know where the responsibility for these sad consequences rest."

On a somewhat loftier plane, Chief Justice Warren E. Burger stated the dilemma in his dissent: "In this case, the imperative of a free and unfettered press comes into collision with another imperative, the effective functioning of a complex modern government, and specifically the effective exercise of certain constitutional powers of the executive. Only those who view the First Amendment as an absolute in all circumstances—a view I respect, but reject— can find such a case as this to be simple or easy."

CBS News conducted its survey on public attitudes toward the Bill of Rights in March 1970, before publication of the Pentagon Papers and the Supreme Court nominations. The study was prompted by Bill Leonard, CBS News Vice President, with the observation that many people had speculated that if the Bill of Rights were presented for ratification today, it would be defeated. At that time, CBS News had established its public opinion polling operations, and Leonard suggested we attempt to measure public attitudes to confirm or refute the speculation. The findings were subsequently broadcast on the "60 Minutes" series on CBS Television.

If the Supreme Court hearings and the Pentagon Papers case were still in the future, legislation covering preventive detention, no-knock entry, and wiretapping was under consideration or already law, and the questions of civil disorder, campus unrest, and antiwar demonstrations were very much before the public eye. The survey was undertaken during a period of considerable stress and conflict.

Because this was the case, the CBS News Poll staff made two critical decisions, both with the purpose of eliciting realistic responses from the sample. The first was to avoid all reference in any of the questions to the Bill of Rights itself. Experience in public opinion studies is that "labels" or symbols in themselves produce preconditioned biases, and it was felt that the very phrase might summon a favorable response even though some respondents might respond negatively to a specific application.

The second related decision was to pose the questions in the form of problems in the application of specific provisions of the Bill of Rights. Again, experience has indicated that unless the respondent in public opinion surveys is forced to make a choice, is required to think about his answer, the results all too often are superficial and meaningless. So our approach, as in the case of the freedom of the press question ("Except in time of war, do you think newspapers, radio and television should have the right to report any story, even if the government feels it's harmful to our national interest?"), was to pose the conflict in terms of the right, in this case the First Amendment, pitted against "the national interest."

In forcing the respondent to make the choice, we attempted to pose situations as realistic as we could, many of them growing out of hours of depth interviewing with small groups where the then-current issues of law and order and group violence were discussed. If some of the questions turned out to anticipate some of the issues in recent headlines, it is because we attempted deliberately to deal with issues and not with abstractions.

In the end, it is apparent that public opinion does not exist in, or grow out of, a vacuum. Nor is it realistic to assume that it exists as a great, silent beast bearing little relation to reality. Public opinion is molded, not necessarily by manipulation, but by a dynamic interlacing of emotion, experience, communications, and background. Not the least of the contributors to this mix is the very leadership of the country itself. The public and their leaders interact in the formation and distillation of their respective attitudes. We cannot say which bears the greatest influence, but it should be apparent that each helps mold the other.

BACKGROUND AND METHODOLOGY

These pages present the findings* from a national sample of adults on their feelings about certain basic concepts embodied in the Bill of Rights of the Constitution. Naturally, the questions asked could not be phrased in the terminology of the original writing; rather, they were written in contemporary language. Because of the inherent danger of trying to interpret the public's responses to questions dealing with their constitutional rights, we tried to make the questions as direct and meaningful as possible.

Before undertaking the study, we conducted five separate depth-interview sessions in which different groups of six to eight people—young men, working women, suburban housewives, etc.—were interviewed intensively for two or three hours each. Later, the tape recordings from those interviews were analyzed for several days to see if we could determine what people's answers meant, and the reasons underlying those answers.

*These findings are based on a national random telephone sample of 1,136 adults, conducted on March 10–12, 1970, with an associated sampling error of up to plus or minus three percentage points.

Most of the questions deal with semiabstractions such as "national interests" and "serious crimes" in order to allow the respondent to provide his own frame of reference in answering a given question. That is, we permitted the individual to make his own interpretation of Bill of Rights concepts as we structured them, because his particular interpretation guides his day-to-day actions and feelings with respect to the rights of others. Naturally, although two people may answer "yes" to a question about trial by jury, chances are they may do so for somewhat different reasons.

Findings from the depth interviews were incorporated into a small-scale (127 people) pre-test in three regions of the country about one week in advance of the major study itself. Findings from the pre-test convinced us the survey was feasible. In addition, the final questionnaire was reviewed by a constitutional lawyer for expert insight into the sense of the questions. His appraisal was that although there are many qualifications for any legal interpretation of articles of the Bill of Rights, in each instance the questions in the study were directly to the point at issue.

SUMMARY OF FINDINGS

The majority of adults in America seem willing to restrict some of the basic freedoms constitutionally guaranteed by the Bill of Rights. Specifically, about three-fourths (76%) of the 1,136 people interviewed in the nationwide CBS News telephone survey believe extremist groups should not be permitted to organize demonstrations against the government, even if there appeared to be no clear danger of violence. Moreover, well over one-half of the people (54%) would not give everyone the right to criticize the government if the criticism were thought to be damaging to our national interest; a comparable number (55%) feel newspapers, radio, and television should not be permitted to report some stories considered by the government to be harmful to our national interests (wartime censorship was excluded in the question).

Two additional freedoms that people would restrict involve "double jeopardy" and "preventive detention." In the case of the former, nearly three out of every five adults (58%) feel that if a person is found innocent of a serious crime, but new evidence is uncovered after the trial, he should be tried again. In the case of the latter, three out of every five adults (58%) also feel that if a person is suspected of a serious crime, the police should be allowed to hold him in jail until they can get enough evidence to charge him with the crime.

These findings suggest that group protests, vocal dissent, and the publicity given to them have surpassed the public's level of tolerance. Moreover, the general concern for law and order seems to have led people to a willingness to curtail the rights of the individual criminal should there be strong indication of his probable guilt.

On the other hand, other constitutional guarantees involving the judicial process appear to be so deeply embedded in our way of life that Americans emphatically uphold them. In particular, four out of five people (82%) feel that guilt or innocence in a criminal case should be decided by a jury, not by the judge alone; three out of four (75%) believe that the government should never be allowed to hold a secret trial; and two out of three (66%) feel that the police should not be allowed to enter someone's home without a search warrant even if they suspect that drugs, guns, or other criminal evidence is hidden there.

Less strongly felt, but nonetheless acceptable to most people, are the rights of defendants in criminal cases to avoid self-incrimination and to confront witnesses against them. In both cases, more than one-half of the people (54%) feel that the individual should have the right to refuse to answer questions if he feels his answers may be used against him, and that the prosecution should never be allowed to keep the identity of witnesses secret during a trial.

Before looking at the specific findings for different groups making up the national population, let us point out that the people most frequently opposed to various freedoms guaranteed to Americans by the Bill of Rights are women, older people, and people with relatively low levels of education. One caution should be raised about interpreting findings for Jewish people; the findings are not necessarily representative of this group because such a small number (48) appeared in the sample.

BILL OF RIGHTS CONCEPTS THAT PEOPLE OPPOSE

The following pages show the basic concepts embodied in the Bill of Rights that the American public rejects, at least in the terms of the questions we asked. The exact question wording is shown for each concept.

Peaceful Assembly

Article I. "Congress shall make no law respecting an establishment of religion, or prohibiting the free exercise thereof; or abridging the freedom of speech or of the press; *of the right of the people peaceably to assemble* and to petition the government for a redress of grievances."

Question. As long as there appears to be no clear danger of violence, do you think any group, no matter how extreme, should be allowed to organize protests against the government?

Results

	Percent of People
Yes	21%
No	76
Sometimes	—
No response	3

In intensive depth interviewing done prior to the study, we found that people tend to think in terms of the Black Panthers, SDS, and other extremist ("radical left" not "radical right") groups as the kinds of groups demonstrating against the government. Altogether, three-fourths of the public would prohibit anti-government demonstrations, often because they fear that no matter how well-intended, such demonstrations invariably disintegrate into violence.

Women are somewhat more likely than men to oppose organized demonstrations even where there is no clear danger of violence. Not surprisingly, older people are much more opposed to demonstrations than are younger people; Republicans and Democrats are more often opposed than are people who claim no political party affiliation or else identify with a political group outside the two-party system.

People with less education and lower income are more likely to oppose demonstrations than are those in the higher education and income groups. Protestants, Catholics, and whites are more frequently opposed to demonstrations than are the few Jews studied, members of other faiths, or secularists, and nonwhites. Southerners are more likely to be against antigovernment demonstrations than are people in other parts of the country, particularly those in the Western states.

Free Press

Article I. "Congress shall make no law respecting an establishment of religion, or prohibiting the free exercise thereof; *or abridging the freedom of speech or of the press*; or the right of the people peaceably to assemble and to petition the government for a redress of grievance."

Question. Except in time of war, do you think newspapers, radio, and television should have the right to report any story, even if the government feels it's harmful to our national interest?

Results

	Percent of People
Yes	42%
No	55
Sometimes	1
No response	2

The findings here closely parallel those for opposition to antigovernment demonstrations. That is, women, Republicans and Democrats, older people, Protestants and Catholics, the less-educated, and those in lower income groups are most likely to oppose the mass media having the freedom to report any story they wish, even in times of relative peace (undeclared war), if the "government" feels the report is inimical to our "national interests."

Only in the Western states do a majority of people favor the free press concept; there are no real differences among people in other regions of the country. Finally, whether a person is white or nonwhite makes no difference in his feelings about press freedom—a majority of both groups oppose the reporting of any or all stories that the government defines as against the nation's best interests.

Free Speech

Article I. "Congress shall make no law respecting an establishment of religion, or prohibiting the free exercise thereof; *or abridging the freedom of speech or of the press*; or the right of the people peaceably to assemble and to petition the government for a redress of grievances."

Question. Do you think everyone should have the right to criticize the government, even if the criticism is damaging to our national interest?

Results

	Percent of People
Yes	42%
No	54
Sometimes	1
No response	3

In this case, men are more likely than women to oppose free criticism of the government. Of all the questions explored in the lengthy depth interview sessions, this one produced the most internal conflict. That is, while people often recognize the right involved and see the implications of the alternative to free speech, they feel that dissent has gone "too far" and that a line somehow must be drawn somewhere. Who should draw the line and how is the problem that produces the mental conflict. The concept of free speech blurs with that of the free press; people tend to feel that criticism of the government in personal conversations among friends and family members is not the same as publicizing that criticism in the mass media.

A person's race, political party affiliation, or region of the country has little bearing on his feelings about the exercise of free speech. But, as we saw before, Protestants and Catholics, older people, poorer people, and less-educated people are most likely to be against giving everyone the right to criticize the government if the criticism purports to be damaging to our national interests.

Reviewing the three concepts thus far, it is not surprising to find that—with the exception of income which is highly correlated with educational attainment— the groups most likely to oppose the unrestricted exercise of free speech, free press, and peaceful assembly are older and are members of the majority parties and religions. In effect, these are the members of the system under attack.

Double Jeopardy

Article V. "No person shall be held to answer for a capital or other infamous crime unless on a presentment or indictment of a Grand Jury, except in cases arising in the land or naval forces, or in the militia, when in actual service in time of war or public danger; nor *shall any person be subject for the same offense to be twice put in jeopardy of life or limb*; nor shall be compelled in any criminal case to be a witness against himself, nor be deprived of life, liberty, or property, without due process of law; nor shall private property be taken for public use without just compensation."

Question. If a man is found innocent of a serious crime, but new evidence is uncovered later, do you think he should be tried again for the same crime?

Results

	Percent of People
Yes	58%
No	38
Sometimes	1
No response	3

Those Bill of Rights guarantees that most people would restrict tend to divide into two groups. The first group, the exercise of dissent, has already been described. The second group is made up of two concepts involving the probable guilt of a suspected criminal. The depth interviews suggested that, while people recognize the danger to the individual of being "hounded for life" for the same crime, there nonetheless is a feeling that if the individual has the right to appeal a conviction the government should have the right to re-try on acquittal. Moreover, the sentiment for retrial grows stronger as the crime becomes more serious, e.g., murder, rape, child molestation, trafficking in narcotics among young people, and espionage.

Not unexpectedly, women are much more likely than men to wish to re-try suspects after acquittal on the basis of new evidence. Women feel, of course, more vulnerable to the commission of crime than do men and have a heightened concern for the safety of their children. Whites and people in Western states, particularly as compared with people in the East, are most likely to want to re-try suspects for the same crime. Age, political affiliation, income, and education have little to do with people's feelings.

Jewish people (at least the small number studied) seem more likely than Protestants and Catholics—who are in turn more likely than members of other faiths and secularists—to abridge the double jeopardy clause. This finding is inconsistent with most findings for Jews, who by the large tend to be civil libertarians in outlook.

Preventive Detention

Article VI. "In all criminal prosecutions, the accused shall enjoy the *right to a speedy* and public trial, by an impartial jury of the State and district, wherein the crime shall have been committed, which districts shall have been previously ascertained by law, and *to be informed of the nature and cause of the accusation;* to be confronted with the witnesses against him; to have compulsory process for obtaining witnesses in his favor, and to have the assistance of counsel for his defense.

Question. If a person is suspected of a serious crime, do you think the police should be allowed to hold him in jail, until they can get enough evidence to officially charge him?

Results

	Percent of People
Yes	58%
No	38
Sometimes	1
No response	2

The findings are substantially the same on this question as for previous ones; namely that women, Republicans and Democrats, older people, members of the major religions, people in lower education groups, and people in lower income brackets are most likely to wish to hold the suspected criminal in jail without a formal charge until sufficient evidence can be brought against him for a serious crime. The issue is not clear-cut, of course. Depth interviews indicated that while people realize that the individual's rights are being compromised, they frequently express concern that "dangerous criminals" on the loose will commit more crimes or else flee the country. Here, again, people feel a line somehow should be drawn with respect to the seriousness of the crime and the length of time a suspect could be held without charge, but have no idea as to how and who could make the distinction.

A person's race has no relationship to his answer to this question; but people in the Midwest are more likely than people in the rest of the country—especially more so than people in the West— to agree to hold suspected criminals without formal charge.

BILL OF RIGHTS CONCEPTS THAT PEOPLE UPHOLD

The following pages show the basic concepts embodied in the Bill of Rights that the American public upholds, at least in terms of the question we asked them. The exact question wording is shown for each concept.

Trial by Jury

Article VII. "In suits at common law, where the value in controversy shall exceed twenty dollars, *the right of trial by jury shall be preserved*, and no fact tried by a jury shall be otherwise reexamined in any court of the United States than according to the rules of the common law.

Question. In most criminal cases, the judge conducts the trial and a jury decides guilt or innocence. Instead of the jury, would it be better if the judge alone decided guilt or innocence?

Results

	Percent of People
Yes	14%
No	82
Sometimes	1
No response	3

The American public is strongest in its support of trial by jury; four-fifths reject the idea of a judge deciding verdicts instead of a jury. In the depth interviews, however, we found that a hypothetical panel of three judges would be acceptable to a number of people who rejected the idea of only one judge deciding guilt or innocence in criminal cases.

Preference for a single judge deciding the outcome of criminal cases increases as age increases and as income and education decrease. Surprisingly, people in the Eastern states are more likely than people in other parts of the country— particularly those in the West—to favor decisions by a judge instead of a jury. Equally surprising, nonwhites are more likely than whites to prefer a single judge. This may be due to the feeling among minority group members that they cannot get an impartial verdict from predominantly white juries.

Political party affiliation, religious preference, and the individual's sex have little relationship to people's feelings about trial by juries.

Public Trial

Article VI. "In all criminal prosecutions, *the accused shall enjoy the right to a speedy and public trial,* by an impartial jury of the State and district, wherein the crime shall have been committed, which districts shall have been previously ascertained by law, *and to be informed of the nature and cause of the accusation*; to be confronted with the witnesses against him; to have compulsory process for obtaining witnesses in his favor, and to have the assistance of counsel for his defense."

Question. In criminal cases, do you think the government should ever have the right to hold a secret trial?

Results

	Percent of People
Yes	20%
No	75
Sometimes	1
No response	4

In the military, trials can be conducted secretly and transcripts withheld from public scrutiny when it is determined that national security would be jeopardized by public disclosure. In civil and criminal cases, however, there is no circumstance in which a trial's transcripts are not public record. The concept of secret trials meets with great resistance, three-fourths of the American public opposing the idea. Opposition cuts uniformly across most subgroups, in that people's sex, age, party affiliation, religion, income, and education have little bearing on their answers. Whites, however, are more likely than nonwhites to be willing to give the government the right to conduct confidential trials. And, while people in the Midwest, South, and West tend to answer about the same way, a noticeably higher proportion of people in the Eastern states than in the Midwestern states would permit secret trials.

Search and Seizure

Article IV. "The right of the people to be secure in their persons, houses, papers, and effects, against unreasonable searches and seizures, shall not be violated, *and no warrants shall issue but upon probable cause, supported by oath or affirmation,* and particularly describing the place to be searched, and the persons or things to be seized."

Question. If the police suspect that drugs, guns, or other criminal evidence is hidden in someone's house, should they be allowed to enter the house without first obtaining a search warrant?

Results

	Percent of People
Yes	32%
No	66
Sometimes	1
No response	1

This particular question was revised many times before reaching its final form. In this case we specified "drugs, guns, or other criminal evidence" in the question; normally we would have preferred to permit the individual to interpret "criminal evidence" without specific examples. In the pre-test and the depth interviews, however, we found that drugs and guns are the two most salient concerns with respect to search and seizure. Asking the question in more vague terms produced confusion between illegal entry and legal entry in "hot pursuit."

Two-thirds of the public reject the idea of the police entering private residences without search warrants. While recognizing that criminals may dispose of evidence during the time lost obtaining search warrants, people nonetheless prefer the right of security in their homes. A number of people interviewed prior to the study itself expressed concern for the police "planting" incriminating evidence in the homes of suspected criminals.

As age increases and education decreases, people are more likely to favor permitting the police to enter homes without search warrants; whites are more likely than members of minority groups to permit the police to enter without warrants. Curiously enough, Jewish people and people in the Eastern states—typically bastions of civil libertarianism—are more likely than their counterparts in other faiths or other regions to be willing to permit entry and search without formal search warrants. Also, people in the $5,000 to $10,000 income range are more permissive than those in higher and lower income groups with respect to search and seizure. People's sex and party affiliation have no relationship to their answers to this question.

Self-Incrimination

Article V. "No person shall be held to answer for a capital or other infamous crime unless on a presentment or indictment of a Grant Jury, except in cases arising in the land or naval forces, or in the militia, when in actual service in time of war or public danger; nor shall any person be subject for the same offense to be twice put in jeopardy of life or limb; *nor shall be compelled in any criminal case to be a witness against himself,* nor be deprived of life, liberty, or property, without due process of law; nor shall private property be taken for public use without just compensation."

Question. At their trials, do you think suspected criminals should have the right to refuse to answer questions if they feel their answers may be used against them?

Results

	Percent of People
Yes	54%
No	42
Sometimes	1
No response	3

In our exploratory research before the survey, we found many people felt that only the guilty take the Fifth Amendment to avoid self-incrimination. A number felt that the Fifth Amendment has been misused, by Mafia members in particular, and is not serving the ends of justice. Consequently, it perhaps is not too startling to find that just over a majority of the public upholds the individual's right to protect himself from self-incrimination.

Opposition to use of the Fifth Amendment is higher among older people, people with less education, and people with less than $15,000 annual income. Opposition also is higher among whites, Protestants, and Republicans. One finding out of character is that proportionately more people in the Eastern states than in other parts of the country oppose the use of the Fifth Amendment to avoid self-incrimination. There is no difference between the answers of men and women.

Confronting Witnesses

Article VI. "In all criminal prosecutions, the accused shall enjoy the right to a speedy and public trial, by an impartial jury of the State and district, wherein the crime shall have been committed, which districts shall have been previously ascertained by law, and to be informed of the nature and cause of the accusation; *to be confronted with the witnesses against him*; to have compulsory process for obtaining witnesses in his favor, and to have the assistance of counsel for his defense."

Question. During court trials, do you think the government should ever be allowed to keep the identity of witnesses secret from the defendant?

Results

	Percent of People
Yes	40%
No	54
Sometimes	2
No response	4

Here, again, the findings of the pre-study research might aid in interpreting the responses to this question. Many people felt that the government should be allowed to protect the identity of its witnesses in two cases: the first being trials involving the Mafia when the life of the witness would be endangered by his testimony, and the second being espionage cases involving undercover agents for the FBI and the CIA. While recognizing the dangers to the defendant with respect to the adequacy of his defense preparation as well as realizing that informers might falsely testify because of personal grudges, there remained nonetheless a rather strong core of sentiment favoring secrecy of witnesses.

Women, whites, and Republicans are more willing than men, nonwhites, and non-Republicans to permit the government to mask the identity of witnesses. There is no difference in people's feelings when compared by their religious preference. There is no clear relationship to education or income; people in the middle income and education groups are more likely to favor the use of secret witnesses than are those at the higher and lower levels of income and education.

One unanticipated finding is that young people are more receptive to the idea of secret witnesses than are older people. And people outside the South are more likely to permit the use of secret witnesses than are people in the South.

In reviewing the findings in this last section, it appears that certain aspects of the judicial process are so ingrained in our lives that considering alternatives to jury trials, public trials, and search warrants is anathema to a substantial majority of Americans. Because of the "abuse" of the Fifth Amendment and because of fear of the Mafia as well as people's willingness to accept secrecy in espionage cases, only somewhat more than a simple majority of the public uphold the rights to avoid self-incrimination and to confront one's accusers.

Black
and White Attitudes

Public opinion polling functionally divides into five general parts—sampling, questionnaire design and testing, interviewing, tabulation, and analysis of the data. It is this last function, reaching conclusions from the survey results, that often requires the greatest judgment and discipline from the polltaker.

There is a particularly relevant aphorism that can characterize the difficulties sometimes encountered in analysis of survey data. It is the old but perceptive saw about the difference between the optimist and the pessimist. When each of them describes a half-glass of water, the optimist describes it as half full, the pessimist as half empty.

In survey analysis, too, there are different ways of interpreting the same data. Because quite frequently the person who conducts the survey brings only a single point of view to his analysis, it is incumbent on the user to be able to look at the findings and examine the other possible interpretations that can be supported by the data. This is particularly essential in the case of studies on subjects of great sensitivity, or on issues which can profoundly affect the popular perception of an important problem.

It was such a sensitive situation with which CBS News found itself confronted in the late spring of 1968, following the completion of a study by the Opinion Research Corporation of Princeton on white and Negro attitudes toward race and related issues. The study had been commissioned by CBS News to form the basis of the final broadcast in a series of 7, "Of Black America," a wide-ranging exploration of the role of the black in American life.

The background is essential to the discussion. Just a month prior to the time the study was launched, Martin Luther King was assassinated, and the assassination touched off a new wave of ghetto riots. These, as it turned out, were the culmination of some four years of riots in the nation's ghettos. While interviewing was in progress, the "Poor People's March" had encamped on Washington's Mall under the leadership of Dr. King's successor, the Reverend Ralph Abernathy. During the later stages of the interviewing, Senator Robert Kennedy, whom many blacks had considered their best white hope, was assassinated.

Earlier in the year, the Kerner Commission report on ghetto disorders had been published, concluding from its exhaustive examination of the riots that the races were drifting further apart and urging programs and attitudes to reverse the trend. It was a period of some despair and confusion. The stridency of black militancy was peaking and the voice of black moderation could hardly be heard in the background.

Beyond this, there was little in the way of hard information about the way people, particularly black people, really felt about racial problems. While there was a considerable amount of data on white attitudes toward race, there was little on black attitudes, and no way to compare black and white views on the same questions and issues. There had been a number of surveys of blacks on the question of black leadership, generally finding that the militants had the allegiance of only small numbers of blacks. But in the volatile situation of 1968, nobody really knew whether even those findings had changed.

As a consequence, the Opinion Research study, using nearly equal samples of blacks and whites, assumed some importance. It was in many respects the first major study of black and white attitudes toward each other and on the same questions; at the very least it would provide new data in a dangerous and volatile time.

When the study was completed, however, CBS News came face to face with the unanticipated problem of the half-glass of water. The data invited several perspectives, but in particular, it raised the question of which of two equally compelling points of view should be utilized:

On the one hand, the data turned up striking differences in the attitudes of whites and blacks. It turned up as well substantial numbers of whites who could, on the basis of their answers to certain questions, be characterized as "racists." At the same time, the data pointed to large areas of agreement among whites and blacks on racial issues.

Perhaps the easiest way to illustrate is with the findings on Question 35 of the study, dealing with relative perceptions of who is to blame for racial problems in the country. The results, as illustrated in the table, indicate sharp differences in perception. Forty-two percent of the blacks see "just the whites" or "mostly whites" as responsible; 31% of whites see "just the Negroes" or "mostly Negroes" as responsible. By the same token, only 1% of the blacks see Negroes as responsible for racial problems, and only 9% of the whites see whites as responsible. Therefore, substantial numbers—nearly half the blacks and nearly a third of the whites—blame the opposite race for the country's racial problems.

It would be quite logical to stress in the analysis of the results that there is a significant degree of polarity between the races in their perception of the blame for racial problems. Yet, the same table reveals that the largest segments of both blacks and whites say that both races ("about half and half"

is the wording) are to blame—48% of the blacks and 54% of the whites take
that position. When one eliminates the "no opinion" responses, both percentages
go higher, the blacks to 53% and the whites to 58%.

Thus, one could state with equal persuasiveness that most people, black and
white, feel that both races are equally to blame for racial differences and
problems. While the differences in perceptions are significant and striking, the
commonality in perception is equally, if not more persuasive.

Another example of the problem—and the study as a whole is replete with
these difficulties—can be found in the responses to Question 3, a commonly
used measure of racial feeling: "Are Negroes in this community making too
much progress or not enough progress in getting the things that they want?"

The most striking response is in the "not enough" category; 78% of the blacks
believe that blacks are not making enough progress, while only 28% of the
whites feel that way. The difference is striking, but not so disparate as a casual
reading might indicate. For one thing, 28% of the whites had no opinion; if
these are removed from the percentage base, then 40% of whites with an opinion
agree that blacks are not making enough progress.

Turning to the negative side, less than 1% of blacks feel they are making too
much progress, while 12% of whites feel they are. Again, removing the white
"no opinions," the 12% rises to 20% of whites. So one could argue that while
20% of whites with an opinion on the matter feel that blacks are making too
much progress, one could also argue that 80% of whites do not think along
these lines, that whites by a four to one majority take a moderate position on
the question of black progress. The key, of course, is in the middle ground:
32% of whites feel blacks are making "about the right amount" of progress. It
is true that only 14% of blacks feel that way, but if one adds the responses in
the "right amount" or "not enough" categories (which reflects a moderate
position), one finds 92% of blacks and 60% of whites in this area.

The problem grows particularly difficult when dealing with questions measur-
ing potential areas of white racism—questions dealing with feelings of superiority.
Question 16 deals with whether white babies have more innate intelligence
than black babies: 14% of whites feel that white babies are born with more
intelligence, while 58% of whites disagree. A more troublesome example is
Question 18: "As a race, Negroes are not as civilized as whites. Would you
agree or disagree?" Forty-three percent of whites agree with the statement;
48% disagree. Among blacks, 10% agree, 83% disagree. Again, taking out the no-
opinion responses, the white measure goes to 47% agree, 53% disagree. Is the
glass half-empty or half-full?

Question 23 gives perhaps a clearer picture of the dilemma. It lists a series
of undesirable traits and asks each race whether the trait is more true of blacks,
more true of whites, true of both blacks and whites or not true of either.
Again, striking differences appear, but so do striking similarities.

For example, 40% of whites believed that lower moral standards were more
typical of blacks than of whites; only 10% of blacks agreed. But 50% of
whites and 68% of blacks felt that lower moral standards were equally true for
both races or untrue of either. The same pattern of sharp differences between
the races but even larger similarities revealed itself throughout the list of items—

cleanliness, child care, poor students, laziness, high crime rates, rundown neighborhoods, and job success.

As noted earlier, the problem asserts itself throughout the study. It presented a problem for the analyst and a problem for the user. In particular, in this case, the user had ordered the study for "publication," in the form of a broadcast, and the sense of responsibility for the interpretation weighed heavily. There was little question that the differences in attitudes and perceptions between the races were striking and disturbing, a cause for the deepest concern and pessimism. Yet, the similarities were also significant and persuasive, an indicator of moderation and optimism.

Given the context of the broadcast and the times, along with the absence of any other detailed data, how should the study be interpreted on the broadcast? This became a matter of considerable discussion among the management of CBS News and the broadcast's producers, writers, and correspondents. In the end, the broadcast, "A Portrait in Black and White," took the most sensible and responsible approach; it pointed to both parts of the glass, to the differences as a sign that the country had serious difficulties to face up to in race relations, and to the similarities as an indication that there was a substantial voice for moderation among both races and that there could be reason for optimism and progress.

The tables which are published here are stripped of analysis, in one direction or another. The reader is invited to study and analyze them, and in the process, perhaps discover whether he is an optimist or a pessimist.

The survey questionnaire was designed jointly by CBS News and the Opinion Research Corporation. Survey interviews were conducted throughout the United States between May 22, and June 16, 1968. To minimize bias in the taking of the poll, black interviewers questioned blacks in the sample, and white interviewers questioned whites.

The sample was composed of 587 whites and 478 blacks. The most advanced probability sampling procedures were used to select interviewees so that the sample fairly represented the nation-wide adult population of whites and blacks. In all samples there is a margin for possible statistical error. In a sample of this size the margin is approximately six percentage points. That is: a difference between any two answers reported in this survey is meaningful if it is greater than six percentage points. If there is less than six percentage points difference, the answers then are meaningful as indicating an even split.

In the reporting of results, a zero (0) indicates no response by an individual, an asterisk (*) indicates less than ½ percent responded in this manner.

THE NEGRO AS HE SEES HIMSELF AND AS HE THINKS WHITES SEE HIM. HOW WHITES FEEL ABOUT NEGROES

The Negro in the Community

Question 2. First, which do you think is the main reason that Negroes (black people)† have not made more progress in this city (town): discrimination against

†Interviewers were instructed to use the term "Negro" or "black," whichever seemed more comfortable to the interviewer.

them because of their race or because Negroes (blacks) have not worked very hard at the opportunities available to them?

	Negro	White
Discrimination because of their race	45%	15%
Negroes haven't worked hard enough	22	49
Both	18	15
Other	3	10
No opinion	12	11

Question 3. Do you think that the Negroes (black people) in this community are making too much progress or not enough progress in getting the things that they want?

	Negro	White
Too much progress	*%	12%
About the right amount	14	32
Not enough	78	28
No opinion	8	28

Question 4. In your opinion is the local government here—that is, the people who run things—fair to both blacks and whites or do they favor one race over the other? (Which race?)

	Negro	White
Fair to both races	21%	56%
Favor blacks over whites	1	12
Favor whites over blacks	60	12
No opinion	18	20

Question 5. Regardless of how much or how little the local government actually does, do you think that the Negroes (black people) who live here *think* that the government is fair or unfair to the Negroes (black people) in town?

	Negro	White
Think it is fair	16%	25%
Think it is unfair	60	41
Other answer	4	3
No opinion	20	31

Question 6. Which of these groups in town seem to be most interested in helping the Negroes (black people): the local government, the white religious leaders, the white businessmen, or the labor unions?

	Negro	White
Local government	20%	26%
White religious leaders	23	25
White businessmen	12	8
Labor unions	19	9
Other answer	6	7
No opinion	22	33

Question 7.† Which group in town do you think the Negro (black) community is most dissatisfied with: the local government, the white religious leaders, the white businessmen, or the labor unions?

†Totals are greater than 100% in Questions 6 and 7 as a result of some respondents giving more than one answer.

	Negro	White
Local government	23%	18%
White religious leaders	4	2
White businessmen	23	19
Labor unions	13	9
Other answer	3	9
No opinion	35	45

Questions Related to White Racism

These next few questions are about natural born differences between whites and blacks because of their race. These are *not* differences between blacks and whites as a result of schooling or where they live. Just race differences.

Tell me if you agree or disagree with each statement.

Question 16. First, when black babies and white babies are examined right after they are born, the white babies usually have more natural intelligence than the black babies. From what you know or have heard, would you agree or disagree with that statement?

Agree	5%	14%
Disagree	83	58
No opinion	12	28

Question 18. As a race, Negroes are not as civilized as whites. Would you agree or disagree?

Agree	10%	43%
Disagree	81	48
No opinion	9	9

Question 23. I'm going to name some things that have been said about Negroes (blacks) and have also been said about whites. After I say each thing, please tell me if you think it is more true of Negroes (blacks), more true of whites, true of *both* blacks and whites, or *not true of either* blacks or whites.

	Negroes	Whites	Both	Neither	No Opinion
WHITES					
Low moral standards	40%	1%	42%	8%	9%
Keep body clean	8	39	39	6	8
Do not take good care of their children	28	3	41	19	9
Poor students who keep back the rest of the class	24	1	39	15	21
Tend to be lazy and would rather not work	53	*	30	10	7
Run down the neighborhoods in which they live	57	1	25	8	9
Have a high crime rate	48	3	36	3	10
If given a good job will probably make a success of it	5	34	52	2	7

	Negroes	Whites	Both	Neither	No Opinion
NEGROES					
Low moral standards	10%	11%	59%	9%	11%
Keep body clean	11	5	72	3	9
Do not take good care of their children	10	12	56	11	11
Poor students who keep back the rest of the class	13	4	47	12	24
Tend to be lazy and would rather not work	13	10	52	9	16
Run down the neighborhoods in which they live	29	4	40	10	17
Have a high crime rate	11	24	50	2	13
If given a good job will probably make a success of it	29	7	52	2	10

A Measure of Racism

Using four questions which have face validity as indicators of racism, a simple index was constructed. These four questions are:

	Whites agreeing
A separate Negro country is a good idea (Q. 41)	33%
White babies are smarter than black babies (Q. 16)	14
Negroes are not as civilized as whites (Q. 18)	43
After warnings, police should shoot one or two rioters as examples (Q. 30)	35

Given the assumption that each of these items reflects a degree of racist sentiment, we can rank the white public on the number of those questions answered in the racist direction.

		Percent of white public
lower racism	0	34%
	1	28
	2	21
	3	12
higher racism	4	5

On the President's Commission Report and Racism

Question 24. Recently the President's Commission on Civil Disorders published a report on what's wrong between the Negro (black) and the white races. By any chance, did you happen to know that there is this report, or didn't you happen to know about it?

	Negro	White
Yes, knew about it	31%	34%
No, didn't know about it	63	65
Other answer	*	*
No opinion	6	1

Question 25. In the report it says that white racism is essentially responsible for the conditions in which Negroes live in American cities. Do you agree or not agree with that statement?

Percentage base†	326	406
Agree	74%	31%
Disagree	9	55
Other	2	5
No opinion	15	9

Responsibility for Race Relations Problems

Question 35. Use this card to tell me how you feel about who is to blame for the problems that Negroes (blacks) and whites are having with each other in this country: just the whites who are to blame, or just the Negroes (blacks) or what?

	Negro		White	
Just the whites	12%	} 42%	1%	} 9%
Mostly whites	30		8	
Half and half	48		54	
Mostly Negroes	1	} 1	28	} 31
Just the Negroes	*		3	
No opinion	9		6	

Skin Color

Question 42. When it comes to getting what he wants out of life, do you think it is easier for a Negro if he has darker skin or lighter skin or doesn't it make any difference?

	Negro	White
Darker	2%	2%
Lighter	15	27
Depends	7	2
Makes no difference	67	63
Other	1	1
No opinion	8	5

Perceptions of White Attitudes toward Negroes

Question 20. Do you think that most whites in this country are sympathetic to or are not sympathetic to the problems of Negroes (blacks)?

	Negro	White
Yes, whites are sympathetic	28%	51%
No, whites are not sympathetic	59	38
No opinion	13	11

†These bases are smaller than the full sample because a revised wording was wired to interviewers after the interviewing started and some respondents had already been interviewed with the original question wording.

Question 21. Do you think that most whites in this country do or do not want complete equality between the races?

	Negro	White
Whites do want equality	19%	34%
Whites do not want equality	67	54
No opinion	14	12

Question 22. Please take a guess on this one: how long do you think it will be before there is complete equality between Negroes (blacks) and whites in this country?

Under 10 years	15%	11%
10 to 20 years	25	15
21 to 30 years	9	11
31 to 50 years	5	8
51 to 100 years	4	9
Over 100 years	5	5
Never	21	28
Already in equality	0	1
No opinion	16	12

Assessment of Negro in American History

Question 36. Would you say that Negroes (blacks) have played an important part or not a very important part in the history of this country?

	Negro	White
Important	80%	52%
Not important	5	32
No opinion	15	16

Question 43. Do you think that Negroes (blacks) should be taught subjects in school that add to their feeling of pride in being Negro (black) or would it be better if the schools did not try to increase this feeling of pride?

	Negro	White
Should be taught subjects that add to feeling of pride	86%	56%
Should not be taught such subjects	7	29
Other	1	6
No opinion	6	9

Analysis by Subgroups of Whites

The tables which follow reflect patterns found among whites with different characteristics. Three specific race-oriented questions are utilized, and while the differences within a given category are not always statistically meaningful, the direction of response is indicated over the three questions.

Whites	Percentage base	White babies are smarter (Q. 16)	
		Agree	Disagree
Total	587	14%	58%
18–29	142	6	76
30–49	217	10	67
50 and over	224	23	39
Not high school graduate	228	22	46
High school graduate	350	10	65
South	148	24	39
Non-South	439	10	65

Whites	Negroes not as civilized (Q. 18)		Negroes have not progressed because— (Q. 2)	
	Agree	Disagree	Discrimination	Not Worked Hard Enough
Total	43%	48%	15%	49%
18–29	37	60	25	45
30–49	38	52	14	49
50 and over	50	38	11	51
Not high school graduate	50	41	14	55
High school graduate	37	53	16	44
South	63	24	6	62
Non-South	35	57	19	44

The percentages for each question do not add across to 100 because the "No opinion" category has been left out.

NEGRO WANTS AND NEEDS. PROTEST AND ITS CONSEQUENCES

Degree of Personal Satisfaction in Four Key Areas

Question 1. I would like to ask you if you are satisfied or dissatisfied with some things in your life. For example, would you say you are satisfied or dissatisfied with the kind of education that your children are getting? (For each item below ask "Would you say you are satisfied or dissatisfied with . . . ")

	Satisfied		Dissatisfied		No opinion	
	Negro	White	Negro	White	Negro	White
Kind of education children are getting	42%	59%	29%	14%	29%	27%
Your family income	43	67	50	30	7	3
The kind of work you have to do on your job	50	72	20	7	30	21
The neighborhood you live in	70	87	25	10	5	3

Questions 38, 39. Which of the things on this list would you be in favor of? Choose as many as you wish and just read me the numbers.
Which of the items on this list, if any, are not such good ideas? Choose as many as you wish. Just read me the numbers.

	In favor of		Object to	
	Negro	White	Negro	White
More government job training programs for Negroes	89%	52%	1%	16%
Improving schools and teaching in Negro areas	79	71	2	4
More low-cost housing for Negroes	79	37	5	25
More effort by Negroes to help themselves	78	85	1	*
Better police protection for Negro neighborhoods	78	33	3	16
More effort by Negroes to participate in government	77	41	1	12
A guaranteed minimum family income	77	20	5	50
More attention by local government to solve Negro problems	74	51	2	10
Stronger enforcement of present antidiscrimination laws	65	31	4	19
Busing Negro students to better schools	62	18	17	40
Birth control clinics for Negroes	51	58	25	10
Housing for Negro families in present all-white neighborhoods	49	14	24	48
Black control of black communities	22	26	51	26
Give Negroes preference over whites in jobs	18	*	54	77
Whole new communities built just for Negroes	17	21	59	42
No choice made	2	3	10	4
No answer	1	*	5	1

Question 40. Some people feel that the best way to solve the race problem would be for the Negroes (blacks) to have a completely separate country of their own, made up of some of the states in the United States. If this were possible, do you think it would be a good idea or not a good idea?

	Negro	White
Good idea	3%	23%
Not a good idea	87	69
Depends	1	2
Other	1	1
No opinion	8	5

Question 41. How about if Negroes had a completely separate country of their own some place away from the United States? If this were possible, do you think it would be a good idea or not a good idea?

Good idea	5%	33%
Not a good idea	84	56
Depends	1	2
Other	1	2
No opinion	9	7

How Negroes Are Covered by the Media

Question 13. Now, let's talk about the amount of attention and the kind of attention that newspapers, radio, and television give to the race relations problems. First, do you think that they give too much attention or not enough attention to Negro (black) activities?

	Negro	White
Too much attention	10%	64%
About right amount	28	21
Not enough	46	8
Other answer	2	2
No opinion	14	5

Question 14. Do you feel that newspapers and television report the Negro (black) story accurately and fairly, or not?

	Negro	White
Yes, fairly	29%	47%
No, not fairly	52	34
Other answer	3	5
No opinion	16	14

Awareness of and Support for Negro Leadership

Questions 8, 9, 10, 11. Please read over this list of people and tell me which of them you have heard about or read about. Be careful, these are not all real people. Which one or two people on this list seem to feel the way that you yourself feel about things? Which of these people do you disagree with most? Which, if any of these, is a leader to whom you would give active support?

	Heard about		Feel same way		Disagree with		Would give active support	
	Negro	White	Negro	White	Negro	White	Negro	White
Ralph Abernathy	83%	76%	53%	13%	4%	7%	49%	13%
Stokely Carmichael	76	84	6	1	38	44	4	1
H. Rap Brown	72	75	5	*	35	44	2	*
Roy Wilkins	67	42	25	8	4	1	16	5
Elijah Muhammad	57	39	2	1	16	6	3	1
Carl Stokes	48	41	12	5	2	2	11	4
Whitney Young	46	18	10	2	1	*	10	2
Edward Brooke	35	30	6	13	1	*	6	12
Floyd McKissick	34	19	4	1	2	1	3	1
Bayard Rustin	11	8	1	1	1	*	1	1
Ron Karenga	4	4	1	0	0	1	1	0
Perry Wolff	4	2	*	0	*	0	*	0
All of these	1	*	1	0	*	8	1	0
None of these	4	7	2	38	9	6	3	44
No opinion	2	1	19	31	23	22	18	25

Attitudes toward Forms of Protest Activity

Question 26. Now let's turn to some of the things that have been going on in this country lately. There have been many types of action aimed at the problem of equal rights for Negroes (blacks)—both whites and Negroes (blacks) have participated in these actions. As I read some of these actions to you, tell me if you think they are good ways or not good ways for people to use to get what they want.

	Good way		Not good way		No opinion	
	Negro	White	Negro	White	Negro	White
Holding meetings	89%	88%	4%	10%	7%	2%
Peaceful demonstrations	68	32	22	64	10	4
Boycotting stores	71	29	19	66	10	5
Picketing stores and businesses	59	17	30	78	11	5
Demonstrations that might lead to violence	6	2	86	97	8	1

Question 27. I am going to read the list again. This time tell me if you would or would not do each of these things for a cause that you thought was very important.

	Would do		Would not do		No opinion	
	Negro	White	Negro	White	Negro	White
Going to meetings	86%	78%	9%	21%	5%	1%
Peaceful demonstrations	63	22	27	76	10	2
Boycotting stores	65	23	27	74	9	2
Picketing stores or businesses	48	8	42	89	9	2
Demonstrations that might lead to violence	3	1	88	98	8	1

Question 28. If you were a Negro, and you thought that rioting was a way to help get action on the Negro's problems, do you think you probably would or probably would not join in a riot or violent demonstration? (Asked of whites only.)

Probably would	15%
Probably would not	76
Other answer	2
No opinion	7

Causal Factors Related to Violence

Question 29. I'm going to read you some possible causes of the riots in the cities. Please tell me which things, in your opinion, had a lot to do with causing the riots, which had something to do with causing the riots but not a lot, and which had nothing to do with the riots.

	White			
	A Lot	Some- thing	Nothing	No opinion
Overcrowding in Negro areas	40%	40%	16%	4%
Mostly young kids looking for excitement	44	41	10	5
A way for Negroes to help get equal rights for themselves	30	38	26	6
Part of a nationwide Communist plan to make trouble	35	30	24	11
A way for Negroes to get back at some businessmen who cheat them	11	38	39	12
A way for Negroes to steal things and not get caught	29	36	27	8
A Negro rebellion against the way they are being treated	39	41	14	6
A way for the black people to take over the cities	21	28	42	9

	Negro			
	A Lot	Some- thing	Nothing	No opinion
Overcrowding in Negro areas	45%	28%	17%	10%
Mostly young kids looking for excitement	24	43	23	10
A way for Negroes to help get equal rights for themselves	31	30	28	11
Part of a nationwide Communist plan to make trouble	4	12	57	27
A way for Negroes to get back at some businessmen who cheat them	22	33	31	14
A way for Negroes to steal things and not get caught	7	18	61	14
A Negro rebellion against the way they are being treated	56	28	8	8
A way for the black people to take over the cities	3	6	75	16

How Best to Handle Riots Once They Start

Question 30. We would like your opinion on what should be done after a riot starts. Is this a good idea or not a good idea: for the police to warn the rioters and then shoot one or two as an example to the rest?

	Good idea		Not a good idea		No opinion	
	Negro	White	Negro	White	Negro	White
Police warn, then shoot one or two as examples	7%	35%	86%	59%	7%	6%

cont.

	Good idea		Not a good idea		No opinion	
	Negro	White	Negro	White	Negro	White
Police should not use guns, but use other means to stop the riot	79%	54%	14%	39%	7%	7%
Let the riot continue, just keep it from getting bigger	14	8	74	88	12	4
Police should arrest riot leaders and instigators	70	91	17	6	13	3
Arrest those who are looting or burning	88	96	5	1	7	3
Arrest everybody	9	30	80	64	11	6

Other Violence Related Issues

Question 31. In handling riots, do you think the police should be tougher than they have been, or should they be easier than they have been, or what?

	Negro	White
Should be tougher	17%	70%
Should go easier	45	5
They are about right	20	16
No opinion	18	9

Question 32. In general, what do you think of the treatment of Negroes (blacks) by the police? Have the police been too brutal, or too soft, or have they been generally fair?

Brutal	59%	6%
Soft	2	27
Fair	24	58
No opinion	15	9

Question 33. Do you think that people like yourself have to be prepared to defend their homes against crime and violence, or can the police take care of that?

Defend homes	65%	52%
Leave to police	23	40
Other	3	3
No opinion	9	5

Question 34. A last question about the riots. Do you think there is a good chance or not a very good chance that there will be a riot around here in the next few months?

Good chance	19%	26%
Not good chance	44	63
Don't know	36	11
No answer	1	*

Question 50. Do you happen to know of anyone who bought a gun within the past year or two in order to defend his own house and himself?

Yes	7%	12%
No	88	86
Not sure, no answer	5	2

Question 51. Do you happen to own a gun?

	Negro	White
Yes	24%	34%
No	70	65
No answer	6	1

Question 52. Does anyone in this household own a gun? †

	70%	65%
Yes	7	12
No	57	47
No answer	6	6

Questions Reflecting a Consistency of Attitudes Related to Age, Education and Place of Residence

Question 41.

| | A separate Negro country ||
Whites	Good idea	Not a good idea
Total	33%	56%
18–29	28	66
30–49	28	58
50 and over	41	47
Not high school graduate	43	40
High school graduate	27	66
South	51	36
Non-South	27	63

Question 32.

| | Treatment of Negroes by police ||
Whites	Too brutal	Too soft
Total	6%	27%
18–29	11	21
30–49	7	29
50 and over	3	29
Not high school graduate	4	32
High school graduate	7	25
South	2	37
Non-South	8	24

Question 30. What should be done after riot starts?

Whites	Warn, then shoot	Stop riot, but don't use guns
Total	35%	54%
18–29	29	63
30–49	33	47
50 and over	40	54
Not high school graduate	40	49

cont.

†Asked of people who answered "no" on preceding question.

Whites	Warn, then shoot	Stop riot, but don't use guns
High school graduate	31%	56%
South	47	41
Non-South	30	58

RESPONDENT CHARACTERISTICS

	Negro	White
Percentage base	478	587

How many different people in this household have a job where they work for pay?

	Negro	White
1	48%	50%
2	23	27
3	5	5
4	1	1
5 or more	1	*
No one working	18	16
No answer	4	1

Which member of the household gives the most money to running the house?

Female head	28%	14%
Male head	56	70
Other	7	7
No answer	9	9

What kind of work does the chief wage earner in this household do?

Service worker	42%	8%
Operator	10	13
Craftsman	7	18
Sales worker	1	7
Clerical	2	9
Manager	1	7
Small business owner	2	5
Professional	6	11
Other	24	21
No answer	5	1

In which age group do you fall?

18–20	5%	4%
21–29	17	20
30–39	21	19
40–49	18	18
50–59	13	18
60 and over	24	21
No answer	2	*

What was the last grade you completed in school?

8th grade or less	37%	21%
Some high school but did not graduate	27	18

cont.

	Negro	White
Graduated from high school	18%	28%
Some college but did not graduate	8	13
Graduated from college	4	12
Vocational, trade, or business school		
after high school	3	6
No answer	3	2

COMMENT SUMMARY ON QUESTION 37

The following is a representative sample of answers to the question:

Would you say that Negroes (blacks) have played an important part or not a very important part in the history of this country? Why do you feel that way?

Negroes Who Think Negroes Have Played an Important Part in the History of This Country

"I fought in Korea, Germany and the Philippines, and I think when a Negro gives up his life for this country he should be a part of the history."

"Our Negro leaders, Dr. King and Elijah Mohammad have contributed a lot."

"There are great Negroes who are outstanding: Carver, Washington, and King."

"Before there were machines, the Negro had to do the work that made the country rich."

"I think they have played an important part but have received no credit for it. In my opinion, if a Negro has the ability, the white man will pull him down. A Negro would be more decent than a white man, more fair because he would realize that he isn't the only one that has to live."

"We have cooperated in everything, but we have benefited nothing—except a lot of promises. A lot of Negroes looked up to Martin Luther King. There are so many Negroes in Vietnam, dying, and I don't know what they are fighting for. So many of them are right on the front line."

"They were the ones who did the work down South, in the fields for the white man. That was important—doing the work."

"I go back to the time . . . say, here in Boston . . . a colored man played a part in the Tea Party. In the 92nd and 125th Divisions overseas, there were a lot of Negroes. The Negroes have played their part."

"We've made many contributions but somehow we were just left out of the history books."

"The Negro's labor helped to build this country to where it is now. We have great Negro scientists in this country. Other professional Negroes have played a great part in the success of this country. Negroes always defended this country and still defend it, keeping it a free country for all mankind and for equality."

Whites Who Think Negroes Have Played an Important Part in the History of This Country.

"Well, they are willing to fight for the country. There are probably other things, but I can't think of any right now."

"They were slaves who helped make the South. They are an important part now —about dividing the nation, it looks like."

"The South would have starved if it hadn't been worked by Negroes in the fields and generally around the plantations. Some have risen to great prominence."

"They've been in all the wars we've been in, have volunteered and have been drafted. Booker T. Washington's importance to Negro education (Tuskegee Institute) is historical. Their work has always been slighted. Now the Supreme Court judges and Senators are doing something about it."

"They are as good as anyone else is, and all people contribute to our country just by being a part of it."

"They have contributed to the culture of this country. They have contributed to getting work done. They have helped in homes, raised our children and many other things that wouldn't have gotten done. Early life in the South wouldn't have flourished as fast without them."

"To a certain extent they have been important because they were a source of cheap labor, years ago. They helped our country to grow and develop. But, of course, Negroes didn't help as much as the rest of the people."

"We gave them everything they have today. They always got everything for nothing; now they expect it."

"They have served in four wars. Sports is a big thing in the U.S. We have good athletes that are Negro."

"I've read certain things. You study history. If we didn't have Negroes to help with the labor, business wouldn't be where it is today. I can't remember names. We have had Negro inventors, and so on. Secretaries. It's like an office—without the secretaries the business wouldn't run."

Negroes Who Do Not Think Negroes Have Played an Important Part in the History of This Country

"The part they have played is not necessarily important. The Negro has helped shape the country as it is in the form of cheap labor down South. As far as leadership, he hasn't had the opportunity."

Whites Who Do Not Think Negroes Have Played an Important Part in the History of This Country

"I suppose the opportunity wasn't as great for them to contribute anything. There just aren't any outstanding Negroes in our history that I know of."

"Their make-up isn't among the most ambitious. They don't have leadership personalities or qualifications. They don't hold enough respect to be leaders."

"Was there ever a Negro President? All you hear about is *Uncle Tom's Cabin* and *Black Sambo* and those kinds of things. They are just here and we're stuck with them. They don't do much of anything."

"Except for the war in Vietnam they haven't done anything. They didn't do anything in World War I and World War II. I think if they took the Negro out of Vietnam, they'd end the war sooner. They need someone to move them all the time and they only cost the government a lot of money. It takes six Negroes to do one white man's job."

"I think so mainly because in all my history reading at school I heard of almost no part the Negro did play except for precipitating the Civil War. According to what history has to say, they didn't do that much in such things as helping to develop the West and other new territories."

"I have had contact with some who steal. As a result, I feel that since they cannot be trusted, they cannot play a prominent part in making worthwhile decisions."

"For the last few years they have tried to destroy what our country has done. Certainly they did not play an important part in building it."

"Negroes weren't here for a long time and have been backward, not smart enough to do anything important."

"They haven't made an important contribution because of their suppression."

COMMENT SUMMARY ON QUESTION 15

The following is a representative sample of answers to the question:

What are you thinking about when you say the newspapers and television are *not fair* in reporting the Negro story accurately?

Negroes

"Too much was said about the riots and Negro crimes—they are overdramatized."

"The war has been overdramatized. Too much emphasis has been put on the black man in Vietnam."

"News as a whole is what I think about. Any ugly thing that can paint the Negro as a bad character is there."

"There is the Poor People's March. Rape cases."

"They never show how it really happened on TV or in the newspapers."

"Sometimes a policeman starts beating a Negro who isn't doing a thing but standing there, looking. The paper doesn't even say anything about that and they don't show much of it on TV."

"They don't tell the cause of the trouble; sometimes, only that there was trouble."

"They should show some Negro homes under good circumstances sometimes. We do have some intelligent Negroes."

"They never said enough about the guy who killed Martin Luther King. They only showed the picture of the guy they think did it."

Whites

"They are white and they can't report the Negro story accurately. They are giving a one-sided opinion. They may not even mean to be that way, but I think only a colored person could report it as it really is."

"They told a lot of lies, and things that were not even close to the truth. I was at Orangeburg, South Carolina and saw what went on. They reported that students were non-violent and didn't use firearms. I know that wasn't true. The students also threw things at the homes of innocent people."

"I think overemphasis on what the Negroes consider inadequacies is the worst thing. It encourages rebellion, and gives them the attention they are looking for."

"I believe the TV or newspapers blow these race riots and demonstrations out of proportion for the sake of publicity or big newscasts. The company I worked for was United Press."

"All I can say is that they report the misdeeds of the colored people and do not do the same for the low-grade white people."

"The Negroes could all have a good job if they wanted it. All they want is welfare."

"They don't have enough coverage of racial problems. It is too limited. The riots and protests are reported, but only the violent things—never the full story."

"They don't put the real truth in everything. They always favor the Negroes when reporting the news."

"All they do is show the really bad stuff. When there was a riot in Denver, they didn't even publicize it and rioting wasn't tried again."

Women's Lib

"Are Little Girls Being Harmed by 'Sesame Street'?" demanded the headline in the Sunday section of the *New York Times.* The headline style was, for the *Times,* surprising in itself; but the very notion that "Sesame Street," the darling of the critics, the educators, and the right-thinking, could be dangerous to anyone, let alone the very tots it was designed to educate, was outright astonishing.

Yet there was Mrs. (or more properly Ms.) Jane Bergman, the mother of a four-year-old viewer, accusing the program and its producers of "tokenism," of limiting the number of female characters, of constricting and typecasting them, of inculcating and perpetuating "sexist stereotypes" among its eager young viewers. "As a feminist," Ms. Bergman wrote, "I am engaged in an effort to make our home a place where sexist stereotypes will not be perpetuated, where our children can feel free to learn about becoming not agressively 'masculine' or passively 'feminine' as defined by a hideous cultural stereotype, but human. For my husband and me, it is very much an ongoing struggle with our own conditioning, and we are trying, always, to make whole people out of the male and female puppets we once felt ourselves to be. For our daughter, we want a life truly full of the joy of knowing herself to be *real.* We want her to have a continuing sense of the options involved in self-definition." "Sesame Street," she concluded, was negating these efforts.

If the article left some angry and some simply amused, it nevertheless appeared to be totally appropriate to its place on the television page of the *Times'* Sunday entertainment section. Feminist literature and protest have become acceptable commodities in the mass media; indeed, the feminist movement, or Women's Liberation, as it has come to be known, is perhaps the very first large-scale social movement to have achieved its success through the use of mass media.

Consider for a moment the speed with which Women's Liberation has established itself throughout the country as an acceptable subject. Had Ms. Bergman written her article five years ago, the responsible editor at the *Times* would have shaken his head in utter mystification, wondering what in the world it was she was complaining about. Yet in the very short period of four or five years, the outlines of a complex new approach to the human condition are generally recognized (if not necessarily understood or accepted) by the lay public, and its proponents have had wide access to the mass media—to the public consciousness—to promote their theories.

The phenomenon is truly remarkable, particularly if one regards Women's Liberation as a radical movement. No other radical political or social movement has been able to gain acceptance by what we call the communications establishment, which is another way of saying access to the public consciousness, so rapidly or readily. Nor has any other movement been so spectacularly successful in creating a recognition of (if not necessarily agreement with) its particular set of credos and philosophies in so short a time.

There are probably two reasons for this spectacular success. One lies with the ability of the feminists to use the mass media more skillfully than any other comparable movement in the past. Many of the leaders of the movement are of the media themselves—they are sophisticated in the ways of access. A "raid" to "liberate" a heretofore men-only bar is an obvious candidate for coverage by television and the newspapers, especially when the organizers know exactly how to arrange for coverage. So is a sit-in at a national news magazine, or a nude swim-in at a society party. The use of forceful, uncompromising spokeswomen on television panels, the creation of striking catchwords (sexism, male chauvinism), even the more esoteric (and erotic) forays into subjects like the advantages of the clitoral orgasm, have all combined into an enormously successful mass assault on public consciousness.

The second, more durable reason, is that for all of the feminists' semantic excesses, there are fundamental inequities in the social structure which the public has come to regard as unjust. If some of the sexual, psychological, and cultural theories of the feminists are beyond the ability or willingness of the general public to accept, their basic complaints about inequalities in the economic and social scheme of things find wide agreement.

If many of the feminist solutions seem unacceptable, the problems for which the solutions are formulated are recognized as legitimate and serious ones. The complaints about unequal opportunity in training, occupations, and compensation strike a sympathetic chord among a majority of people. Their complaints about the traditional marital relationships, the division of labor and responsibilities outside and in the home, strike notes of unease if not agreement among both women and men. At a time when it has become increasingly difficult for most individuals to define their own aspirations, it is not surprising that questions about the role of women in society and in the family should be greeted as legitimate areas of inquiry.

So, in the curious way that so many social movements have registered themselves on the public consciousness and conscience, Women's Liberation has found an audience and some acceptance through a combination of the outlandish and the mundane. Although the tactics and the techniques have tended toward the more spectacular, their real effect has been to focus attention on the more universal and basic imbalances in the family/societal roles of women.

This can help to explain what would appear to be a basic discrepancy in the findings of the CBS News Poll on Women's Lib. Although a majority of the public (55%) disapproves of the methods of Women's Lib, and a greater number (63%) claim they do not take Women's Lib seriously, an equal number (58%) believe that the movement will cause real changes in society in the next ten years.

What those changes will be, however, is another question. For the public, at least as reflected in this survey, is open-handed and liberal in the abstract but holds tenaciously to its traditional values in the specific. A majority favored an Equal Rights Amendment to the Constitution. A majority would encourage a daughter who wants a full-time career, even after marriage. In terms of specific occupations, on the other hand, the public tended to place its trust overwhelmingly in male doctors, lawyers, and accountants.

Similarly, a majority held for equal pay and equal consideration for promotion for women, while the public split nearly evenly on the question of preferential hiring for women. By two to one, it agreed with the statement that "an employer is better off to hire a man instead of a woman because a woman will quit if she gets married." The public also split evenly on whether women in business can hold up under pressure as well as men. Even on the question of day care centers for working women, while the public favored such centers by a three-to-one margin, a majority felt such centers should be financed by the working women themselves, in preference to financing through taxes or employers.

In general, the survey results indicate a climate of sympathy for some of the more realistic objectives of Women's Lib, but some difficulty in overcoming long-held values. The public showed less sympathy for the organizational and tactical aspects of Women's Lib, but recognized their inevitable impact.

And last but hardly least, the survey results indicate that the segment of the public most hostile to the movement and to its complaints and objectives is—that's right—women. Perversity, is thy name still woman?

BACKGROUND AND METHODOLOGY

The national study was conducted by telephone September 8-10, 1970, with a random sample of 1,312 people, 18 years or older. To make the questions as sensitive and pertinent as possible, the CBS News Poll staff spent over two months in background research on Women's Liberation.

To supplement personal interviews with women in feminist groups, and with sociologists, we conducted in-depth interviews with five separate groups of six to eight women each. Each session lasted two to three hours. The groups were composed of suburban housewives, young professionals, older marrieds, and successful businesswomen. Later, the tape recordings from these interviews were analyzed for several days to see if we could determine what the women's answers meant and the reasons underlying these answers.

Findings from the depth interviews and the background research were incorporated into a small-scale pre-test of 144 men and women in five areas of the country about one week prior to the actual study. The pre-test results were used to shape the final questionnaire. The findings in this report are based on a random sample of 1,312 people in 105 areas of the country. The areas, telephone numbers, and respondents within each household all were chosen randomly. The sample results were adjusted statistically (weighted) to give a representative cross section of the American public.

SUMMARY OF FINDINGS

The Impact of Women's Liberation*

One of the major interests of the study was to determine the degree to which people favor equal rights for women; how many know about Women's Liberation; whether they know people in the movement or, in the case of women, would join the movement; how they feel about Women's Liberation; and their image of women involved in the movement. Below are some brief highlights of the findings.

1. One of the goals of some Women's Liberation groups is Congressional passage of the "Equal Rights" Amendment guaranteeing women equal rights with men. A majority of people (56%) support the amendment, but men are surprisingly more likely than women to support it.

2. About four out of every five people (78%) has "heard or read" about Women's Liberation, meaning that still today one-fifth of the public does not know about Women's Liberation.

3. Of those who know about Women's Liberation, people are evenly divided in terms of their sympathy with the goals of Women's Liberation (47% for and 46% against), and men are more likely to say they are sympathetic toward the movement than are women.

4. A majority of people (55%) oppose the tactics of Women's Liberation groups. Again, women are more likely than men to disapprove of the tactics of the feminist groups.

5. An overwhelming number of people, three out of every four (75%), feel that a woman individually can achieve the goals of Women's Liberation without having to join a fem-lib group.

6. Nearly seven out of ten people (68%) do not take the Women's Liberation movement "seriously"; women are more likely than men to say the movement is not serious.

7. Despite the feeling that the movement is not really serious, a substantial majority of people (58%)—in this case women more often than men—feel that Women's Liberation will make "real changes" in society within the next ten years.

*All findings in this section, specifically about Women's Liberation, are based on the 78% of the people who have heard or read about the movement. Findings in the following two sections are for all 1,312 respondents.

8. Only a handful (8%) of both men and women say they personally know someone who belongs to a fem-lib group. Altogether, more than nine-tenths of the public (92%) do not know anyone connected with Women's Liberation.

9. Less than one percent (a total of four women) of the women interviewed said that they presently are members of Women's Liberation groups. Four out of every five women (80%) said they would not join such groups.

10. A majority of both men and women (from 52% to 68%) disagree with negative statements about women involved in Women's Liberation—that they are overly masculine, maladjusted, or man-haters.

Women—The Family and the Career

One of the major complaints of fem-lib groups is that women are so restricted by housework and child-rearing that they are denied the freedom, the right, or the encouragement to earn a living. Thus, another area of interest in the study was to determine whether women would like jobs outside the home, whether they would encourage their daughters to have careers, how they view the working woman as a mother, and whether they would approve of child-care centers for working mothers.

1. Nearly one-half (48%) of the women interviewed already have some kind of part-time or full-time job outside the home. The jobs were not distinguished, however, in terms of continuity, hours worked, or wages.

2. Of the women who do not have part-time or full-time jobs outside the home, two-thirds do not want jobs.

3. About two-thirds (64%) of both men and women would encourage their daughter to have a full-time career after marriage.

4. Three-tenths (30%) of both men and women say that having a full-time job outside the home interferes "very much" with the wife's responsibilities at home. The majority of people (56%) say a wife's full-time job interferes "a little" or "somewhat" with her home life, and about one-tenth say a wife's job doesn't interfere at all.

5. If both a husband and wife have full-time jobs, a majority of people (52%) feel that the husband should do at least "some" of the housework, but men are much more likely than women to say that the husband should do "as much" of the cooking, cleaning, and child-caring as the wife.

6. Just about one-half (48%) of the people say that working women make worse mothers than women who don't work outside the home.

7. About three out of four people (74%)—women much more so than men—would favor setting up child-care centers to accommodate women who want to work during the day.

8. About one-half (53%) say that, if child-care centers were established in their area, the centers should be financed by the working mothers themselves. Another one-fourth (24%) feel the centers should be supported by the companies that employ the women.

Employment Opportunities for Women

We know that most of the women who work do so because of economic necessity. The survey indicates that most of the women who do not work presently do not want to work outside the home. A major objective of Women's Liberation is to achieve equal employment opportunities and "equal pay for equal work." In this section of the study, we tried to find out something about the stereotypes of women in occupations that would serve to lessen their chances for employment. We asked about people's trust in women in certain occupations, whether they felt men should have preference over women in hiring and promotions, and whether they felt women function as well as men in executive positions.

1. If given a choice, about seven out of ten men and women would trust a man more than a woman to be their doctor (68%) or their lawyer (70%). Less than one-tenth would choose a woman in either case.

2. About one-half (53%) would choose a male accountant instead of a woman, but men are much more likely than women to say sex would make no difference in choosing an accountant.

3. Because a man is expected to make a living for his family, a majority of people (52%) would give preference to men over women in hiring for jobs.

4. But anywhere from two-thirds to four-fifths of the people do not think it is necessary to pay men more than women for doing the same work (80%), would not consider men first for promotion (63%), and would not give men preference over women in admitting them to universities and professional schools (68%).

5. In hiring for executive positions, about three out of every five people disagree that an employer is better off to hire a man instead of a woman because women "don't think as logically" (57%) or "can't make big decisions" (59%) as well as men do.

6. The public is evenly split, however, over the question of whether women hold up under work pressure as well as men do. Just about half agree (47%) and half disagree (49%). Men are more likely to say that women don't hold up well under pressure.

7. About three-fifths of all people (61%)—primarily men—agree that an employer is better off hiring a man instead of a woman because "a woman will quit if she gets married."

DIFFERENCES BETWEEN MEN AND WOMEN

A prominent columnist has written that the most infuriating thing to Women's Liberation leaders is that men shrug off Fem-Lib with condescension and patronizing humor. The editors of the national newspapers are laughing at Women's Liberation, says Representative Martha Griffiths (D-Mich),—they're "treating this thing as a joke." Rather, the findings of this national survey suggest that the American male's acceptance of Women's Liberation is more in keeping with what many of the newspaper editorial pages are saying: it is a serious social and political movement that may have a profound effect on this society.

As the data here suggest, men overall are more inclined than women to accept Women's Liberation and seem more willing to relax some of the traditional prescriptions for male and female roles. Naturally, some of this largess may be tongue in cheek, if not just superficial tolerance for a set of issues that have not as yet directly touched the male.

Men are more likely than women to say they favor the "Equal Rights" Amendment. Also, men are more likely than women to say they are sympathetic with the goals of Women's Liberation, that they approve of the methods of the feminists, and that they take the movement seriously. On the other hand, although they typically dismiss the movement as not serious, women are more likely than men to say that Women's Liberation will in fact cause "real changes" in society within the next ten years. In short, although men seem more willing to show a tolerance for the goals and tactics of Women's Liberation, they are less willing to concede that the movement will have any real effects.

Men seem more relaxed than women even in those areas of their lives in which women could be a direct threat to their livelihood. Specifically, men are more likely to say that sex would make no difference and that they would choose equally between a man and a woman when it comes to selecting their doctor, lawyer, or accountant. A sizeable majority of women in each case say they would trust a man before a woman.

Men also are more likely to say that a husband should do as much of the housework—cooking, cleaning, and taking care of the children—as a working wife does. More women tend to be tradition-bound; that is, if they had full-time jobs outside the home, they still wouldn't expect the man to do as much housework as they do, although they would want him to do at least some.

As it seems to prevail in the home, tradition also seems to prevail for women in at least one social area. Women are more likely than men to say that a cocktail lounge should have the right to refuse to serve a woman unescorted by a man.

Even when considering equal occupational and educational opportunities for women, the male characteristically shows less resistance to women's equality than do women. Both sexes feel it is necessary to give preference to men over women in hiring, because the man is expected to earn a living for his family. But, if the woman is employed, neither men or women feel it is necessary to pay a man more for doing the same kind of work. Although both sexes typically would not give preferences to men, women nonetheless are somewhat more likely than men to say that it is necessary to consider men first for promotion and to give preference to men in admitting students to universities and professional schools.

It is only in the area of stereotyped differences between men and women that men are more severe with women than are women themselves. For example, in considering women for executive positions in business, men are somewhat more likely to agree with the negative stereotypes that women "don't think as

logically as men," that women "can't make big decisions as well as men," and
that women "don't hold up under pressure as well as men do." Too, men
are more likely to agree that an employer is better off hiring a man instead of a
woman because a woman "will quit when she gets married."

Other than the kind of ingrained adherence to the stereotypical superiority
of the man over the woman in decision-making and under pressure, men routinely are more willing than women to accept the rationale for women's equality
on the job, in the home, and socially. This was, of course, a general population
survey, and not a study of the men who make the laws in state legislatures or
who control labor unions.

The only time women seem more in accord with the goals of Women's Liberation than men is with their feelings toward the establishment of child day-care
centers for women who want to work. Although large majorities of both sexes
favor the idea, women are more likely to favor establishing child-care centers
than are men. On the other hand, there is essentially no difference between the
feelings of men and women as to whether a wife's full-time job interferes with
her responsibilities at home or whether working mothers make "worse" mothers
than those who don't have jobs outside the home.

With the exception that men are less likely than women to predict that
Women's Liberation will have major effects on society within the next ten
years, the data in this survey nonetheless indicate that the male's reaction to
Women's Liberation is not, as characterized, universally derisive and flip. On
the other hand, the data do indicate that the number of women presumed to be
eager to overthrow the "yoke of male supremacy" is exaggerated.

Many women, it appears, are not willing today—as one career woman put it—
"to lose their femininity for vague promises of equality and self-determination."
With this in mind, let us look now at the kind of woman who opposes Women's
Liberation.

WOMEN AGAINST WOMEN'S LIBERATION

The in-depth interviews with more than 30 women produced a number of
themes. Many women, especially those in professional occupations, uniformly
shrugged off Fem-Lib as a movement of a "bunch of weak sisters" who are
unable and unwilling to cope with the challenges of life individually. Second,
the women—whether housewife or actress—disdained the feminists as "scraggy-
haired freaks who don't speak for us as women." And third, many of the
women—although basically sympathetic with the goals of abortion, equal employment opportunities, equal pay for equal work, child-care centers, and the
like—rejected women's new role as defined by Women's Liberation in favor of
preserving their "femininity" and the notion that they are the center, if not the
"traffic director," of the home.

An abundance of evidence in the depth interviews suggests, then, that there is
a strong core of resentment among women to Women's Liberation as they
understand it. In studying this section, it should be kept in mind that men and
women alike tend to blur the distinction between some of the goals of Women's

Liberation and some of the tactics. They react initially to the popular image of the more radical liberationists they read about or see on television. For the most part, however, the women we interviewed supported many of the goals of the movement.

Data from the depth interviews are only impressionistic. The following findings are for the 563 women in the National Survey who knew about Women's Liberation.

The Housewife

Women who don't work and don't want to work are most likely to resist Women's Liberation. By and large these women classify themselves as house-wives. As compared with women who already have full-time or part-time jobs and women who do not but who would like to work, the housewife:

is less likely to sympathize with the goals of Women's Liberation.

is more likely to disapprove of the methods the feminists use to achieve their goals.

is less likely to take the movement seriously.

is a little less likely to feel that Women's Liberation will cause any real changes in society within the next ten years.

is more likely to say she would not belong to a Women's Liberation group.

is more likely to see women in Fem-Lib as more masculine than feminine.

is more likely to agree that women in Fem-Lib are maladjusted.

Of all the characteristics analyzed, the fact that a woman is not employed and does not want to be employed is the clearest indicator of resistance to Women's Liberation.

Wealthier Women

Another rather clear indicator of which kinds of women are most likely to resist Women's Liberation is the amount of money in the family. Even grouping women broadly as being in families where the total annual income is more or less than $10,000, there are consistent differences between the higher and lower income groups.

Beyond the fact that they are much more likely even to know about Women's Liberation, women in higher-income families are—on almost all measures—less kindly disposed to the movement than are women in lower-income families. The wealthier woman is less likely to sympathize with either Fem-Lib goals or tactics. Although she is more likely to take the movement seriously and feels it will cause real social changes, she is more inclined to feel that a woman could accomplish the same goals of Fem-Lib on her own.

The wealthier woman is a little more likely to know someone in Women's

Liberation, but is less likely to want to join. She also is more likely to disagree that Fem-Lib women are maladjusted.

Older Women

Women between the ages of 18 and 29 years typically are most likely to be receptive to Women's Liberation, and women 50 years old or older typically are least sympathetic. Women in their 30s and 40s usually fall between the youngest and oldest age groups, but women 40 to 49 years old are as likely as the youngest group to say that Women's Liberation will cause real changes in society. And, women 30 to 39 years of age are more likely than any other group to say they would not join a Fem-Lib group.

Generally, however, the older the woman is, the less likely she is to sympathize with the goals of Women's Liberation or the methods used by the feminists. Too, she is less likely to take the movement seriously or to know anyone involved in Women's Liberation. The older woman generally has the most negative stereotypes—i.e., that Fem-Lib women are overly masculine, are maladjusted, and are women who really dislike men.

Married Women and Widows

Unattached women—single, divorced, or separated—characteristically are more favorable toward Women's Liberation than are married women or widows; they are more often sympathetic with the goals and less likely to disapprove of Fem-Lib tactics.

Single women are most likely to know someone involved in Women's Liberation, and to disagree that they are women who really dislike men. Divorced and separated women are most likely to feel a woman could achieve the same goals for herself without joining the movement, to take the movement seriously, and to say they would join a Fem-Lib group if they had a chance to. On the other hand, possibly as a result of frustration with their own circumstances, divorced and separated women are more likely than all other women to say that Women's Liberation will not cause any real changes in society.

On most questions, married women tend to fall between the answers of the (usually younger) unattached women and the widows. For their part, the widows are most likely to have the negative impressions that women in the Fem-Lib movement are masculine, maladjusted, and man-haters.

Better Educated Women

Generally speaking, the higher the woman's educational attainment, the less likely she is to support Women's Liberation. This parallels a finding in the depth interviews that women who see themselves as "already liberated" typically are those with the highest levels of education. Such women felt their individuality and resourcefulness were adequate for the challenges of life, and no group movement would achieve for them what they had "made on their own."

Thus, the higher the woman's education the less likely she is to sympathize with the goals of Women's Liberation and the more likely she is to disapprove of the public tactics of the groups. Too, she is convinced that women can achieve the goals of Fem-Lib on their own without joining a group. These latter two findings are especially true of women with some college training.

The better educated woman is more likely as well to see Women's Liberation as a serious movement, but is less likely than women with less education to feel that the movement will cause any real social changes in the next ten years. Finally, she is more likely to know someone involved in Women's Liberation and is less likely to say she would join a Fem-Lib group if she had a chance to.

One unexpected set of findings was that women with college training are just as likely as women with only a grade school or some high school education to have negative stereotypes of feminists. That is, between the group with the lowest education and those with the highest education, high school graduates are most likely to disagree with the idea that Fem-Lib women are overly masculine, maladjusted, or man-haters.

Other Characteristics

A woman's religion and the region of the country in which she lives have no bearing at all on her feeling about Women's Liberation. Nor does the age of a woman's children or her place of residence—in a city, suburb, or rural area— have much to do with her feelings about Women's Liberation. There are some indications that women in large cities are least likely to be sympathetic to the Fem-Lib movement and most likely to feel a woman could accomplish the same objectives alone, but the findings generally are weak or inconsistent with other measures. There are no firm bases for conclusions.

When analyzed by whether they have children and the children's ages, differences among women's feelings toward Women's Liberation also are tentative. There is some indication that younger mothers with children under six years of age are a little more likely to think that the movement is serious and will change society, and to reject unfavorable stereotypes about the kind of woman involved in Fem-Lib groups. But they are no more likely than other women to sympathize with the movement or to want to join it. They are, moreover, a little more likely than others to disapprove of the feminists' methods, and noticeably more likely to feel that women individually can achieve the goals of the movement for themselves.

In a number of surface respects, it appears that while Women's Liberation is a movement among women, it is viewed by many women as a movement against women.

Although equality is the objective of Women's Liberation, it is the female more often than the male who seems to resist the objective. It is the female outside the movement, more so than the male, who personalizes the implications of liberation and is perplexed. It is the female, more so than the male, who seems uneasy about liberation and fears she may forfeit more than she gains. It is the female, more so than the male, who seems willing to perpetuate the role assigned to her by tradition and culture.

The contradiction is in the fact that men, while more likely to say they take the movement seriously, are less likely than women to feel that Women's

Liberation will produce any major changes in society within the next ten years. Perhaps men are still so remote from Women's Liberation that they can afford for the moment to be more charitable than women themselves in assessing the role of women in society generally.

The following tables summarize the differences in the responses of men and women on all questions in the study of Women's Liberation.

WOMEN'S LIB SURVEY

1. Recently, it was proposed that an "Equal Rights" amendment be added to our Constitution. This amendment would guarantee that women would have all of the rights that men have. Do you favor or oppose adding such an amendment to the Constitution?

	Total Sample	Percent Men	Percent Women
Favor the amendment	56%	66%	47%
Oppose the amendment	37	28	44
No response	7	7	8

2. Who would you trust more to be your doctor, a man or a woman?

	Total Sample	Percent Men	Percent Women
Would choose a male doctor	68%	66%	70%
Would choose a female doctor	8	4	11
Would choose either	23	28	18
No answer	1	2	1

Who would you trust more to be your accountant, a man or a woman?

	Total Sample	Percent Men	Percent Women
Would choose a male accountant	53%	46%	59%
Would choose a female accountant	19	21	17
Would choose either	26	31	21
No answer	3	2	3

Who would you trust more to be your lawyer, a man or a woman?

	Total Sample	Percent Men	Percent Women
Would choose a male lawyer	70%	66%	73%
Would choose a female lawyer	9	7	10
Would choose either	20	26	14
No answer	2	1	2

3. If you had a daughter who wanted a full-time career—even after she was married—would you encourage her, or not?

	Total Sample	Percent Men	Percent Women
Would encourage her	64%	65%	63%
Would not encourage her	31	29	32
No answer	5	5	5

4. Would you favor or oppose setting up child-care centers in your area, that would take care of the children of women who wanted to work during the day?

	Total Sample	Percent Men	Percent Women
Favor child-care centers	74%	68%	78%
Oppose child-care centers	24	29	20
No answer	2	3	2

5. If child-care centers were set up in your area, do you think they should be financed by taxes, by the companies that employ the women, or by the women themselves?

	Total Sample	Percent Men	Percent Women
Financed by taxes	12%	11%	12%
Financed by the companies	24	23	24
Financed by the women who work	53	51	54
Some combination of all three	7	9	6
No answer	5	5	4

6. If both a husband and wife work full-time, do you think that the husband should do as much as the wife does, at least some, or none of the cooking, cleaning, or taking care of the children?

Should do as much	39%	48%	30%
Should do at least some	52	41	61
Should do none	7	8	7
No answer	2	3	2

7. When married women have full-time jobs outside the home, do you think that their work interferes very much, somewhat, a little, or not at all with their responsibilities at home?

Work interferes very much	30%	33%	27%
Work interferes somewhat	38	35	40
Work interferes a little	18	17	18
No interference at all	10	10	10
No answer	5	6	5

8. Would you say that working women generally seem to make better—or worse mothers—than women who don't work outside the home?

Make better mothers	23%	21%	24%
Make worse mothers	48	50	45
Equally as good mothers	16	16	17
No answer	13	13	13

9. Would you like to have a part-time job outside the home or not?*

Already have a job	—	—	49%
Yes, would like a job	—	—	17
No, would not like a job/Don't know	—	—	33

10. Because the man is expected to make a living for his family:

(A) Do you think it is necessary to give preference to men over women in hiring for jobs?

Yes, would give preference to men	52%	50%	53%
No, would not give preference to men	44	45	42
No answer	5	5	5

(B) Do you think it is necessary to pay a man more than a woman for doing the same kind of work?

Yes, would pay a man more	18%	16%	21%
No, would not pay a man more	80	83	78
No answer	1	1	1

*Asked of women only.

(C) Do you think it is necessary to consider men first for promotion, before women?

	Total Sample	Percent Men	Percent Women
Yes, would consider men first	33%	28%	38%
No, would not consider men first	63	67	60
No answer	4	5	3

(D) Do you think it is necessary to give preference to young men over young women in admitting them to universities and professional schools?

Would give preference to men	28%	25%	31%
Would not give preference to men	68	71	65
No answer	4	4	4

11. In hiring for an executive position in business:

(A) Would you agree or disagree that an employer is better off to hire a man instead of a woman because women usually don't think as logically as men do?

Agree	39%	42%	35%
Disagree	57	53	60
No answer	5	4	5

(B) Would you agree or disagree that an employer is better off to hire a man instead of a woman because women usually can't make big decisions as well as men can?

Agree	37%	40%	34%
Disagree	59	56	63
No answer	4	4	3

(C) Would you agree or disagree that an employer is better off to hire a man instead of a woman because women usually don't hold up under pressure as well as men do?

Agree	47%	51%	43%
Disagree	49	44	53
No answer	4	5	4

(D) Would you agree or disagree that an employer is better off to hire a man instead of a woman because a woman will quit if she gets married?

Agree	61%	67%	56%
Disagree	34	29	39
No answer	5	4	5

12. Here are some different questions . . . do you think that cocktail lounges should have the right to refuse to serve a woman who is not escorted by a man?

Yes, should have the right	31%	25%	35%
No, should not have the right	64	71	59
No answer	5	4	6

13. Have you heard or read anything lately about a movement among women . . . called "Women's Liberation"?

Heard of Women's Liberation	78%	77%	79%
Never heard of Women's Liberation	20	22	19
No answer	1	1	2

Asked Only of Those Who Know of Women's Liberation

(A) Generally, do you sympathize with the overall objectives of Women's Liberation, or not?

	Percent of Those Who Know		
	Total	Men	Women
Sympathize with objectives	47%	55%	41%
Do not sympathize with objectives	46	40	51
No answer	7	5	8

(B) What about their methods, do you approve or disapprove of them? (The methods they use to achieve their goals.)

Approve of methods	35%	42%	29%
Disapprove of methods	55	50	60
No answer	10	8	11

(C) Do you think it is probable, or not . . . that a woman could achieve the same goals of Women's Liberation for herself, without joining the movement?

Can achieve goals by herself	75%	73%	77%
Cannot achieve goals by herself	21	23	19
No answer	4	4	3

(D) Do you, yourself, take the Women's Liberation movement seriously . . . or not?

Believe it is a serious movement	29%	35%	23%
Do not believe it is a serious movement	68	63	73
No answer	3	2	4

(E) Within the next ten years, do you think Women's Liberation will cause any real changes in our society—or not?

Will cause changes	58%	54%	62%
Will not cause changes	36	42	32
No answer	6	4	6

(F) Do you personally know anyone who belongs to a Women's Liberation group?

Yes, know someone	8%	9%	7%
No, do not know anyone	92	91	93

(G) Do you feel that most women involved in Women's Liberation are more masculine than feminine?

Are more masculine than feminine	36%	35%	37%
Are not more masculine than feminine	52	50	53
No answer	12	14	10

(H) Do you feel that most women involved in Women's Liberation are not well-adjusted, emotionally?

Are not well-adjusted	38%	37%	40%
Are well-adjusted	52	52	52
No answer	10	11	8

(I) Do you feel that most women involved in Women's Liberation are women who really dislike men?

| | Percent of Those Who Know | | |
	Total	Men	Women
Are women who dislike men	24%	24%	24%
Are not women who dislike men	68	70	67
No answer	8	6	9

Asked of Women Only

(J) Do you belong to a Women's Liberation group? (IF NO: Would you join such a group, if you had a chance to?)

Yes, belong to a Women's Liberation group	–	–	1%
Yes, would join a Women's Liberation group	–	–	17
No, would not join a Women's Liberation group	–	–	80
No answer	–	–	2

The Generation Gap

If there was a focal point around which the social turbulence of the late sixties converged, it was the young people of the country. The antiwar movement, political radicalism, black militancy, the counterculture, the drug scene, shifting moral values—in all of these social currents, the youth of America seemed to be leading the way.

Campus unrest was at its height, propelled by political radicalism that flailed out at failures of "the system," reaching out to include virtually every aspect of American life among its targets. Campus protest was more than political, in that it reflected a malaise and frustration among the young that extended to basic questions about how life should be lived and for what purpose. Their questions took the form of challenges to traditional American values, to sexual and marital standards, to standards of "success" in one's career, to religion and to authority, and to traditional concepts in interpersonal relationships.

This revolt against tradition was in itself a matter of deep concern to an older generation, but the sense of anger and despair that characterized the revolt was particularly disturbing. What were the kids angry about? The Vietnam war, and their inability to do anything about it, of course. The reaction of authority to student demands and demonstrations. The fact that we live in an imperfect society, with many examples of inequity and injustice.

There were obviously some answers, but there were far more questions. Was this anti-institutional movement confined to college students, or did it extend into the ranks of nonstudents as well? Even among students, was it monolithic, or was there substantial disagreement? Were all "liberal" students revolutionaries, as one might conclude from the turnout at campus demonstrations, or were the radicals a small number who had mobilized support? Were the political aspects of student discontent correlated to the rebellion against cultural and social standards and values?

Equally important, were these changes in student attitudes reflective of a generation gap wider, more scarring and more permanent than any we had known before? The youthful turbulence of the late sixties was too powerful, too extreme, to be dismissed as a modern version of "sowing wild oats."

It was characterized by anger and despair rather than exuberance, by violence rather than prankishness. It represented a depth of feeling unmatched by the superficiality of past generational rebelliousness. In short, it appeared that an intelligent, rather affluent student generation was hurtling toward irreconcilable differences in attitudes and values with adult America.

These were some of the questions that CBS News decided to explore in a series of documentaries, "Generations Apart," broadcast in the spring of 1969. The exploration of generational differences in documentary form would best be served, it was felt, by focusing on individuals rather than through the use of generalizations. So the documentaries took the form of interviews with students and nonstudents and their parents, exploring their differences in attitudes on a variety of subjects, both political and cultural.

At the same time, it was decided that a national study of youth and their parents could be extremely useful to the series. For one thing, it could identify and quantify the various types of youth and their parents, thereby providing answers to some of the questions about the degree and categorization of the youth rebellion. For another, it could permit quantitative comparisons between young people and their parents, overall and by type. And finally, its findings could provide significant guideposts to the editorial thrusts of the series.

Early in 1969, *Fortune* magazine devoted an issue to youth, one of whose highlights was a study of college students conducted by Daniel Yankelovich, Inc. The Yankelovich study covered some of the questions CBS News was asking, and he was thereupon commissioned to conduct a new survey, with added elements—more questions, and a more sophisticated sample, to include nonstudents and parents both of college and noncollege youth. *Fortune* graciously consented to the inclusion of its questions and findings in the wider CBS News study.

The "Generations Apart" study speaks for itself, but in light of subsequent work by Yankelovich it might be well to summarize it briefly here. The survey confirmed a shift of major proportions in youthful attitudes toward societal values—specifically towards sex, drugs, religion, work, patriotism, and authority. It found deep mistrust in the country's social-economic-political institutions. It found a high degree of support among students for political activism.

These traits were found primarily among college students, and at that, only among particular segments of college students. Politically, for example, student radicals were small in number, but because large numbers of "moderate" students shared their frustrations with political and economic institutions, they gave sympathy and support to the extremism of the radicals. One of Yankelovich's major findings, however, was that the differences within the generations seemed wider than those between the generations. Among students, outlook and attitudes ranged from extreme conservatism to extreme liberalism, from firm belief in traditional values to deep mistrust and outright rejection of these values. The distinction between students and nonstudents, as groups, was even sharper, with the working young far more likely to cling to traditional beliefs and to support existing institutions.

Moreover, he found that generation differences between specific youth segments and their respective parental groups were not as great as had been imagined, that youth in particular categories were likely to share a number of their parents' attitudes toward institutions and standards. The tables in the study are formatted to permit this kind of analysis by the reader.

Following the "Generations Apart" study, Yankelovich was commissioned, in 1970 and again in 1971, by the JDR 3rd (John D. Rockefeller 3rd) Fund, to conduct studies of a national sample of college students on many of the same issues covered in the CBS News and *Fortune* studies. As a result, Yankelovich has been able to make comparisons on shifts in attitudes, at least among college students, over a four-year period.

In 1970, he found, political alienation rose to a peak, but in 1971, confirming the casual observations of scores of journalists and others, he found an abrupt shift in the student mood and attitudes. Summarizing it in the published version of his 1971 findings, *The Changing Values on Campus* (New York: Pocket Books, 1972), Yankelovich pointed to an "unlinking of political and cultural attitudes." While noting a continuing upward rise in attitudes challenging traditional ethical, social, and moral behavior, he also found a distinct decline in political activism and involvement. He found more students willing to "work within the system" for change, fewer students willing to support violence as a means toward change, less criticism of political and economic institutions.

He found, as well, that students seemed more content, less angry than in the past. He attributes this, in large part, to an apparent shift in student attitude: they have "sharply divorced their worries about the state of the nation from their own personal fate." By "withdrawing emotional involvement from social and political matters," Yankelovich states, "they have channeled their feelings into their own private lives where they experience more control, less frustration . . . and greater contentment."

Yankelovich also reports greater concern among students about their career objectives and with making money, attributing this trend to the recession and its effect on students and their families during 1971.

Save for these two downward curves, Yankelovich finds that student dissatisfaction with traditional societal and cultural values continues to widen. It is difficult to project into the future, of course, among so volatile an attitudinal group, but it is possible that the events of the late sixties have resulted in a new and permanent outlook among what will surely be the country's leadership elite in the future. We shall simply have to wait and see.

BACKGROUND AND METHODOLOGY

Who are the activists among youth? Are the political radicals also the leaders of the rebellion against traditional values? What kinds of homes do the rebels come from, and is the gap wider between the rebels and their parents or between the nonrebellious youth and their parents? Is this generation gap different in character from a "normal" gap between youth and adult values? Is the gap one of actual differences in values, or only "perceived" differences, or both?

As CBS News began its plans to explore the subject in documentary form, it became apparent that to answer most of the questions, a statistical survey of youth and their parents would be required. To prepare and conduct the study, CBS News selected Daniel Yankelovich, Inc., which months earlier had completed a large-scale study on youth values for *Fortune*. The CBS News Election Unit, which has considerable survey experience, was assigned to supervise the study.

The demands placed on Dr. Yankelovich and his organization were considerable—to select a highly specialized sample segment, to conduct extensive interviews with youth, and then in the case of the college students to contact their parents and question them by telephone, to devise a far-reaching questionnaire, to run detailed tabulations, and to prepare an analysis of the results for CBS News, all in a matter of little more than three months. The Yankelovich organization responded superbly to these deadlines, and CBS News is most grateful for their efforts.

Because the use of survey data on television is at best an uneasy compromise between the demands of the documentary and those of statistics, only a limited amount of the data was used on the broadcast series.

Survey Design

The survey was designed to measure the attitudes, values, and behavior of youth in the age range of 17 through 23. This age group was selected in the belief that public awareness of youth today centers primarily on college age youth, as well as youth immediately preceding and following the college age.

In order to estimate the magnitude of different characteristics in the general population of all youth in this age range, both college and noncollege youth were sampled. For the purpose of analysis the youth sample was divided into those currently enrolled in college and those not enrolled. In addition, youth were also divided into relatively homogeneous groups, discussed in the section "Youth Profiles," for a different analysis.

The concept of a generation gap was viewed as the differences between youth and their parents. For this purpose the parent of the same sex (if available) as the youths selected in a subsample of the youth sample was also interviewed. The generation gap, if any, was viewed as the actual differences in the response of youth and parents about common subjects. In addition an attempt was made to determine perceived differences.

All youth were questioned by personal interview. The parents were interviewed personally when they had the same residence as the youth. When they lived apart the parent was interviewed by telephone. All interviewing took place during March and April 1969.

Sample Design

For the purpose of efficiency, two sampling frames were established. The first was a sample of youth on college campuses, the second, a general household sample. The frames were unduplicated by eliminating from the household frame any college youths living at home.

The college sample was selected in two stages. The first stage consisted of selecting college campuses. All campuses in the country were stratified by geographic region, by public or private type of institution, and by total enrollment over or under 10,000 students. Campuses were selected from each stratum with a probability proportionate to current enrollment. At each of the 30 campuses selected the interviewer was provided with a general procedure to select approximately 33 students from the available listing of students. The interviewer was then told to screen the names selected to determine the age and current enrollment status, and to interview only those students meeting these criteria. Interviews were completed with 723 students.

The noncollege enrolled youth were selected from an area probability sample of the country. Altogether there were 72 segments of approximately 200 housing units each. The sampling procedure was designed to underrepresent rural areas. Rural segments were weighted to account for the difference in the sampling rate. All of the housing units in the 72 segments were canvassed by the interviewers and all youth between the ages of 17 and 23 not currently enrolled in college were interviewed. Interviews were completed with 617 youths.

The parents included in the study were designated by a random selection of one-half of the entire youth sample. Once the parents were selected, an attempt was made to interview the parent of the same sex as the youth interviewed. Of the college youth group, 362 parents were interviewed, and of the noncollege youth group, 301 parents were interviewed.

Tabulation

All tabulations were done with weighted data. The weights were assigned to account for the varying probabilities of selection; there are approximately three times as many noncollege youth in the country as college youth, but there are more college youth in the sample. In order to assure the correct proportions of youth to their representation in the country, it is necessary to inflate the number of noncollege youth to reflect this ratio. Therefore, any sample sizes relating to college youth in the text tables are the actual number of interviews; numbers used to represent noncollege youth have been inflated.

SUMMARY OF FINDINGS

The data in this study can be looked at in two ways—with emphasis on the large majority of youth who retain orthodox and traditional American values, or with emphasis on the minority who are challenging those values. There is no reliable way to state that the rebellious minorities are larger in size than they have ever been in the past. But they *are* large, and they are concentrated in the "youth leadership" communities—the college campuses—where indeed on some issues they actually become majorities.

The findings in the questionnaire sections entitled "Society—Institutions and Restraints" and "Activism and Involvement," dealing with the political and institutional values by which adult America lives, reveal a deep-seated sense of disaffection on the part of the young with these values and institutions. Although, as indicated later in the "Youth Profiles" section of this chapter, "Revolutionaries" and "Radical Reformers" constitute only 11% of all youth and 13% of college students, the quarrel of a significant number of their fellows is not with their objectives so much as with their tactics.

On a wide variety of subjects—war, the draft, civil disobedience, the military, big business, the political parties, the mass media, the distribution of wealth—large minorities of youth (and occasionally, majorities of college youth) are sharply critical of our economic and political systems, the "establishment," and authorities who run them.

Not surprisingly, this disaffection and challenge extends to nonpolitical values as well, to topical subjects such as sex, drugs, dress and grooming, and careers, as well as to traditional values like religion, money, and hard work. Nor is it surprising that with a single exception, the more radical the political values of a youth, the more critical he is of traditional and societal values. The single exception is the noncollege "Radical Reformer," who, while challenging the political institutions, nonetheless clings strongly to traditional American values. The apparent reason is the large number of blacks in the group, who while militant on domestic, political and economic issues, are not challenging other values to the same degree as their white counterparts.

The generation differences are large, not only in political and ideological matters, but in the traditional values as well. They are largest between the radical youth and their parents, smallest between conservative youth and their parents, but they exist and they are significant.

QUESTIONNAIRE AND RESULTS

The following pages contain the questionnaire and results, in percentage form, for all youth and youth by college and noncollege, with comparative tables for all parents interviewed, parents of college students and parents of noncollege youth.

Because most of the interviews of parents of college students had to be accomplished by telephone, the parents were asked fewer questions than the youth. Where the questions were worded differently, both questions are shown.

Because of rounding, the percentages will add vertically on occasion to 101%, and sometimes to 99%. In other cases where the total is less than 99%, the difference is due to "don't know" responses or nonresponses not shown in the tables.

The questions as they appear here have been reordered from the original questionnaire in order to group them by subject matter. Some open-end responses have been omitted.

Traditional Values

1. The following statements represent some traditional American values. Which of them do you *personally believe in* and which do you *not believe in?*

	YOUTH			PARENTS		
	Total Youth	College	Non-college	Total Parents	Parents College Youth	Parents Noncollege Youth

A. Hard work will always pay off

Believe in	74%	56%	79%	83%	76%	85%
Do not believe in	26	43	21	17	24	15

B. Everyone should save as much as he can regularly and not have to lean on family and friends the minute he runs into financial problems

Believe in	86	76	88	96	90	98
Do not believe in	14	24	11	3	10	2

C. Depending on how much strength and character a person has, he can pretty well control what happens to him

Believe in	74	62	77	74	71	75
Do not believe in	26	38	23	24	28	23

D. Belonging to some organized religion is important in a person's life

Believe in	66	42	71	89	81	91
Do not believe in	34	57	28	11	17	9

E. Competition encourages excellence

Believe in	80	72	82	89	84	91
Do not believe in	20	28	18	9	15	7

F. The right to private property is sacred

Believe in	85	75	87	91	83	94
Do not believe in	15	24	12	8	16	5

G. Society needs some legally based authority in order to prevent chaos

Believe in	94	92	94	96	97	96
Do not believe in	6	7	5	3	2	3

H. Compromise is essential for progress

Believe in	87	80	88	84	82	85
Do not believe in	13	19	11	14	17	13

2. Many people feel that we are undergoing a period of rapid social change in this country today, and that people's values are changing at the same time. Which of the following changes would you *welcome*, which would you *reject*, and which would *leave you indifferent?*

A. Less emphasis on money

Would welcome	57%	72%	54%	NOT ASKED OF
Would reject	13	11	13	PARENTS
Leave indifferent	30	17	33	

B. Less emphasis on working hard

Would welcome	30	24	32
Would reject	46	48	45
Leave indifferent	23	28	22

C. More emphasis on law and order

Would welcome	76	57	81
Would reject	10	23	7
Leave indifferent	12	19	11

cont.

	YOUTH			PARENTS		
	Total Youth	College	Non-college	Total Parents	Parents College Youth	Parents Noncollege Youth
D. More emphasis on technological improvement						
Would welcome	62%	56%	63%	NOT ASKED OF		
Would reject	5	10	3	PARENTS		
Leave indifferent	33	33	32			
E. More emphasis on self-expression						
Would welcome	72	84	70			
Would reject	6	3	6			
Leave indifferent	22	13	24			
F. More sexual freedom						
Would welcome	27	43	22			
Would reject	39	24	43			
Leave indifferent	34	33	34			
G. More vigorous protests by blacks and other minority groups						
Would welcome	12	23	9			
Would reject	73	56	77			
Leave indifferent	15	20	14			
H. More acceptance of other people's peculiarities						
Would welcome	64	80	60			
Would reject	8	4	9			
Leave indifferent	28	16	31			
I. More emphasis on friendliness and neighborliness						
Would welcome	93	92	94			
Would reject	1	2	1			
Leave indifferent	5	7	5			
J. More respect for authority						
Would welcome	80	59	86			
Would reject	5	14	3			
Leave indifferent	14	27	11			
K. More emphasis on personal responsibility						
Would welcome	86	84	87			
Would reject	2	2	2			
Leave indifferent	11	14	10			

3. ASKED OF YOUTH: Here are some of the ways others have described how their parents' values and outlook differ from their own. For each of the following statements, tell me whether it is more true of you or your parents.

ASKED OF PARENTS: Here are some of the ways in which other parents have described how their children's values and outlook differ from their own. For each of the following statements, tell me whether you feel it is more true of you or your son/daughter.

A. More likely to accept things as they are						
More true of parents	38%	40%	37%	39%	45%	37%
More true of youth	36	35	37	25	17	27
No difference	26	25	26	35	37	35

cont.

	YOUTH			PARENTS		
	Total Youth	College	Non-college	Total Parents	Parents College Youth	Parents Noncollege Youth
B. More tolerant of other people's views						
More true of parents	24%	11%	28%	37%	32%	38%
More true of youth	49	60	46	22	24	21
No difference	26	29	26	39	43	38
C. More interested in money						
More true of parents	36	44	34	27	34	25
More true of youth	27	17	30	24	21	25
No difference	36	39	36	47	44	49
D. More optimistic about the future						
More true of parents	19	19	19	25	21	26
More true of youth	52	49	52	38	38	38
No difference	29	32	28	36	40	35
E. More fearful of financial insecurity						
More true of parents	44	50	43	53	53	53
More true of youth	28	21	30	14	12	15
No difference	28	28	28	32	35	31
F. More respectful of people in positions of authority						
More true of parents	40	50	37	29	26	30
More true of youth	12	7	14	10	11	10
No difference	47	43	49	60	62	59
G. More likely to do something about what they believe is right						
More true of parents	16	13	17	24	10	28
More true of youth	42	45	42	22	35	19
No difference	41	42	41	53	55	52
H. Have more faith in the democratic process						
More true of parents	39	42	38	32	31	32
More true of youth	13	13	13	9	10	8
No difference	48	45	49	56	58	55
I. More self-centered						
More true of parents	15	12	16	16	18	16
More true of youth	44	53	41	33	36	32
No difference	40	35	42	47	45	48
J. More interested in other people						
More true of parents	14	13	14	24	19	25
More true of youth	40	42	39	26	30	25
No difference	46	44	47	49	51	49
K. More concerned with what is happening to the country						
More true of parents	24	17	26	33	25	36
More true of youth	30	35	29	14	20	12
No difference	45	47	45	52	53	51
L. More honest with themselves						
More true of parents	22	18	23	21	17	23
More true of youth	33	34	32	11	17	9
No difference	45	48	44	66	65	67

4. What role does each of the following values play in your life—that is, as I read off each item, tell me whether it is *very important* to you, *fairly important* to you, or *not very important* to you.

	YOUTH			PARENTS		
	Total Youth	College	Non-college	Total Parents	Parents College Youth	Parents Noncollege Youth
A. Friendship						
Very important	89%	85%	90%	NOT ASKED OF		
Fairly important	10	14	10	PARENTS		
Not very important	1	2	—			
B. Money						
Very important	36	18	40			
Fairly important	53	65	51			
Not very important	11	17	9			
C. Being a leader						
Very important	18	18	18			
Fairly important	40	48	38			
Not very important	42	33	44			
D. Service to others						
Very important	54	51	55			
Fairly important	39	43	38			
Not very important	7	7	7			
E. Doing your own thing						
Very important	61	66	60			
Fairly important	30	27	31			
Not very important	9	7	9			
F. Doing work that is more than just a job						
Very important	71	80	69			
Fairly important	25	17	27			
Not very important	4	2	4			
G. Patriotism						
Very important	55	35	60			
Fairly important	34	42	32			
Not very important	10	23	7			
H. Living a clean, moral life						
Very important	71	45	77			
Fairly important	21	37	17			
Not very important	7	17	5			
I. Education						
Very important	80	80	80			
Fairly important	16	19	15			
Not very important	4	1	4			
J. Privacy						
Very important	71	61	74			
Fairly important	25	34	23			
Not very important	3	4	3			

cont.

	YOUTH			PARENTS		
	Total Youth	College	Non-college	Total Parents	Parents College Youth	Parents Noncollege Youth
K. Changing society						
Very important	29%	33%	29%	NOT ASKED OF		
Fairly important	50	46	51	PARENTS		
Not very important	20	20	20			
L. Love						
Very important	89	85	90			
Fairly important	10	14	9			
Not very important	1	1	1			
M. Religion						
Very important	59	38	64			
Fairly important	25	31	23			
Not very important	16	30	12			

5. What role does religion play in your life? (FREE RESPONSE)

Plays an important role	20%	13%	22%	NOT ASKED OF	
Gives basis for moral code	23	19	24	PARENTS	
I'm an agnostic. Religion plays no role.	10	17	8		
Plays small part	16	15	16		

6. Which of the following statements do you *strongly agree* with, which do you *partially agree* with, and which do you *strongly disagree* with?

A. Most people will go out of their way to help someone else

Strongly agree	14%	6%	16%	NOT ASKED OF	
Partially agree	57	60	56	PARENTS	
Strongly disagree	29	34	28		

B. No sane, normal, decent person could even think of hurting a close friend or relative

Strongly agree	38	18	43
Partially agree	39	45	38
Strongly disagree	23	37	19

C. Anyone who completely trusts anyone else is asking for trouble

Strongly agree	17	15	18
Partially agree	37	43	36
Strongly disagree	46	42	47

D. Most people can be depended on to come through in a pinch

Strongly agree	21	17	22
Partially agree	57	61	55
Strongly disagree	22	22	22

E. Man is basically good, but our society brings out the worst in him

Strongly agree	31	24	33
Partially agree	41	45	40
Strongly disagree	27	30	26

The Generations

7. A. ASKED OF YOUTH: Overall, would you say that differences between your values and those of your parents are *very great, moderate* or *very slight?*

ASKED OF PARENTS: Overall, would you say that differences between your values and those of your son/daughter are *very great, moderate* or *very slight?*

	YOUTH			PARENTS		
	Total Youth	College	Non-college	Total Parents	Parents College Youth	Parents Noncollege Youth
Very great	16%	15%	16%	9%	4%	10%
Moderate	49	55	47	40	42	40
Very slight	35	29	37	51	55	50

B. ASKED OF YOUTH: Would you say that, in general, you want the *same things* for yourself as your parents wanted when they were your own age, or do you want *something different?*

ASKED OF PARENTS: Thinking back to the time when you were your son's/daughter's age, did you want the *same things* out of life that they want now, or were you looking for *something different?*

Same	41	35	43	59	58	59
Different	58	65	57	40	40	40

8. Do you feel that there is a *large* "generation gap" today, that it exists but has been *exaggerated,* or that it *doesn't exist?*

Large generation gap	28%	25%	28%	22%	15%	24%
Exists but exaggerated	67	72	66	70	80	67
No generation gap	4	2	5	6	4	6

9. Which *one* of the following best describes your *present* relationship with your parents?

A. I get along fine with them and enjoy their company	57%	52%	58%	NOT ASKED OF PARENTS
B. I'm fond of them but have trouble communicating with them	31	28	31	
C. I like to go home for a few days, but no longer than that	8	15	6	
D. I do not enjoy spending time with my parents	4	4	4	

10. Which *one* of the following best fits your impressions of your parents' social values?

A. They have strong moral principles and they live by them	65%	64%	65%	NOT ASKED OF PARENTS

cont.

	YOUTH			PARENTS		
	Total Youth	College	Non-college	Total Parents	Parents College Youth	Parents Noncollege Youth
B. They have strong moral principles but they don't always act on them	23%	25%	22%	NOT ASKED OF PARENTS		
C. They usually act out of expediency rather than out of any moral principles	12	11	13			

11. In general, would you say that your son/daughter is *more mature* than you were at his/her age, *about as mature,* or *less mature* than you were?

More mature	NOT ASKED OF	47%	52%	46%
As mature	YOUTH	35	32	35
Less mature		18	17	19

12. In your view, what has your parents' way of life brought them? For example, has it brought them personal fulfillment, material confort, both, or not much of either?

Personal fulfillment	15%	15%	15%	NOT ASKED OF
Material comfort	10	16	9	PARENTS
Both	61	58	61	
Neither	14	10	15	

13. A. ASKED OF YOUTH: Which of the following would describe your parents during your *childhood:* (MORE THAN ONE ANSWER PERMISSIBLE)

Permissive, lenient	39%	43%	38%
Strict, authoritarian	38	31	39
Considered your opinion, gave you a full vote in family matters	37	42	36
Gave you much of r time	53	63	51
Too busy to give much of their time	15	15	15
Old-fashioned in their outlook	33	35	32
Modern, progressive in their outlook	31	37	30
Liberal in their politics	20	27	19
Conservative in their politics	31	49	27

B. ASKED OF PARENTS: When your son/daughter was younger, were you *fairly permissive* with him/her, *fairly strict,* or *somewhere in between?*

| | YOUTH | | | PARENTS | |
	Total Youth	College	Non-college	Total Parents	Parents College Youth	Parents Noncollege Youth
Fairly permissive				12%	15%	12%
Fairly strict				40	30	43
In between				47	55	45

C. ASKED OF PARENTS: Were you able to give him/her a great deal of time and attention, or were you too busy with the day-to-day pressures?

	Total Youth	College	Non-college	Total Parents	Parents College Youth	Parents Noncollege Youth
Gave time and attention				78	77	79
Too busy				19	19	19
Not as much as I would have liked				2	4	1

14. Thinking back to your economic circumstances when you were a child, would you say that you personally felt *very secure* economically, *fairly secure,* or *not very secure?*

	Total Youth	College	Non-college		
Very secure	54%	61%	52%	NOT ASKED OF	
Fairly secure	38	31	39	PARENTS	
Not very secure	8	7	9		

15. What about now—would you say that you feel *very secure* economically, *fairly secure* or *not very secure?*

	Total Youth	College	Non-college		
Very secure	37%	36%	37%	NOT ASKED OF	
Fairly secure	57	54	57	PARENTS	
Not very secure	7	10	6		

16. A. ASKED OF YOUTH: Would you please complete the following sentence for me. The main trouble with the young generation is: (FREE RESPONSE)

	Total Youth	College	Non-college
Immature and naive	21%	25%	20%
Too impatient	13	16	12
Intolerant and close-minded	10	12	10
No respect for authority or parents	10	7	11
Self-centered and lack of responsibility	10	8	11
Doesn't try to communicate with older people	10	11	10
Has too much freedom	9	4	10
Nothing—there is no trouble	9	9	9

B. ASKED OF PARENTS: What is it about the younger generation that bothers you the most? (FREE RESPONSE)

	YOUTH			PARENTS		
	Total Youth	College	Non-college	Total Parents	Parents College Youth	Parents Noncollege Youth
Grooming and appearance				21%	14%	23%
No respect for authority or their elders				20	17	20
Nothing—the majority are good kids				14	16	13
Self-centered and lack of responsibility				11	10	12
Immature and naive				11	11	11
Rebellious—want too much freedom				10	8	10
Use drugs and LSD				11	9	12

17. ASKED ONLY IF ATTENDING COLLEGE: Which of the following two statements comes closer to expressing your own point of view:

For me, college is mainly a practical matter. With a college education I can earn more money, have a more interesting career and enjoy a better position in the society.	11%	53%	—	NOT ASKED OF PARENTS
I'm not really concerned with the practical benefits of college. I suppose I take them for granted. College for me means something more intangible; perhaps the opportunity to change things rather than make out well within the existing system.	9	43		

18. A. ASKED OF YOUTH: Which of the following considerations will have a relatively strong influence on your choice of career:

Your family	35%	31%	36%
The money that you can earn	47	41	49
The prestige or status of the job	21	23	20

cont.

	YOUTH			PARENTS		
	Total Youth	College	Non-college	Total Parents	Parents College Youth	Parents Noncollege Youth
The security of the job	45%	42%	46%			
The ability to express yourself	47	66	43			
The challenge of the job	52	71	47			
The opportunity to make a meaningful contribution	60	76	56			

B. ASKED OF PARENTS: Thinking back to the time when you were your son's/daughter's age, were your economic aspirations *higher, lower,* or *about the same* as your son's/daughter's are now?

Higher				21%	23%	21%
Lower				38	41	37
Same				39	36	40

19. A. Do you have any doubt about being able to make as much money as you may want to, whatever that amount is?

Yes	47%	40%	48%	NOT ASKED OF
No	53	60	52	PARENTS

B. Do you have any doubt about your ability to be successful—as you define success?

Yes	30	33	29
No	70	67	71

20. Many young people today dress and groom themselves quite differently than did young people five years ago. How do you feel about these changes in dress and grooming?

Nothing wrong with them	35%	30%	36%	NOT ASKED OF
It's up to the individual	25	39	21	PARENTS
Dislike long hair and beards	16	7	18	
Dislike mini-skirts	10	3	11	
Dislike the hippie look	9	4	10	
Dislike extremes	9	6	10	
All right if the people are clean	9	13	8	
Change is normal	8	12	7	

Society—Institutions and Restraints

21. A. Which of the following activities do you feel are *morally wrong* from your personal point of view, and which do you feel are *not a moral issue?*

	YOUTH			PARENTS		
	Total Youth	College Youth	Non-college Youth	Total Parents	Parents College Youth	Parents Noncollege Youth
Having an abortion						
Morally wrong	58%	36%	64%	62%	50%	66%
Not a moral issue	40	63	35	36	48	33
Relations between consenting homosexuals						
Morally wrong	66	42	72	75	63	79
Not a moral issue	33	57	27	22	35	19
Pre-marital sexual relations						
Morally wrong	53	34	57	85	74	88
Not a moral issue	46	64	41	14	25	11
Extra-marital sexual relations						
Morally wrong	77	77	77	91	90	92
Not a moral issue	21	22	21	7	9	7

B. Which of these activities do you think your parent (of same sex) would feel are *morally wrong*, and which do you think he would feel are *not a moral issue?*

Having an abortion					
Morally wrong	75	65	78	NOT ASKED OF	
Not a moral issue	19	32	16	PARENTS	
Relations between consenting homosexuals					
Morally wrong	84	74	87		
Not a moral issue	11	23	8		
Pre-marital sexual relations					
Morally wrong	85	80	86		
Not a moral issue	10	17	8		
Extra-marital sexual relations					
Morally wrong	88	91	88		
Not a moral issue	7	6	7		

C. Under which of the following conditions would you approve of abortion:

Recommended by a physician	77	83	76	NOT ASKED OF	
Pregnancy as the result of rape	64	79	60	PARENTS	
Failure of birth control practices in marriage	14	30	10		
Pre-marital pregnancy	21	42	16		
Under no conditions	13	8	15		

22. Some people have said that the present institution of marriage is becoming obsolete. Do you agree or disagree?

Agree	24%	24%	24%	NOT ASKED OF	
Disagree	74	76	74	PARENTS	

23. Which of the following restraints imposed by society and its institutions can

you *accept easily*, which do you *accept reluctantly*, and which do you *reject outright?*

	YOUTH			PARENTS		
	Total Youth	College Youth	Non-college Youth	Total Parents	Parents College Youth	Parents Noncollege Youth
Abiding by laws you don't agree with						
Accept easily	30%	15%	34%	NOT ASKED OF		
Accept reluctantly	59	71	55	PARENTS		
Reject outright	11	14	11			
Conforming in matters of clothing and personal grooming						
Accept easily	50	33	54			
Accept reluctantly	27	29	26			
Reject outright	23	38	19			
The prohibition against marijuana						
Accept easily	67	48	72			
Accept reluctantly	13	20	11			
Reject outright	20	31	17			
The prohibition against LSD						
Accept easily	78	73	79			
Accept reluctantly	8	11	7			
Reject outright	13	16	13			
The prohibition against other drugs						
Accept easily	76	71	77			
Accept reluctantly	10	14	9			
Reject outright	14	14	14			
Outward conformity for the sake of career advancement						
Accept easily	31	14	35			
Accept reluctantly	38	46	36			
Reject outright	30	39	27			
The power and authority of the police						
Accept easily	72	48	78			
Accept reluctantly	22	42	17			
Reject outright	5	10	4			
The power and authority of the "boss" in a work situation						
Accept easily	67	49	71			
Accept reluctantly	29	45	25			
Reject outright	4	6	3			
Having little decision-making power in the first few years of a job						
Accept easily	45	33	50			
Accept reluctantly	39	52	35			
Reject outright	13	15	12			
Being treated impersonally in a job						
Accept easily	18	9	21			
Accept reluctantly	38	35	39			
Reject outright	43	57	39			

cont.

	YOUTH			PARENTS		
	Total Youth	College Youth	Non-college Youth	Total Parents	Parents College Youth	Parents Noncollege Youth

Accepting the authority of the university administration
Accept easily	69%	47%	74%			
Accept reluctantly	23	44	18			
Reject outright	5	9	4			

24. For each of the following, please tell me whether you feel it needs no substantial change, needs moderate change, needs fundamental reform or should be done away with.

Big business
No substantial change	20%	10%	23%	NOT ASKED OF
Moderate change	52	52	52	PARENTS
Fundamental reform	24	34	21	
Done away with	3	3	3	

The military
No substantial change	20	10	23
Moderate change	43	29	46
Fundamental reform	29	49	25
Done away with	7	11	6

The universities
No substantial change	20	11	23
Moderate change	50	56	49
Fundamental reform	28	32	27
Done away with	1	–	1

Trade unions
No substantial change	23	14	25
Moderate change	43	42	44
Fundamental reform	24	32	22
Done away with	7	11	6

The political parties
No substantial change	17	9	18
Moderate change	36	33	37
Fundamental reform	39	48	37
Done away with	7	9	7

The mass media
No substantial change	20	18	21
Moderate change	49	46	50
Fundamental reform	24	33	22
Done away with	4	2	4

25. Which of the following values do you believe are *worth fighting a war for*, which do you believe are *not worth fighting a war for*, and for which would you say it *depends on the specific circumstances?*

Keeping a commitment
Worth fighting for	25%	14%	28%	28%	25%	29%
Not worth fighting for	17	20	17	17	14	17

cont.

	YOUTH			PARENTS		
	Total Youth	College	Non-college	Total Parents	Parents College Youth	Parents Noncollege Youth
Depends on circumstances	58%	65%	56%	54%	61%	52%
Containing the Communists						
Worth fighting for	64	43	69	64	58	66
Not worth fighting for	14	25	11	14	16	14
Depends on circumstances	23	32	20	20	25	18
Maintaining our position of power in the world						
Worth fighting for	46	25	51	53	40	57
Not worth fighting for	23	39	19	19	29	16
Depends on circumstances	31	36	30	26	31	24
Protecting allies						
Worth fighting for	47	38	50	47	40	50
Not worth fighting for	10	12	10	8	11	7
Depends on circumstances	42	50	40	43	48	41
Fighting for our honor						
Worth fighting for	53	25	59	59	46	63
Not worth fighting for	18	38	13	14	19	13
Depends on circumstances	29	37	27	25	35	22
Counteracting aggression						
Worth fighting for	64	56	67	67	66	67
Not worth fighting for	6	6	6	5	5	5
Depends on circumstances	28	37	26	26	29	25
Protecting our national interests						
Worth fighting for	61	39	66	68	55	72
Not worth fighting for	7	14	6	6	10	5
Depends on circumstances	32	48	28	24	34	21

26. Which one of the following statements comes closest to your own point of view:

Resisting the draft is basically wrong—a citizen is obligated to serve his country regardless of his personal views about the justness of a war.	66%	44%	72%
An individual should obey his conscience—if he feels that he is being drafted to fight in a war that is morally wrong, he should resist in any way that he can.	33	55	28

NOT ASKED OF PARENTS

27. Which of the following statements do you *strongly agree* with, which do you *partially agree* with, and which do you *strongly disagree* with?

	YOUTH			PARENTS	
Total Youth	College Youth	Non-college Youth	Total Parents	Parents College Youth	Parents Noncollege Youth

"The Establishment" unfairly controls every aspect of our lives; we can never be free until we are rid of it

Strongly agree	12%	8%	13%	NOT ASKED OF		
Partially agree	45	50	43	PARENTS		
Strongly disagree	41	42	41			

A mass revolutionary party should be created

Strongly agree	4	5	4
Partially agree	12	14	11
Strongly disagree	83	80	84

Authorities must be put in an intolerable position so they will be forced to respond with repression and thus show their illegitimacy

Strongly agree	7	5	8
Partially agree	30	27	31
Strongly disagree	60	68	58

Disruption is preferable to discussing issues for changing our society

Strongly agree	8	4	10
Partially agree	22	22	22
Strongly disagree	69	74	67

Sexual behavior should be bound by mutual feelings, not by formal and legal ties

Strongly agree	35	51	32
Partially agree	27	33	25
Strongly disagree	37	17	42

A minority must never be allowed to impose its will on the majority

Strongly agree	27	18	25
Partially agree	34	44	32
Strongly disagree	42	37	43

There are legitimate channels for reform which must be exhausted before attempting disruption

Strongly agree	55	68	51
Partially agree	33	27	34
Strongly disagree	11	5	12

Today, rebuilding society is of less immediate importance than destroying it

Strongly agree	29	19	31
Partially agree	15	13	13
Strongly disagree	58	68	55

Radicals of the left are as much a threat to the rights of the individual as are radicals of the right

Strongly agree	52	54	51
Partially agree	34	36	33
Strongly disagree	11	10	11

There is too much concern with equality and too little with law and order

Strongly agree	42	17	48	55	42	59
Partially agree	36	40	35	32	37	31
Strongly disagree	22	43	17	11	20	9

cont.

	YOUTH			PARENTS		
	Total Youth	College Youth	Non-college Youth	Total Parents	Parents College Youth	Parents Noncollege Youth

The whole social system ought to be replaced by an entirely new one; the existing structures are too rotten for repair

Strongly agree	9%	7%	10%	10%	5%	11%
Partially agree	30	28	30	22	16	24
Strongly disagree	60	65	59	65	78	62

Computers and other advanced technology are creating an inhuman and impersonal world

Strongly agree	22	18	23	24	16	26
Partially agree	40	46	39	37	34	38
Strongly disagree	37	36	37	38	49	34

Activism and Involvement

29. Which one of the following statements comes closest to expressing your own point of view about civil disobedience—that is, defying a law in the name of principle?

Civil disobedience is never justified	23%	9%	27%	NOT ASKED OF PARENTS	
Under some circumstances, it may be necessary to resort to civil disobedience	65	71	64		
There is nothing wrong with civil disobedience; it's a part of our history	11	20	9		

30. Roy Wilkins of the NAACP recently said that colleges which yielded to the demands for separate facilities made by black students should be sued. Do you agree or disagree?

Agree	41%	41%	42%	NOT ASKED OF	
Disagree	57	58	56	PARENTS	

31. A black leader recently said, "This is a time for hate." Do you agree or disagree with this statement?

Agree	8%	10%	7%	NOT ASKED OF	
Disagree	91	89	92	PARENTS	

32. Do you think that, in general, this country is doing *too much* for black people now, doing *enough*, doing *too little*, or doing *the wrong things?*

Too much	14%	6%	16%	15%	9%	17%
Enough	26	15	29	31	27	32
Too little	17	21	16	10	19	8
Wrong things	43	57	39	41	43	40

33. Which of the following views of American society and American life reflect your own feelings?

	YOUTH			PARENTS		
	Total Youth	College Youth	Non-college Youth	Total Parents	Parents College Youth	Parents Noncollege Youth
The American way of life is superior to that of any other country	30%	18%	33%	28%	21%	29%
There are serious flaws in our society today, but the system is flexible enough to solve them	64	75	62	61	73	58
The American system is not flexible enough; radical change is needed	12	14	12	9	6	10

34. In general, do you feel that your own personal values and points of view are shared by most Americans today?

Yes	49%	33%	53%	67%	52%	71%
Not certain	29	31	28	20	25	19
No	22	36	19	13	24	10

35. If you continue to feel at odds with the majority, which of the following, realistically speaking, are you *most* likely to do?

Change your point of view	—%	—%	—%	NOT ASKED OF PARENTS	
Outwardly accept the majority way of life, but retain your own private values	7	9	7		
Build a private life with like-minded people who share your values, and try to ignore the majority	4	9	2		
Withdraw from the system and drop out	—	1	—		
Continue to fight actively for what you believe is right	11	16	9		

36. A. Which of the following have you yourself been involved in:

Sit-ins	5%	12%	3%	NOT ASKED OF PARENTS	
Strikes	5	11	4		
Riots	3	6	2		
Marches	9	24	6		

cont.

	YOUTH			PARENTS		
	Total Youth	College	Non-college	Total Parents	Parents College Youth	Parents Noncollege Youth
Political campaigns	17%	38%	12%	NOT ASKED OF		
Organization meetings	25	52	18	PARENTS		
Civil rights protests	5	15	3			
Joined organizations like SDS and YAF	1	4	1			
Been arrested	8	9	7			
None	60	30	68			

B. For those activities you have not been involved in, which of these would you like to be involved in?

Sit-ins	11	20	9
Strikes	9	14	8
Riots	3	4	3
Marches	11	20	8
Political campaigns	25	35	22
Organization meetings	12	15	12
Civil rights protests	12	24	9
Join organizations like SDS and YAF	6	8	5
Be arrested	3	3	3
None	59	36	65

37. Which of the tactics listed on this card do you feel are *always* justified, which are *sometimes* justified, and which do you feel are *never* justified?

Sit-ins

Always justified	5%	12%	3%	NOT ASKED OF
Sometimes justified	66	78	63	PARENTS
Never justified	28	10	33	

Ultimatums to those in authority

Always justified	7	6	8
Sometimes justified	65	75	63
Never justified	26	19	28

Blockades of buildings

Always justified	3	2	3
Sometimes justified	36	46	34
Never justified	59	52	61

Destruction or mutilation of property

Always justified	1	—	1
Sometimes justified	12	16	12
Never justified	86	84	87

Resisting or disobeying police

Always justified	3	1	4
Sometimes justified	34	62	27
Never justified	62	37	69

cont.

	YOUTH			PARENTS		
	Total Youth	College Youth	Non-college Youth	Total Parents	Parents College Youth	Parents Noncollege Youth
Assaulting police						
Always justified	2%	– %	3%	NOT ASKED OF		
Sometimes justified	15	20	13	PARENTS		
Never justified	83	79	84			
Assaulting other civil authorities						
Always justified	1	–	1			
Sometimes justified	16	21	15			
Never justified	82	79	83			
Holding an authority captive						
Always justified	2	1	2			
Sometimes justified	13	21	11			
Never justified	84	78	86			
Use of police to control demonstrators						
Always justified	44	24	49			
Sometimes justified	50	70	45			
Never justified	6	6	6			
Use of police to evict those participating in sit-ins						
Always justified	32	12	38			
Sometimes justified	56	67	53			
Never justified	12	21	9			
Use of police to prevent destruction of property						
Always justified	78	70	79			
Sometimes justified	20	28	18			
Never justified	2	2	2			
Using draft resistance as a political weapon						
Always justified	7	10	6			
Sometimes justified	26	39	23			
Never justified	65	50	69			

38. Which, if any, of these criticisms that have been made about the radical student movement do you personally share:

"All they want to do is tear things down— they have no positive program."	30%	22%	32%	NOT ASKED OF PARENTS	
"They are too hostile and antagonistic to be effective."	44	47	43		
"They are not tolerant of anyone but themselves."	43	46	42		
"The radical student movement lacks real leadership."	42	52	40		
None of these criticisms is true.	13	16	13		

39. With respect to your own personal role in seeking to bring about needed changes in colleges or other institutions of our society, which *one* of the following statements best describes your own position?

	YOUTH			PARENTS		
	Total Youth	College Youth	Non-college Youth	Total Parents	Parents College Youth	Parents Noncollege Youth
I consider myself to be an activist.	2%	5%	2%	NOT ASKED OF PARENTS		
I am in sympathy with most of the activists' objectives, but not with all of their tactics.	27	48	22			
I'm not emotionally involved, one way or the other.	35	19	39			
I am not sure that I approve of what the activists are trying to do, but I have no strong objections to letting them try.	19	20	18			
I am in total disagreement with the activists.	16	9	18			

40. With which of the following groups, if any, do you feel a sense of identification? (MULTIPLE RESPONSE PERMISSIBLE)

The middle class	60%	71%	57%	77%	89%	73%
Students	56	88	48	23	44	17
The New Left	5	13	3	1	4	–
Conservatives	16	23	14	32	50	27
The Old Left	3	7	2	5	9	4
Your family	76	78	75	87	92	85
People of your nationality	41	54	38	42	61	36
People of your religion	42	45	41	61	66	59
Other people of your generation	71	83	68	62	80	57
People of your race	51	58	49	51	70	45

41. Which *one* of these candidates did you want to see elected last fall?

Nixon	26%	22%	27%	NOT ASKED OF PARENTS	
Humphrey	10	6	11		
Wallace	7	1	8		
Robert Kennedy	38	35	39		
McCarthy	9	19	7		
Reagan	1	–	1		
Rockefeller	3	8	2		

cont.

	YOUTH			PARENTS	
	Total Youth	College	Non-college	Total Parents	Parents College Youth	Parents Noncollege Youth
Gregory	– %	1%	– %	NOT ASKED OF		
Cleaver	–	1	–	PARENTS		
Johnson	1	1	1			
None of these	4	6	3			

42. Which of the following events, if any, have had a *great effect* on your life and your values, which have had a *moderate effect,* and which have had *little or no effect?*

Your college experience (if any)

Great effect	21%	66%	10%	NOT ASKED OF	
Moderate effect	10	28	6	PARENTS	
Little or no effect	35	66	42		

The Vietnam war

Great effect	35	35	35
Moderate effect	34	40	33
Little or no effect	31	25	33

The civil rights movement

Great effect	20	27	18
Moderate effect	32	43	29
Little or no effect	48	30	53

The New Left

Great effect	4	9	2
Moderate effect	12	25	9
Little or no effect	82	66	86

The invasion of Czechoslovakia

Great effect	8	10	8
Moderate effect	23	32	21
Little or no effect	69	59	71

The Cuban missile crisis

Great effect	10	13	9
Moderate effect	22	28	20
Little or no effect	68	58	71

The death of John F. Kennedy

Great effect	49	50	49
Moderate effect	32	33	31
Little or no effect	19	17	20

The McCarthy campaign

Great effect	10	19	7
Moderate effect	16	30	13
Little or no effect	74	51	80

The death of Martin Luther King

Great effect	25	30	24
Moderate effect	33	41	31
Little or no effect	42	28	45

43. A. What scene stands out *most vividly* in your mind from the TV coverage you saw of: (FREE RESPONSE)

	YOUTH			PARENTS		
	Total Youth	College Youth	Non-college Youth	Total Parents	Parents College Youth	Parents Noncollege Youth
The Vietnam war						
Killing and bodies	41%	38%	42%	NOT ASKED OF		
Fighting and torturing	22	28	21	PARENTS		
No particular scenes	18	10	20			
Hunger and suffering of children	12	17	11			
Riots in ghettos						
Destruction and burning	25	30	23			
Looting	21	23	20			
No particular scenes	21	7	24			
Fighting and shooting	14	17	13			
Police brutality	9	10	9			
Specific areas mentioned (Watts, etc.)	6	10	5			
Poverty and poor living conditions	5	8	4			
Campus demonstrations, such as those at Columbia, Wisconsin, San Francisco State, etc.						
No particular scenes	25	12	28			
Childish actions by students	14	15	14			
Police brutality	12	20	10			
Riots and kids beaten	9	13	8			
Destruction and chaos	7	7	7			
Students taking over buildings	7	10	7			
The Democratic Convention in Chicago						
Police brutality	24	34	22			
No particular scenes	20	7	24			
Violence and bloodshed	18	22	17			
Chaos and confusion	7	9	7			
Demonstrations	6	9	6			
Mayor Daley	4	10	3			

B. What comments would you care to make about TV coverage of these events?

Coverage one-sided	34	45	31
Showed both sides	20	20	20
Good coverage generally	17	13	18
Too much coverage	6	5	6
Too little coverage	2	3	2

Demographic Characteristics

	YOUTH			PARENTS		
	Total Youth	College Youth	Non-college Youth	Total Parents	Parents College Youth	Parents Noncollege Youth
Sex						
Male	45%	56%	42%	38%	46%	36%
Female	55	44	58	62	54	64
Age						
17 years old	18	1	22	—	—	—
18–19 years	35	47	31	—	—	—
20–21 years	25	36	23	—	—	—
22–23 years	23	16	24	—	—	—
under 45 years	—	—	—	33	25	35
45 years or more	—	—	—	67	75	65
Marital Status						
Unmarried	78	93	74	—	—	—
Married	22	7	26	90	92	89
Widowed	—	—	—	4	3	4
Divorced/Separated	—	—	—	6	5	6
Race						
White	91	93	90			
Nonwhite	9	7	10			
Education						
Some college/graduate				30	58	22
Had no college				70	42	78
Religion						
Protestant	58	48	61	66	59	69
Catholic	27	24	28	24	23	24
Jewish	5	10	3	5	13	3
Other	2	2	2	2	2	2
None	8	15	6	2	3	1
Political Affiliation						
Republican	25	27	24	32	41	29
Democrat	47	45	47	50	44	51
Liberal	—	1	—	—	1	—
Independent	3	4	3	6	4	6
Conservative	—	—	1	—	—	—
Other	1	1	1	—	—	—
None	19	20	19	9	5	10
Parents' Occupation						
White collar	41	65	35	43	66	36
Blue collar	46	25	51	51	29	57
Parents' Income						
Under $10,000	48	30	53	44	24	50
$10,000–$14,999	29	32	29	33	35	32
$15,000 or more	22	38	19	23	41	18

cont.

	YOUTH			PARENTS		
	Total Youth	College Youth	Non-college Youth	Total Parents	Parents College Youth	Parents Noncollege Youth
Youths' Occupation						
Not employed	45%	51%	43%			
Employed, white collar	29	30	28			
Employed, blue collar	27	18	29			
Youths' Income						
No income	45	51	43			
Under $3,000	28	41	25			
$3,000–$4,999	14	5	17			
$5,000 or more	13	3	16			
Labor Union Member						
Yes, a member				22%	13%	24%
No, not a member				78	87	76
Region of Country						
Northeast	25	23	26			
Midwest	26	28	26			
South	30	26	31			
West	18	23	17			
Draft Status						
Eligible	19	12	20			
Deferred	45	75	36			
Ineligible	14	6	16			
Indeterminable	22	5	28			
Campus Size						
Under 10,000 students	–	59	–			
Over 10,000 students	–	41	–			

YOUTH PROFILES

One of the prime objectives of the study was to establish the dimensions of rebelliousness and alienation among youth. How large is the radical movement; who are its members? Comparatively, how large is the conservative segment of youth? Do radical youth come from "radical" or highly liberal homes? Do they come from high income families?

Daniel Yankelovich and CBS News agreed to segment the youth into five groups: Revolutionaries, Radical Reformers, Moderate Reformers, Middle-of-the-Roaders, and Conservatives. The criteria for segmentation were set after the interviewing was completed, and were based on responses to several series of questions described below. As a general rule, the questions were selected on the basis of values pertaining to socio-political institutions in order to identify the groups in ideological terms. Once so identified, each group could then be measured in terms of its response to other manifestations of rebellion—to traditional values, to sexual mores, to drug use, to career goals. The questionnaire and results indicate these responses by youth segment, and where available, by parents of each group.

Before presenting the findings, we should specify how the five segments were derived. The first group, the Revolutionaries, are young people who believe that the American social system is "too rotten for repair," that radical change is required, and who want to create a mass revolutionary party. They also believe that destroying and mutilating property, assaulting police, and holding authorities captive are justified tactics. To qualify as a Revolutionary, a young person had to hold *all* of these beliefs. (In the study they were asked as six wholly separate items.)

To qualify for membership in the second group, the Radical Reformers, a young man or woman had to hold just one or another of certain extreme views.

The third group, the Moderate Reformers, are young people who agree with six or more Left-leaning statements out of a possible total of fourteen. These include: endorsing draft resistance, opposing the war in Vietnam on the grounds of its imperialist character, endorsing civil disobedience, and urging that such institutions as our political parties, big business and the military establishment be reformed in fundamental ways.

Young people who agreed with fewer than six of the fourteen statements were classified as Middle-of-the-Road, so that in this study even a Middle-of-the-Roader may hold one or several beliefs that might be considered Liberal or Left-Wing.

At the other end of the spectrum, to classify as a Conservative a young person had to subscribe to a coherent pattern of beliefs, including the view that the American way of life is superior to all others, that we are too concerned with equality and not sufficiently concerned with law and order, too concerned with the "welfare bum" and not sufficiently concerned with the hard-working person struggling to make a living, and that destroying and mutilating property, assaulting police, and holding authorities captive are never justified under any circumstances.

The breakdown of youth by ideology follows:

	Total Youth	College	Noncollege
Revolutionaries	1.0%	3.3%	0.4%
Radical Reformers	9.7	9.5	9.8
Moderate Reformers	23.0	39.3	18.9
Middle-of-the-Road	47.7	37.1	50.3
Conservatives	18.6	10.8	20.6

Profile of a Revolutionary

This group is so small that it should be looked at in combination with the Radical Reformer. This is particularly true of noncollege Revolutionaries. Obviously, most of the Revolutionaries are college students.

The college Revolutionary is disproportionately higher than other college students in the following characteristics: nonwhite, male, age 20 to 23. One striking characteristic is that very few revolutionaries come from the 10 to 15 thousand dollar income bracket. They cluster about evenly above and below this range.

They have about the same proportion as other college students in relation to marital status and father's occupation, which is white collar. There are proportionately fewer Protestants and Catholics. Unlike other college students, a majority of the Revolutionaries have no religious preference.

	Total Youth	Total Revolutionary	Total College	College Revolutionary	Non-college Revolutionary
Sex					
Male	45%	71%	56%	67%	*
Female	55	29	44	33	*
Marital Status					
Married	22	7	7	8	*
Not married	78	93	93	92	*
Age					
17 years old	18	2	1	—	*
18–19 years old	35	29	47	31	*
20–21 years old	25	49	36	44	*
22–23 years old	23	20	16	25	*
Race					
White	91	81	93	81	*
Nonwhite	9	19	7	19	*
Parents' Income					
Under $10,000	49	36	30	40	*
$10,000–$14,999	29	20	32	13	*
$15,000 or more	22	44	38	47	*
Father's Occupation					
White collar	41	58	65	69	*
Blue collar	46	31	25	23	*
Other	13	11	10	8	*
Religion					
Protestant	58	7	48	8	*
Catholic	27	7	24	4	*
Jewish	5	12	10	15	*
Other	2	14	2	10	*
None	8	61	15	63	*
Education					
College	20	81			
Noncollege	80	19			

*Base too small to be meaningfully percentaged.

Profile of a Radical Reformer

The radicals have one striking characteristic: blacks are disproportionately represented in both the college and noncollege groups. The college radicals have proportionately fewer Protestants and more with no religious preference than the college youth as a whole. In most other respects they are like other college students.

The noncollege youth have proportionately more 20 and 21 year olds and fewer 22 and 23 year olds. They tend to a greater degree than other non-college youth to come from lower income parents, but this is probably due to the large proportion of nonwhites. As a group they have proportionately fewer fathers in blue collar occupations, but this is probably due to the unemployment of a large proportion of this group. They also have a larger proportion married than other noncollege youth.

The composition of the radical group among noncollege youth, and the weight of this group on the overall radical category, produces some startling results in the tables. While holding radical views on most ideological questions, the noncollege radicals (and therefore total radicals) appear more like middle-of-the-roaders on traditional values like patriotism, sex and religion, and are not totally consistent on political matters. The principal reason appears to be the disproportionate number of blacks. Considering the nature of many black militant groups today—radical in domestic issues, but highly disciplined in terms of upholding certain standards of personal morality, the results should not be altogether surprising.

	Total Youth	Total Radical Reformer	Total College	College Radical Reformer	Total Non-college	Non-college Radical Reformer
Sex						
Male	45%	44%	56%	58%	42%	40%
Female	55	56	44	42	58	60
Age						
17 years old	18	18	1	1	22	22
18–19 years old	35	33	47	46	31	29
20–21 years old	25	34	36	30	23	36
22–23 years old	23	15	16	23	24	13
Race						
White	91	74	93	83	90	72
Nonwhite	9	26	7	17	10	28
Parents' Income						
Under $10,000	49	55	30	29	53	61
$10,000-$14,999	29	24	32	29	29	23
$15,000 or more	22	21	38	42	19	16
Father's Occupation						
White collar	41	46	65	71	35	40
Blue collar	46	27	25	20	51	29
Other	13	27	10	9	14	31
Religion						
Protestant	58	50	48	28	61	55
Catholic	27	25	24	25	28	25
Jewish	5	8	10	10	3	8
Other	2	5	2	7	2	5
None	8	12	15	30	6	7

cont.

	Total Youth	Total Moderate Reformer	Total College	College Moderate Reformer	Total Non-college	Non-college Moderate Reformer
Marital Status						
Married	22%	15%	7%	9%	26%	16%
Not married	78	85	93	91	74	84
Education						
College	20	20				
Noncollege	80	80				

Profile of a Moderate Reformer

Numerically there are more noncollege than college moderate reformers. However, there are proportionately more in the college group.

The college reformer is an excellent cross section of all college youth, that is, the proportions of age, sex, and other demographic characteristics is the same as total college youth.

The noncollege reformers differ from all noncollege youth in that they are disproportionately fewer in the younger ages, and fewer Protestants, and slightly more Catholics. There is a proportionately higher parent income in this group than parents of all noncollege youth; however, a plurality is low income. Marital status and race are about the same as other noncollege youth.

	Total Youth	Total Moderate Reformer	Total College	College Moderate Reformer	Total Non-college	Non-college Moderate Reformer
Sex						
Male	45%	50%	56%	52%	42%	49%
Female	55	50	44	48	58	51
Age						
17 years old	18	13	1	–	22	20
18–19 years old	35	30	47	47	31	21
20–21 years old	25	34	36	37	23	33
22–23 years old	23	23	16	16	34	26
Race						
White	91	93	93	91	90	94
Nonwhite	9	7	7	9	10	6
Parents' Income						
Under $10,000	49	35	30	28	53	39
$10,000–$14,999	29	34	32	33	29	34
$15,000 or more	22	31	38	39	19	27
Father's Occupation						
White collar	41	44	65	66	35	32
Blue collar	46	47	25	23	51	60
Other	13	9	10	11	14	8
Religion						
Protestant	58	49	48	43	61	52
Catholic	27	29	24	20	28	34
Jewish	5	9	10	16	3	5
Other	2	1	2	3	2	*
None	8	12	15	18	6	9

cont.

	Total Youth	Total Middle Road	Total College	College Middle Road	Total Non-college	Non-college Middle Road
Marital Status						
Married	22%	19%	7%	7%	26%	25%
Not married	78	81	93	93	74	75
Education						
College	20	34				
Noncollege	80	66				

*Base too small to be meaningfully percentaged.

Profile of a Middle-of-the-Roader

There are numerically and proportionately more noncollege than college youth. Both college and noncollege moderates are a cross section of the youth population except for having proportionately more noncollege females, and proportionately more college Protestants.

	Total Youth	Total Middle Road	Total College	College Middle Road	Total Non-college	Non-college Middle Road
Sex						
Male	45%	38%	56%	56%	42%	34%
Female	55	62	44	44	58	66
Age						
17 years old	18	20	1	1	22	24
18–19 years old	35	38	47	53	31	34
20–21 years old	25	20	36	33	23	18
22–23 years old	23	22	16	13	24	24
Race						
White	91	91	93	97	90	90
Nonwhite	9	9	7	3	10	10
Parents' Income						
Under $10,000	49	53	30	29	53	58
$10,000–$14,999	29	24	32	35	29	22
$15,000 or more	22	23	38	36	19	20
Father's Occupation						
White collar	41	41	65	62	35	37
Blue collar	46	47	25	29	51	51
Other	13	12	10	9	14	12
Religion						
Protestant	58	61	48	57	61	62
Catholic	27	30	24	29	28	30
Jewish	5	3	10	5	3	3
Other	2	1	2	1	2	1
None	8	5	15	8	6	4
Marital Status						
Married	22	23	7	7	26	26
Not married	78	77	93	93	74	74
Education						
College	20	16				
Noncollege	80	84				

Profile of a Conservative

Conservatives as a group tend to be proportionately more male and Protestant. There are numerically and proportionately more noncollege than college conservatives. Noncollege conservatives come predominantly from a blue collar background, but to the same degree as other noncollege youth. College conservatives are predominantly from white collar background, but to the same degree as other college youth.

The noncollege group is proportionately more middle income and fewer high income than other noncollege youth. A majority of all noncollege youth and noncollege conservatives are low income.

The college youth has proportionately more youth age 20 to 23 in the conservative group as well as a proportionately lower average parent income and a proportionately smaller group with no religious preference.

	Total Youth	Total Conserv- ative	Total College	College Conserv- ative	Total Non- college	Non- college Conserv- ative
Sex						
Male	45%	58%	56%	64%	42%	57%
Female	55	42	44	36	58	43
Age						
17 years old	18	18	1	3	22	20
18–19 years old	35	33	47	35	31	33
20–21 years old	25	21	36	40	23	19
22–23 years old	23	28	16	22	24	28
Race						
White	91	94	93	97	90	94
Nonwhite	9	6	7	3	10	6
Parents' Income						
Under $10,000	49	48	30	38	53	50
$10,000–$14,999	29	41	32	31	29	42
$15,000 or more	22	11	38	31	19	8
Father's Occupation						
White collar	41	33	65	67	35	29
Blue collar	46	50	25	22	51	54
Other	13	17	10	11	14	17
Religion						
Protestant	58	70	48	62	61	72
Catholic	27	21	24	28	28	20
Jewish	5	2	10	5	3	1
Other	2	2	2	1	2	2
None	8	5	15	4	6	5
Marital Status						
Married	22	30	7	6	26	33
Not married	78	70	93	94	74	67
Education						
College	20	12				
Noncollege	80	88				

Augmented Sample

It was anticipated early in the study that the extreme "Revolutionary" group of youth would be extremely small. This constituted no problem in the measurement of its size.

However, for purposes of study of the group itself, to contrast, for example, responses among Revolutionaries on different questions, it was necessary to augment the number of cases in this category.

To do so, the Yankelovich organization selected 100 students known to hold radical views. After subjecting them to the questionnaire and the segmentation criteria described above, 24 students among the 100 qualified as Revolutionaries. These additional cases were added, not to the overall totals, but to the tabulations for responses by Revolutionaries in order to have a sufficient number of cases to make these responses somewhat more meaningful.

QUESTIONNAIRE AND RESULTS BY YOUTH PROFILES

This section contains the same questionnaire printed earlier, but with the tabulations by the five youth groups. Tabulations for parents of youths in each of the groups are shown where they were asked the same questions and where time permitted the appropriate tabulations.

Because the number of parents of Revolutionary youth is so small, parental responses for Revolutionary and Radical Reformer youth groups should be looked at together. There are too few cases in the Revolutionary parents group to make the data reliable.

Traditional Values

1. The following statements represent some traditional American values. Which of them do you *personally believe* in and which do you *not believe in*?

| | YOUTH | | | | | PARENTS OF | | | | |
	Revolution-ary	Radi-cal Re-former	Mod-erate Re-former	Mid-dle Road	Con-serv-ative	Revo-lution-ary	Radi-cal Re-former	Mod-erate Re-former	Mid-dle Road	Con-serv-ative
A. Hard work will always pay off										
Believe in	12%	57%	58%	84%	83%	91%	79%	77%	85%	86%
Do not believe in	86	43	42	16	17	9	19	21	15	14
B. Everyone should save as much as he can regularly and not have to lean on family and friends the minute he runs into financial problems										
Believe in	47	81	76	89	94	91	95	93	97	100
Do not believe in	51	19	24	11	6	9	5	6	3	—
C. Depending on how much strength and character a person has, he can pretty well control what happens to him										
Believe in	39	77	67	76	77	82	68	75	74	78
Do not believe in	61	23	33	24	23	18	32	25	24	19
D. Belonging to some organized religion is important in a person's life										
Believe in	8	58	47	70	84	73	94	85	88	91
Do not believe in	92	42	53	30	16	27	6	13	11	9

cont.

	YOUTH					PARENTS OF				
	Revolution-ary	Radical Reformer	Moderate Reformer	Middle Road	Conserv-ative	Revolution-ary	Radical Reformer	Moderate Reformer	Middle Road	Conserv-ative
E. Competition encourages excellence										
Believe in	31%	67%	77%	81%	89%	91%	81%	89%	91%	91%
Do not believe in	69	32	22	19	11	9	19	8	7	9
F. The right to private property is sacred										
Believe in	31	70	78	90	92	73	95	85	93	94
Do not believe in	69	29	22	10	8	27	3	12	7	6
G. Society needs some legally based authority in order to prevent chaos										
Believe in	41	82	95	96	97	100	98	99	95	96
Do not believe in	59	17	4	4	3	—	—	1	4	4
H. Compromise is essential for progress										
Believe in	29	82	90	85	92	82	92	73	87	87
Do not believe in	71	17	10	14	7	18	5	24	12	12

2. Many people feel that we are undergoing a period of rapid social change in this country today, and that people's values are changing at the same time. Which of the following changes would you *welcome*, which would you *reject*, and which would *leave you indifferent*?

A. Less emphasis on money						
Would welcome	81%	54%	75%	51%	53%	NOT ASKED OF
Would reject	10	19	10	11	17	PARENTS
Leave indifferent	8	26	16	37	39	
B. Less emphasis on working hard						
Would welcome	63	40	24	30	32	
Would reject	17	37	52	46	44	
Leave indifferent	20	22	24	24	23	
C. More emphasis on law and order						
Would welcome	8	68	57	86	83	
Would reject	78	15	17	5	9	
Leave indifferent	14	16	23	8	8	
D. More emphasis on technological improvement						
Would welcome	44	68	61	58	69	
Would reject	31	9	7	4	3	
Leave indifferent	24	23	32	37	27	
E. More emphasis on self-expression						
Would welcome	97	84	82	67	67	
Would reject	—	2	3	5	11	
Leave indifferent	3	14	15	27	21	

3. ASKED OF YOUTH: Here are some of the ways others have described how their parents' values and outlook differ from their own. For each of the following statements, tell me whether it is more true of you or of your parents.

ASKED OF PARENTS: Here are some of the ways in which other parents have described how their children's values and outlook differ from their own.

For each of the following statements, tell me whether you feel it is more true of you or of your son/daughter.

	YOUTH					PARENTS OF				
	Revo-lution-ary	Radi-cal Re-former	Mod-erate Re-former	Mid-dle Road	Con-serv-ative	Revo-lution-ary	Radi-cal Re-former	Mod-erate Re-former	Mid-dle Road	Con-serv-ative
A. More likely to do something about what they believe is right										
More true of parents	17%	19%	15%	18%	13%	18%	27%	29%	23%	19%
More true of youth	63	49	45	43	32	45	13	22	25	19
No difference	20	33	40	39	54	36	60	49	51	58
B. Have more faith in the democratic process										
More true of parents	73	50	52	36	24	82	43	34	34	17
More true of youth	8	10	11	13	17	9	3	8	10	10
No difference	19	40	37	51	59	9	43	53	56	69
C. More self-centered										
More true of parents	22	19	12	15	17	9	29	17	14	15
More true of youth	44	29	50	44	41	55	32	31	35	31
No difference	34	46	38	40	42	36	26	52	49	48
D. More interested in other people										
More true of parents	12	18	13	13	16	36	38	29	22	14
More true of youth	56	55	46	37	30	9	35	19	25	33
No difference	32	25	41	50	54	55	27	52	53	49
E. More concerned with what is happening to the country										
More true of parents	8	31	23	25	21	18	32	28	37	31
More true of youth	54	28	39	27	30	45	9	15	15	12
No difference	37	41	38	48	49	36	58	58	48	53
F. More honest with themselves										
More true of parents	14	21	17	24	24	36	20	19	23	19
More true of youth	58	44	43	30	19	18	23	12	10	4
No difference	29	35	41	45	57	15	56	69	66	73

4. What role does each of the following values play in your life—that is, as I read off each item, tell me whether it is *very important* to you, *fairly important* to you, or *not very important* to you.

A. Friendship						
Very important	83%	93%	85%	90%	89%	NOT ASKED OF
Fairly important	17	6	14	9	10	PARENTS
Not very important	–	1	2	–	1	
B. Money						
Very important	5	36	30	39	38	
Fairly important	46	43	54	53	59	
Not very important	49	21	16	8	4	
C. Being a leader						
Very important	10	22	20	17	16	
Fairly important	36	36	38	40	46	
Not very important	54	42	42	43	38	

cont.

	YOUTH					PARENTS OF				
	Revo-lution-ary	Radi-cal Re-former	Mod-erate Re-former	Mid-dle Road	Con-serv-ative	Revo-lution-ary	Radi-cal Re-former	Mod-erate Re-former	Mid-dle Road	Con-serv-ative
D. Service to others										
Very important	53%	63%	54%	54%	50%	NOT ASKED OF				
Fairly important	41	30	38	42	37	PARENTS				
Not very important	7	7	7	4	13					
E. Doing your own thing										
Very important	86	81	75	51	59					
Fairly important	7	13	20	39	30					
Not very important	7	6	4	10	11					
F. Doing work that is more than just a job										
Very important	90	74	72	73	65					
Fairly important	10	26	27	23	26					
Not very important	–	–	–	4	9					
G. Patriotism										
Very important	2	53	26	63	73					
Fairly important	27	27	54	30	20					
Not very important	71	20	20	6	3					
H. Living a clean, moral life										
Very important	37	70	46	79	83					
Fairly important	20	19	41	15	13					
Not very important	42	11	12	6	3					
I. Education										
Very important	61	84	76	82	80					
Fairly important	31	11	21	15	14					
Not very important	8	5	3	3	5					
J. Privacy										
Very important	63	75	76	69	69					
Fairly important	32	18	22	27	29					
Not very important	5	8	2	3	2					
K. Changing society										
Very important	93	51	34	22	27					
Fairly important	5	41	53	50	52					
Not very important	2	7	12	26	21					
L. Love										
Very important	97	88	89	89	89					
Fairly important	3	10	10	10	11					
Not very important	–	–	1	1	–					
M. Religion										
Very important	12	56	43	65	68					
Fairly important	25	16	30	24	25					
Not very important	63	28	27	11	7					

5. What role does religion play in your life? (FREE RESPONSE)

	YOUTH					PARENTS OF				
	Revo-lution-ary	Radi-cal Re-former	Mod-erate Re-former	Mid-dle Road	Con-serv-ative	Revo-lution-ary	Radi-cal Re-former	Mod-erate Re-former	Mid-dle Road	Con-serv-ative
Plays an important role	−%	17%	10%	23%	29%	NOT ASKED OF PARENTS				
Gives basis for moral code	5	23	18	24	26					
I'm an agnostic. Religion plays no role	46	17	16	7	5					
Plays small part	14	13	22	15	14					

6. Which of the following statements do you *strongly agree* with, which do you *partially agree* with, and which do you *strongly disagree* with?

A. Most people will go out of their way to help someone else

Strongly agree	8%	21%	5%	16%	15%	NOT ASKED OF PARENTS
Partially agree	53	46	60	59	56	
Strongly disagree	39	33	35	26	29	

B. No sane, normal, decent person could even think of hurting a close friend or relative

Strongly agree	10	42	26	38	50
Partially agree	39	33	47	38	36
Strongly disagree	51	24	27	23	14

C. Anyone who completely trusts anyone else is asking for trouble

Strongly agree	7	21	19	15	18
Partially agree	36	36	42	34	38
Strongly disagree	58	43	39	51	43

D. Most people can be depended on to come through in a pinch

Strongly agree	14	31	15	22	21
Partially agree	58	37	60	58	59
Strongly disagree	29	32	24	19	21

E. Man is basically good, but our society brings out the worst in him

Strongly agree	63	51	31	29	27
Partially agree	20	27	48	40	46
Strongly disagree	15	21	21	31	27

The Generations

7. A. ASKED OF YOUTH: Overall, would you say that differences between your values and those of your parents are *very great, moderate* or *very slight*?

Very great	54%	38%	17%	11%	12%
Moderate	41	39	54	51	43
Very slight	5	23	29	38	45

B. ASKED OF YOUTH: Would you say that, in general, you want the *same things* for yourself as your parents wanted when they were your own age, or do you want *something different*?

	YOUTH					PARENTS OF				
	Revo-lution-ary	Radi-cal Re-former	Mod-erate Re-former	Mid-dle Road	Con-serv-ative	Revo-lution-ary	Radi-cal Re-former	Mod-erate Re-former	Mid-dle Road	Con-serv-ative
Same	10%	34%	37%	44%	45%					
Different	90	66	63	55	55					

8. Do you feel that there is a *large* "generation gap" today, that it exists but has been *exaggerated*, or that it *doesn't exist*?

Large generation gap	66%	38%	37%	21%	26%	NOT TABULATED	
Exists but exagger-ated	25	53	62	72	70		
No generation gap	7	9	1	5	3		

9. Which *one* of the following best describes your *present* relationship with your parents?

A. I get along fine with them and en-joy their company	15%	38%	47%	60%	74%	NOT ASKED OF	
B. I'm fond of them but have trouble communicat-ing with them	36	43	36	29	21	PARENTS	
C. I like to go home for a few days, but no longer than that	32	12	12	6	4		
D. I do not enjoy spending time with my parents	12	4	5	4	1		

10. Which *one* of the following best fits your impressions of your parents' social values?

A. They have strong moral prin-ciples and they live by them	34%	51%	58%	71%	69%	NOT ASKED OF	
B. They have strong moral prin-ciples but they don't always act on them	31	26	27	19	23	PARENTS	
C. They usually act out of expediency rather than out of any moral principles	36	23	16	10	7		

12. In your view, what has your parents' way of life brought them? For example, has it brought them personal fulfillment, material comfort, both, or not much of either?

	YOUTH					PARENTS OF				
	Revolution-ary	Radi-cal Re-former	Mod-erate Re-former	Mid-dle Road	Con-serv-ative	Revo-lution-ary	Radi-cal Re-former	Mod-erate Re-former	Mid-dle Road	Con-serv-ative
Personal fulfillment	8%	15%	13%	16%	13%	NOT ASKED OF				
Material comfort	39	15	14	8	7	PARENTS				
Both	29	44	56	63	72					
Neither	24	24	17	13	8					

13. ASKED OF YOUTH: Which of the following would describe your parents during your *childhood*: (MORE THAN ONE ANSWER PERMISSIBLE)

Permissive, lenient	47%	35%	48%	35%	41%
Strict, authoritarian	36	42	27	40	43
Considered your opinion, gave you a full vote in family matters	27	27	32	40	42
Gave you much of their time	42	40	52	52	67
Too busy to give much of their time	36	12	21	12	14
Old-fashioned in their outlook	46	28	39	33	28
Modern, progres-sive in their outlook	36	29	28	32	34
Liberal in their politics	41	22	23	20	17
Conservative in their politics	34	25	34	31	33

14. Thinking back to your economic circumstances when you were a child, would you say that you personally felt *very secure* economically, *fairly secure*, or *not very secure*?

Very secure	54%	56%	56%	53%	53%	NOT ASKED OF
Fairly secure	29	27	37	39	41	PARENTS
Not very secure	17	16	8	8	6	

15. What about now—would you say that you feel *very secure* economically, *fairly secure* or *not very secure*?

Very secure	34%	40%	26%	43%	31%	NOT ASKED OF
Fairly secure	39	42	68	52	63	PARENTS
Not very secure	25	17	6	5	6	

16. ASKED OF YOUTH: Would you please complete the following sentence for me. The main trouble with the young generation is: (FREE RESPONSE)

| | YOUTH | | | | | PARENTS OF | | | | |
	Revo-lution ary	Radi-cal Re-former	Mod-erate Re-former	Mid-dle Road	Con-serv-ative	Revo-lution ary	Radi-cal Re-former	Mod-erate Re-former	Mid-dle Road	Con-serv-ative
Immature and naive	24%	22%	20%	20%	23%					
Too impatient	3	15	12	13	11					
Intolerant and close-minded	2	8	14	10	6					
No respect for authority or parents	5	13	7	10	15					
Self-centered and lack of responsibility	7	6	4	11	19					
Doesn't try to communicate with older people	3	6	7	11	14					
Has too much freedom	2	11	8	7	12					
Nothing—there is no trouble	20	9	13	8	6					

17. ASKED ONLY IF ATTENDING COLLEGE: Which of the following two statements comes closer to expressing your own point of view:

For me, college is mainly a practical matter. With a college education I can earn more money, have a more interesting career and enjoy a better position in the society.	6%	30%	43%	69%	73%	NOT ASKED OF PARENTS	
I'm not really concerned with the practical benefits of college. I suppose I take them for granted. College for me means something more intangible; perhaps the opportunity to change things rather than make out well within the existing system.	92	65	53	27	24		

18. ASKED OF YOUTH: Which of the following considerations will have a relatively strong influence on your choice of career:

	YOUTH					PARENTS OF				
	Revolution-ary	Radi-cal Re-former	Mod-erate Re-former	Mid-dle Road	Con-serv-ative	Revo-lution-ary	Radi-cal Re-former	Mod-erate Re-former	Mid-dle Road	Con-serv-ative
Your family	17%	25%	31%	38%	36%					
The money that you can earn	12	42	47	47	55					
The prestige or status of the job	10	16	22	20	26					
The security of the job	12	37	42	46	52					
The ability to express yourself	76	45	68	42	35					
The challenge of the job	54	38	63	52	46					
The opportunity to make a meaningful contribution	78	53	70	58	54					

19. A. Do you have any doubt about being able to make as much money as you may want to, whatever that amount is?

Yes	39%	40%	41%	49%	50%	NOT ASKED OF
No	61	60	58	50	50	PARENTS

B. Do you have any doubt about your ability to be successful—as you define success?

Yes	25	35	30	27	34
No	71	65	70	73	66

20. Many young people today dress and groom themselves quite differently than did young people five years ago. How do you feel about these changes in dress and grooming?

Nothing wrong with them	34%	38%	40%	33%	31%	NOT ASKED OF
It's up to the individual	49	32	33	23	14	PARENTS
Dislike long hair and beards	—	7	7	21	20	
Dislike mini-skirts	—	11	8	11	8	
Dislike the hippie look	—	4	13	7	11	
Dislike extremes	—	10	3	10	13	
All right if people are clean	2	3	9	8	16	
Change is normal	5	9	8	7	7	

Society—Institutions and Restraints

21. A. Which of the following activities do you feel are *morally wrong* from your personal point of view, and which do you feel are *not a moral issue*?

	YOUTH					PARENTS OF				
	Revo-lution-ary	Radi-cal Re-former	Mod-erate Re-former	Mid-dle Road	Con-serv-ative	Revo-lution-ary	Radi-cal Re-former	Mod-erate Re-former	Mid-dle Road	Con-serv-ative
Having an abortion										
Morally wrong	14%	56%	38%	65%	68%	NOT TABULATED				
Not a moral issue	85	44	61	34	26					
Relations between consenting homosexuals										
Morally wrong	7	69	35	75	83					
Not a moral issue	90	31	63	25	15					
Pre-marital sexual relations										
Morally wrong	—	47	32	61	63					
Not a moral issue	100	52	67	38	34					
Extra-marital sexual relations										
Morally wrong	19	69	70	81	83					
Not a moral issue	81	30	29	18	14					

B. Which of these activities do you think your parent (of same sex) would feel are *morally wrong*, and which do you think he would feel are *not a moral issue*?

Having an abortion							
Morally wrong	51	78	67	78	79	NOT ASKED OF	
Not a moral issue	36	18	31	16	13	PARENTS	
Relations between consenting homosexuals							
Morally wrong	66	86	80	85	88		
Not a moral issue	24	11	17	9	7		
Pre-marital sexual relations							
Morally wrong	54	85	84	84	90		
Not a moral issue	37	11	13	10	5		
Extra-marital sexual relations							
Morally wrong	85	89	92	87	86		
Not a moral issue	7	7	6	7	7		

C. Under which of the following conditions would you approve of abortion:

Recommended by a physician	88	72	84	77	72
Pregnancy as the result of rape	86	65	69	63	61
Failure of birth control practices in marriage	66	20	25	9	10
Pre-marital pregnancy	71	28	40	14	11
Under no conditions	2	15	10	12	21

22. Some people have said that the present institution of marriage is becoming obsolete. Do you agree or disagree?

	YOUTH					PARENTS OF				
	Revo-lution-ary	Radi-cal Re-former	Mod-erate Re-former	Mid-dle Road	Con-serv-ative	Revo-lution-ary	Radi-cal Re-former	Mod-erate Re-former	Mid-dle Road	Con-serv-ative
Agree	68%	42%	30%	19%	18%	NOT ASKED OF				
Disagree	32	57	68	79	80	PARENTS				

23. Which of the following restraints imposed by society and its institutions can you *accept easily*, which do you *accept reluctantly*, and which do you *reject outright*?

Abiding by laws you don't agree with
Accept easily	−%	26%	10%	36%	44%	NOT ASKED OF
Accept reluctantly	32	50	70	58	51	PARENTS
Reject outright	68	24	20	6	5	

Conforming in matters of clothing and personal grooming
Accept easily	5	55	33	55	58
Accept reluctantly	15	11	31	28	27
Reject outright	80	34	36	16	15

The prohibition against marijuana
Accept easily	5	47	43	77	85
Accept reluctantly	3	8	25	10	8
Reject outright	92	45	32	13	7

The prohibition against LSD
Accept easily	24	58	68	83	91
Accept reluctantly	8	10	16	5	3
Reject outright	68	30	15	11	6

The prohibition against other drugs
Accept easily	22	52	67	81	87
Accept reluctantly	20	16	19	6	6
Reject outright	58	31	14	12	7

Outward conformity for the sake of career advancement
Accept easily	2	48	20	30	39
Accept reluctantly	29	15	37	42	42
Reject outright	69	37	41	27	18

The power and authority of the police
Accept easily	—	56	52	80	91
Accept reluctantly	37	32	40	17	7
Reject outright	63	11	8	3	2

The power and authority of the "boss" in a work situation
Accept easily	3	66	56	70	76
Accept reluctantly	54	25	39	27	22
Reject outright	42	8	5	3	2

Having little decision-making power in the first few years of a job
Accept easily	5	56	36	50	46
Accept reluctantly	44	29	46	36	43
Reject outright	51	15	18	11	9

cont.

	YOUTH					PARENTS OF				
	Revo-lution-ary	Radi-cal Re-former	Mod-erate Re-former	Mid-dle Road	Con-serv-ative	Revo-lution-ary	Radi-cal Re-former	Mod-erate Re-former	Mid-dle Road	Con-serv-ative
Being treated impersonally in a job										
Accept easily	3%	22%	13%	20%	21%	NOT ASKED OF				
Accept reluctantly	22	27	29	45	41	PARENTS				
Reject outright	75	50	58	35	38					
Accepting the authority of the university administration										
Accept easily	2	63	46	77	82					
Accept reluctantly	42	30	40	17	12					
Reject outright	56	6	12	3	1					

24. For each of the following, please tell me whether you feel it needs no substantial change, needs moderate change, needs fundamental reform or should be done away with.

	YOUTH					PARENTS OF				
Big business										
No substantial change	2%	20%	13%	25%	19%	NOT ASKED OF				
Moderate change	12	43	40	57	61	PARENTS				
Fundamental reform	44	28	43	16	17					
Done away with	42	9	4	–	1					
The military										
No substantial change	–	10	6	29	22					
Moderate change	3	42	20	50	55					
Fundamental reform	51	29	57	20	19					
Done away with	46	18	18	1	3					
The universities										
No substantial change	–	22	14	24	21					
Moderate change	14	48	44	55	51					
Fundamental reform	83	28	41	21	28					
Done away with	3	1	2	–	–					
Trade unions										
No substantial change	3	18	14	30	19					
Moderate change	25	43	45	41	47					
Fundamental reform	63	31	32	21	18					
Done away with	8	6	6	6	10					

cont.

	YOUTH					PARENTS OF				
	Revo-lution-ary	Radi-cal Re-former	Mod-erate Re-former	Mid-dle Road	Con-serv-ative	Revo-lution-ary	Radi-cal Re-former	Mod-erate Re-former	Mid-dle Road	Con-serv-ative
The political parties										
No substantial change	2%	9%	6%	22%	21%	NOT ASKED OF				
Moderate change	10	32	20	44	39	PARENTS				
Fundamental reform	42	45	63	28	34					
Done away with	46	13	11	5	4					
The mass media										
No substantial change	7	21	14	23	21					
Moderate change	24	48	44	51	52					
Fundamental reform	66	17	37	20	19					
Done away with	3	13	2	3	5					

25. Which of the following values do you believe are worth *fighting a war for,* which do you believe are *not worth fighting a war for,* and for which would you say it *depends on the specific circumstances?*

Keeping a committment										
Worth fighting for	5%	33%	10%	30%	28%	27%	29%	19%	33%	23%
Not worth fighting for	47	30	28	10	15	18	19	23	13	16
Depends on circumstances	47	37	62	60	58	55	39	58	53	60
Containing the Communists										
Worth fighting for	10	48	35	75	81	55	53	48	69	78
Not worth fighting for	71	33	26	5	7	27	16	27	11	5
Depends on circumstances	19	18	39	20	12	18	18	25	19	16
Maintaining our position of power in the world										
Worth fighting for	10	52	19	54	56	55	45	47	57	54
Not worth fighting for	80	30	40	14	21	36	29	25	18	11
Depends on circumstances	10	18	41	32	24	9	13	28	25	32
Protecting Allies										
Worth fighting for	10	45	32	52	59	36	46	37	50	56
Not worth fighting for	49	26	12	7	6	18	6	18	6	2
Depends on circumstances	39	28	56	41	35	45	34	45	44	42

cont.

	YOUTH					PARENTS OF				
	Revo-lution-ary	Radi-cal Re-former	Mod-erate Re-former	Mid-dle Road	Con-serv-ative	Revo-lution-ary	Radi-cal Re-former	Mod-erate Re-former	Mid-dle Road	Con-serv-ative
Fighting for our honor										
Worth fighting for	3%	59%	21%	62%	66%	45%	41%	50%	64%	71%
Not worth fighting for	90	23	37	9	10	18	29	23	10	4
Depends on circumstances	7	17	42	28	24	36	17	27	26	24
Counteracting aggression										
Worth fighting for	22	50	59	68	73	64	72	53	71	71
Not worth fighting for	31	27	6	4	1	9	3	15	2	1
Depends on circumstances	46	20	35	28	24	27	12	12	26	25
Protecting our national interests										
Worth fighting for	7	63	39	66	75	91	66	61	70	75
Not worth fighting for	58	19	14	3	3	—	8	9	4	7
Depends on circumstances	36	19	46	31	22	9	14	30	25	18

26. Which one of the following statements comes closest to your own point of view:

Resisting the draft is basically wrong —a citizen is obligated to serve his country regardless of his personal views about the justness of a war.	—%	45%	33%	82%	83%	NOT ASKED OF PARENTS
An individual should obey his conscience—if he feels that he is being drafted to fight in a war that is morally wrong, he should resist in any way that he can.	98	55	67	17	17	

27. Which of the following statements do you *strongly agree* with, which do you *partially agree* with, and which do you *strongly disagree* with?

	YOUTH					PARENTS OF				
	Revo-lution-ary	Radi-cal Re-former	Mod-erate Re-former	Mid-dle Road	Con-serv-ative	Revo-lution-ary	Radi-cal Re-former	Mod-erate Re-former	Mid-dle Road	Con-serv-ative

"The Establishment" unfairly controls every aspect of our lives; we can never be free until we are rid of it.

Strongly agree	53%	35%	11%	8%	9%	NOT ASKED OF				
Partially agree	47	48	53	42	38	PARENTS				
Strongly disagree	—	15	36	46	52					

A mass revolutionary party should be created.

Strongly agree	61	26	1	1	3
Partially agree	39	22	15	11	3
Strongly disagree	—	51	83	87	92

Authorities must be put in an intolerable position so they will be forced to respond with repression and thus show their illegitimacy.

Strongly agree	32	26	3	5	6
Partially agree	51	34	36	29	24
Strongly disagree	17	36	57	64	69

Disruption is preferable to discussing issues for changing our society.

Strongly agree	22	26	8	5	6
Partially agree	54	25	23	23	12
Strongly disagree	24	47	69	70	80

Sexual behavior should be bound by mutual feelings, not by formal and legal ties.

Strongly agree	90	64	48	29	18
Partially agree	7	12	30	29	27
Strongly disagree	3	24	22	41	54

A minority must never be allowed to impose its will on the majority.

Strongly agree	10	28	17	24	26
Partially agree	29	32	48	32	26
Strongly disagree	61	40	34	43	47

There are legitimate channels for reform which must be exhausted before attempting disruption.

Strongly agree	24	36	56	54	67
Partially agree	49	44	32	34	22
Strongly disagree	27	13	11	10	9

Today, rebuilding society is of less immediate importance than destroying it.

Strongly agree	32	23	29	32	23
Partially agree	22	18	14	12	8
Strongly disagree	46	59	56	55	68

Radicals of the left are as much a threat to the rights of the individual as are radicals of the right.

Strongly agree	15	42	54	52	55
Partially agree	25	37	37	31	35
Strongly disagree	59	16	8	12	6

cont.

	YOUTH					PARENTS OF				
	Revo-lution-ary	Radi-cal Re-former	Mod-erate Re-former	Mid-dle Road	Con-serv-ative	Revo-lution-ary	Radi-cal Re-former	Mod-erate Re-former	Mid-dle Road	Con-serv-ative

The American system of representative democracy can respond effectively to the needs of the people.

Strongly agree	3%	43%	19%	53%	51%	NOT ASKED OF	
Partially agree	20	32	67	41	41	PARENTS	
Strongly disagree	76	25	13	4	7		

28. Following are a number of criticisms that have been made in recent years about American society. For each one tell me whether you *strongly agree, partially agree*, or whether you *strongly disagree.*

Our foreign policy is based on our own narrow economic and power interests.

Strongly agree	88%	45%	41%	19%	22%	18%	33%	19%	20%	9%
Partially agree	12	40	50	52	38	73	45	55	40	42
Strongly disagree	—	13	8	27	36	9	20	23	32	43

Business is overly concerned with profits and not with public responsibility.

Strongly agree	90	72	63	40	53	45	60	45	46	57
Partially agree	10	23	34	48	40	36	25	33	38	27
Strongly disagree	—	5	3	11	7	18	15	20	16	16

The individual in today's society is isolated and cut off from meaningful relationships with others.

Strongly agree	63	38	17	9	14	27	34	21	12	11
Partially agree	36	37	55	35	37	45	28	34	35	37
Strongly disagree	2	25	28	53	49	27	38	42	53	52

There is more concern today for the "welfare bum" who doesn't want to work than for the hard-working person who is struggling to make a living.

Strongly agree	3	51	37	53	71	55	64	62	68	72
Partially agree	10	24	40	29	29	36	23	21	22	22
Strongly disagree	86	25	22	17	—	9	12	17	10	5

Economic well-being in this country is unjustly and unfairly distributed.

Strongly agree	88	42	41	24	28	27	45	40	25	23
Partially agree	12	45	48	45	43	55	22	36	42	44
Strongly disagree	—	11	10	31	28	18	21	22	32	33

Basically, we are a racist nation.

Strongly agree	85	51	42	18	22	27	60	46	28	19
Partially agree	14	32	47	48	48	55	20	28	34	19
Strongly disagree	2	17	11	32	29	18	20	25	35	61

Most of what is taught in universities is not relevant to today's needs.

Strongly agree	68	33	17	14	11	18	24	26	9	12
Partially agree	27	48	52	37	39	64	43	39	50	28
Strongly disagree	3	19	28	48	49	18	19	32	36	55

Morally and spiritually our country has lost its way.

Strongly agree	54	36	22	17	20	18	22	32	23	27
Partially agree	32	46	50	38	40	64	47	32	38	32
Strongly disagree	14	18	28	45	40	18	31	34	39	41

cont.

	YOUTH					PARENTS OF				
	Revo-lution-ary	Radi-cal Re-former	Mod-erate Re-former	Mid-dle Road	Con-serv-ative	Revo-lution-ary	Radi-cal Re-former	Mod-erate Re-former	Mid-dle Road	Con-serv-ative

The war in Vietnam is pure imperialism.

Strongly agree	75%	34%	20%	7%	8%	9%	33%	29%	7%	5%
Partially agree	25	42	61	34	35	36	25	26	37	21
Strongly disagree	–	23	19	57	56	55	38	40	48	66

Today's American society is characterized by "injustice, insensitivity, lack of candor and inhumanity."

Strongly agree	81	42	21	7	10	–	27	10	11	10
Partially agree	17	44	63	36	43	82	24	38	40	30
Strongly disagree	–	13	16	57	46	18	40	48	47	58

There is too much concern with equality and too little with law and order.

Strongly agree	2	44	24	42	63	64	56	49	59	53
Partially agree	2	18	37	39	37	36	28	37	34	22
Strongly disagree	97	34	39	19	–	–	16	14	6	22

Activism and Involvement

33. Which of the following views of American society and American life reflect your own feelings?

The American way of life is superior to that of any other country.	–%	11%	6%	18%	76%	NOT TABULATED
There are serious flaws in our society today, but the system is flexible enough to solve them.	–	40	84	75	23	
The American system is not flexible enough; radical change is needed.	100	49	9	7	1	

34. In general, do you feel that your own personal values and point of view are shared by most Americans today?

Yes	–%	40%	37%	54%	60%	NOT TABULATED
Not certain	17	28	31	29	24	
No	83	32	31	17	16	

35. If you continue to feel at odds with the majority, which of the following, realistically speaking, are you *most* likely to do?

	YOUTH					PARENTS OF				
	Revolutionary	Radical Reformer	Moderate Reformer	Middle Road	Conservative	Revolutionary	Radical Reformer	Moderate Reformer	Middle Road	Conservative
Change your point of view	−%	−%	−%	−%	−%	NOT ASKED OF PARENTS				
Outwardly accept the majority way of life, but retain your own private values.	−	3	9	8	6					
Build a private life with like-minded people who share your values, and try to ignore the majority.	19	8	6	1	3					
Withdraw from the system and drop out.	10	1	1	−	1					
Continue to fight actively for what you believe is right.	53	19	15	8	7					

36. A. Which of the following have you yourself been involved in:

Sit-ins	63%	13%	10%	2%	1%	NOT ASKED OF PARENTS				
Strikes	53	8	8	3	2					
Riots	39	3	5	1	2					
Marches	73	26	18	3	3					
Political campaigns	64	22	28	14	8					
Organization meetings	66	25	35	23	16					
Civil rights protests	64	9	12	1	3					
Joined organizations like SDS and YAF	44	4	2	1	−					
Been arrested	19	7	12	6	5					
None	12	55	42	65	76					

B. For those activities you have not been involved in, which of these would you like to be involved in?

Sit-ins	12	10	18	9	8
Strikes	17	11	11	7	9
Riots	27	2	1	3	5
Marches	10	10	16	9	9

cont.

	YOUTH					PARENTS OF				
	Revo-lution-ary	Radi-cal Re-former	Mod-erate Re-former	Mid-dle Road	Con-serv-ative	Revo-lution-ary	Radi-cal Re-former	Mod-erate Re-former	Mid-dle Road	Con-serv-ative
Political campaigns	7%	24%	31%	24%	20%	NOT ASKED OF PARENTS				
Organization meetings	2	8	18	11	13					
Civil rights protests	19	13	23	9	6					
Join organizations like SDS and YAF	22	12	5	4	6					
Be arrested	17	2	1	3	4					
None	37	52	42	65	70					

37. Which of the tactics listed on this card do you feel are *always* justified, which are *sometimes* justified, and which do you feel are *never* justified?

Sit-ins
Always justified	56%	17%	7%	2%	1%	NOT ASKED OF PARENTS				
Sometimes justified	39	67	82	63	53					
Never justified	5	12	10	34	46					

Ultimatums to those in authority
Always justified	49	18	5	7	6					
Sometimes justified	51	62	83	62	55					
Never justified	–	15	12	30	38					

Blockades of buildings
Always justified	31	18	1	2	–					
Sometimes justified	66	43	65	29	13					
Never justified	3	30	32	68	85					

Destruction or mutilation of property
Always justified	12	5	–	1	–					
Sometimes justified	88	39	16	8	–					
Never justified	–	56	83	90	100					

Resisting or disobeying police
Always justified	37	18	1	2	–					
Sometimes justified	63	47	62	25	15					
Never justified	–	36	37	73	84					

Assaulting police
Always justified	19	10	1	2	–					
Sometimes justified	81	34	23	11	–					
Never justified	–	56	77	86	100					

cont.

	YOUTH					PARENTS OF				
	Revo-lution-ary	Radi-cal Re-former	Mod-erate Re-former	Mid-dle Road	Con-serv-ative	Revo-lution-ary	Radi-cal Re-former	Mod-erate Re-former	Mid-dle Road	Con-serv-ative
Assaulting other civil authorities										
Always justified	8%	5%	1%	1%	–%	NOT ASKED OF PARENTS				
Sometimes justified	88	41	20	13	3					
Never justified	3	54	79	85	97					
Holding an authority captive										
Always justified	8	12	1	1	–					
Sometimes justified	92	27	19	11	–					
Never justified	–	59	80	87	100					
Use of police to control demonstrators										
Always justified	–	45	23	48	59					
Sometimes justified	47	48	70	46	35					
Never justified	53	7	6	6	6					
Use of police to evict those participating in sit-ins										
Always justified	–	35	12	36	49					
Sometimes justified	27	48	66	55	50					
Never justified	73	18	23	8	1					
Use of police to prevent destruction of property										
Always justified	–	65	67	82	91					
Sometimes justified	63	32	32	15	6					
Never justified	34	3	1	3	1					
Using draft resistance as a political weapon										
Always justified	56	18	9	5	3					
Sometimes justified	31	35	42	22	12					
Never justified	14	42	45	73	83					

38. Which, if any, of these criticisms that have been made about the radical student movement do you personally share:

"All they want to do is tear things down—they have no positive program."	–%	22%	22%	32%	41%	NOT ASKED OF PARENTS				
"They are too hostile and an-tagonistic to be effective."	5	24	34	47	61					

cont.

	YOUTH					PARENTS OF				
	Revo-lution-ary	Radi-cal Re-former	Mod-erate Re-former	Mid-dle Road	Con-serv-ative	Revo-lution-ary	Radi-cal Re-former	Mod-erate Re-former	Mid-dle Road	Con-serv-ative
"They are not tolerant of anyone but themselves."	7%	49%	40%	42%	47%	NOT ASKED OF PARENTS				
"The radical student movement lacks real leadership."	49	43	48	42	35					
None of these criticisms is true.	47	21	15	13	8					

39. With respect to your own personal role in seeking to bring about needed changes in colleges or other institutions of our society, which *one* of the following statements best describes your own position?

I consider myself to be an activist.	63%	4%	4%	1%	1%	NOT ASKED OF PARENTS				
I am in sympathy with most of the activists' objectives, but not with all of their tactics.	32	32	43	23	16					
I'm not emotionally involved, one way or the other.	2	31	23	41	36					
I am not sure that I approve of what the activists are trying to do, but I have no strong objections to letting them try.	5	26	20	18	14					
I am in total disagreement with the activists.	—	6	9	16	32					

40. With which of the following groups, if any, do you feel a sense of identification? (MULTIPLE RESPONSE PERMISSIBLE)

The middle class	15%	44%	59%	60%	71%	NOT TABULATED				
Students	69	55	61	56	48					
The New Left	69	14	13	—	1					
Conservatives	2	6	9	17	26					
The Old Left	15	6	7	1	1					
Your family	51	55	80	78	78					
People of your nationality	25	25	45	41	44					

cont.

	YOUTH					PARENTS OF				
	Revo-lution-ary	Radi-cal Re-former	Mod-erate Re-former	Mid-dle Road	Con-serv-ative	Revo-lution-ary	Radi-cal Re-former	Mod-erate Re-former	Mid-dle Road	Con-serv-ative
People of your religion	17%	21%	33%	47%	52%	NOT TABULATED				
Other people of your generation	68	56	75	73	70					
People of your race	25	45	52	50	54					

41. Which *one* of these candidates did you want to see elected last fall?

Nixon	–%	7%	16%	32%	33%	NOT ASKED OF	
Humphrey	–	1	9	12	11	PARENTS	
Wallace	–	–	5	9	9		
Robert Kennedy	27	64	40	34	34		
McCarthy	29	22	17	5	4		
Reagan	–	–	–	1	2		
Rockefeller	–	1	6	3	1		
Gregory	2	1	–	–	–		
Cleaver	27	1	–	–	–		
Johnson	–	–	1	1	4		
None of these	12	4	6	3	2		

42. Which of the following events, if any, have had a *great effect* on your life and your values, which have had a *moderate effect*, and which have had *little or no effect*?

Your college experience (if any)							
Great effect	64%	23%	33%	19%	11%	NOT ASKED OF	
Moderate effect	14	9	16	9	7	PARENTS	
Little or no effect	20	36	27	38	39		
The Vietnam war							
Great effect	68	32	47	34	22		
Moderate effect	12	36	36	32	37		
Little or no effect	20	32	17	34	41		
The civil rights movement							
Great effect	59	37	23	17	14		
Moderate effect	22	40	35	28	33		
Little or no effect	19	23	41	55	52		
The New Left							
Great effect	61	10	3	2	2		
Moderate effect	14	21	19	8	10		
Little or no effect	25	69	73	87	87		
The invasion of Czechoslovakia							
Great effect	17	15	8	8	6		
Moderate effect	31	13	34	21	18		
Little or no effect	53	73	58	70	76		

cont.

	YOUTH					PARENTS OF				
	Revo-lution-ary	Radi-cal Re-former	Mod-erate Re-former	Mid-dle Road	Con-serv-ative	Revo-lution-ary	Radi-cal Re-former	Mod-erate Re-former	Mid-dle Road	Con-serv-ative
The Cuban missile crisis										
Great effect	24%	14%	9%	10%	7%	NOT ASKED OF				
Moderate effect	14	19	23	21	25	PARENTS				
Little or no effect	63	66	67	69	68					
The death of John F. Kennedy										
Great effect	42	65	47	48	49					
Moderate effect	31	21	36	36	22					
Little or no effect	27	14	17	16	30					
The McCarthy campaign										
Great effect	41	24	17	5	4					
Moderate effect	20	12	29	12	13					
Little or no effect	39	64	55	82	83					
The death of Martin Luther King										
Great effect	53	46	27	22	17					
Moderate effect	24	29	41	32	29					
Little or no effect	24	25	32	46	54					

43. A. What scene stands out *most vividly* in your mind from the TV coverage you saw of: (FREE RESPONSE)

The Vietnam war										
Killing and bodies	39%	47%	39%	40%	44%	NOT ASKED OF				
Fighting and torturing	29	25	22	23	18	PARENTS				
No particular scenes	8	13	14	19	22					
Hunger and suffering of children	8	16	9	15	8					
Riots in ghetto										
Destruction and burning	14	17	28	25	25					
Looting	8	15	18	23	20					
No particular scenes	5	19	10	24	27					
Fighting and shooting	8	11	15	15	9					
Police brutality	36	19	15	7	2					
Specific areas mentioned (Watts, etc.)	12	1	8	7	5					
Poverty and poor living conditions	12	4	4	5	4					

cont.

	YOUTH					PARENTS OF				
	Revo-lution-ary	Radi-cal Re-former	Mod-erate Re-former	Mid-dle Road	Con-serv-ative	Revo-lution-ary	Radi-cal Re-former	Mod-erate Re-former	Mid-dle Road	Con-serv-ative

Campus demonstrations, such as those at Columbia, Wisconsin, San Francisco State, etc.

No particular scenes	10%	25%	19%	27%	28%	NOT ASKED OF
Childish actions by students	7	9	15	14	15	PARENTS
Police brutality	46	15	17	8	15	
Riots and kids beaten	17	9	11	9	6	
Destruction and chaos	–	5	7	8	4	
Students taking over buildings	3	13	6	8	6	

The Democratic Convention in Chicago

Police brutality	42	15	41	21	17
No particular scenes	5	27	12	23	21
Violence and bloodshed	14	14	23	17	16
Chaos and confusion	–	8	6	8	8
Demonstrations	5	8	7	6	7
Mayor Daley	7	3	7	4	4

B. What comments would you care to make about TV coverage of these events?

Coverage one-sided	44	32	42	32	28
Showed both sides	14	18	26	19	19
Good coverage generally	15	16	14	17	18
Too much coverage	2	5	7	6	2
Too little coverage	7	1	1	3	3

Demographic Characteristics

Characteristic:		Youths classified as:					
	Total Youth	Rev	Rad	Ref	Mod	Con	Total Parents
Sex							
Male	45%	71%	44%	50%	38%	58%	38%
Female	55	29	56	50	62	42	62

cont.

Characteristic:	Total Youth	Youths classified as:					Total Parents
		Rev	Rad	Ref	Mod	Con	
Age							
17 years old	18%	2%	18%	13%	20%	18%	– %
18–19 years	35	29	32	30	38	33	–
20–21 years	25	49	34	34	20	21	–
22–23 years	23	20	15	23	22	28	–
under 45 years	–	–	–	–	–	–	33
45 years or more	–	–	–	–	–	–	67
Marital Status							
Unmarried	78	7	15	19	23	30	–
Married	22	93	85	81	77	70	90
Widowed	–	–	–	–	–	–	4
Divorced/ Separated	–	–	–	–	–	–	6
Race							
White	91	81	74	93	91	94	
Nonwhite	9	19	26	7	9	6	
Education							
Some college/graduate							30.
Had no college							70
Religion							
Protestant	58	7	50	49	61	71	66
Catholic	27	7	25	29	30	21	24
Jewish	5	12	8	9	3	2	5
Other	2	14	5	1	1	2	2
None	8	61	12	12	5	5	2
Political Affiliation							
Republican	25	–	9	22	30	26	32
Democrat	47	20	52	43	46	51	50
Liberal	–	–	–	–	–	–	–
Independent	3	3	3	3	4	2	6
Conservative	–	–	–	1	–	1	–
Other	1	34	4	1	–	–	–
None	19	31	22	27	16	15	9
Parents' Occupation							
White collar	41	58	46	44	41	33	43
Blue collar	46	31	27	47	47	50	51
Parents' Income							
Under $10,000	48	36	55	35	53	48	44
$10,000–$14,999	29	20	24	34	24	41	33
$15,000 or more	22	44	21	31	23	11	23
Youths' Occupation							
Not employed	45	54	45	36	45	52	
White collar	29	39	15	33	31	24	
Blue collar	27	7	40	31	24	24	

cont.

| Characteristic: | Total Youth | Youths classified as: | | | | | Total Parents |
		Rev	Rad	Ref	Mod	Con	
Youths' Income							
No income	45%	54%	45%	36%	45%	52%	
Under $3,000	28	42	34	34	29	16	
$3,000–$4,999	14	3	17	12	15	13	
$5,000 or more	13	—	3	18	11	19	
Labor Union Member							
Yes, a member							22%
No, not a member							78
Region of Country							
Northeast	25	24	25	30	26	16	
Midwest	26	24	23	28	28	20	
South	30	17	26	19	32	44	
West	18	36	26	22	14	20	
Draft Status							
Eligible	19	36	26	23	18	11	
Deferred	45	50	38	52	41	50	
Ineligible	14	2	7	12	13	21	
Indeterminable	22	12	29	14	27	19	

Marijuana

Amid the swirling cultural, social, and political currents of the sixties, the emergence of widespread drug use, particularly among the young, was a development that literally stunned the consciousness of America. The so-called "drug culture" actually comprised two separate subcultures, each quite different from the other, but with enough similarities to make it impossible for many people to discriminate between them.

First, of course, and most troublesome, was the culture and the problems of the narcotics addicts, the heroin users. The "hard" drugs, addictive, expensive, and therefore linked to criminality among their users, a product of international criminal traffic, had been known to the public in a remote sort of way prior to the sixties. Recently, the staggering increase in the use of heroin, along with a wider awareness of its implications in a decade alarmed by increases in crime and disorder, brought the problem closer to home. Moreover, heroin use, long confined to the ghetto, began to evidence itself in white, middle class neighborhoods, and the proximity of human tragedy also served to heighten awareness of the problem.

Even more stunning in its impact on middle America was the emergence of the casual use of hallucinogens as an element of the "youth culture." First appearing among the so-called "hippies," on campuses and off, the use of hallucinogens rapidly spread throughout the country, to high schools, even junior high schools.

Unlike heroin, the "soft" drugs were easy to come by and were comparatively inexpensive. For one thing, they need not be imported. Marijuana, the most frequently used drug of the group, could be locally grown in most parts of the country; of the synthetics, most were available as household commodities, particularly the amphetamines and the barbiturates, while some of the newer "mind drugs" such as LSD could be manufactured in crude laboratories by amateur chemists.

So the homegrown "soft" drugs were cheap and available, and their use spread rapidly among young people, whether students or not. No community was immune from the traffic. If heroin was a big-city problem, marijuana evidenced itself just as strongly in rural, small-town America as it did in the cities and the suburbs. Indeed, most of the illicit cultivation of marijuana was undertaken in the fertile prairie states, in the heart of middle America.

Middle America was scared, frightened enough not to be able to discriminate between addictive and nonaddictive drugs, between casual use or youthful experimentation and commitment and dependency. To some extent this was understandable—the frightening effects in some LSD cases involved more than a simple "high," and who could tell whether a youngster who had tried marijuana might not also want to experiment with something more potent—not just another hallucinogen, but even, eventually, an addictive drug like heroin?

Drug use was against the law, as was possession, and the laws were harsh. The public awoke to another difficult problem, though. The nice kid next door, or even the one upstairs in the bedroom, was hardly a hardened criminal, nor was he an addict whose habit led him into other types of crime. Shouldn't the law and the courts differentiate between the types? Shouldn't they discriminate between the user, merely a customer, even a victim, and the "pusher," who was spreading the stuff around?

Even more compelling a question, particularly to the young, was the difference in effect among drugs. Marijuana, it was argued, had no residual aftereffects. Among youth convinced of the lack of understanding, or hypocrisy of the older generation, the use of marijuana appeared no more dangerous, perhaps less so, than the use of alcohol or cigarettes. After all, argued the kids, medical authorities had proved the relationship between alcohol and a variety of diseases, and between cigarettes and lung cancer and heart disease. Why condemn and punish the use of a drug which had no provable harmful effects?

Thus, the public debate, which continues to rage, began. Should possession and use of marijuana be legalized? Or at the least, should penalties be lightened? Did it make sense to impose sentences in marijuana cases equal to or greater than those imposed in cases of criminal assault on people or property?

Unfortunately, it was not, nor is it today, a debate based solely on the merits of the legal and medical facts. For one thing, little medical information was available. The little research and experimentation done in the field was fragmentary and contradictory in nature; although experts agreed that marijuana was nonaddictive and not immediately harmful, there was a difference of opinion both as to whether its use led to a need for addictive drugs, and as to whether longtime use created psychological if not medical damage.

The debate was also colored by a host of emotional hangups, with political, social, racial, and cultural attitudes and fears playing an important role. Combined with the public's lack of specific knowledge of the subject, it was to be expected that the public's basic attitudes toward drugs should reflect fear, and therefore harshness.

It was to explore these attitudes that the CBS News Poll staff set about its public opinion survey in the summer of 1970. We found that concern and fear was even greater than we expected, that the public generally favored harsh treatment for offenders. Yet, at the same time, perhaps because the problem struck so close to home, there was an element of honest doubt and confusion about the penalties, and an occasional display of tolerance.

Two years after the survey, other studies by public opinion firms and by government show marijuana use still on the increase. Federal studies early in 1972 reported that nearly 25,000,000 Americans had tried it and that more than 8,000,000 were current users. Among college students, use was estimated at 44% by the National Institute of Mental Health, and Gallup reported that 51% of students have tried marijuana and that 30% are current and frequent users. Meanwhile, few of the social, medical, and legal problems associated with marijuana use have begun to be resolved.

SUMMARY OF FINDINGS*

A CBS News national telephone poll of 1,128 people, 18 years old and older, finds 6% of them saying that they have used marijuana. By a six to one ratio, however, many more people (36%) say they have friends whom they think have tried marijuana.

In addition to the 6% acknowledging the use of marijuana, another 6% say they have wanted to try marijuana to see what it would be like. Altogether, then, about one person out of every ten (or 12% of the sample) says he or she has tried or would like to try marijuana, as compared with 88% disclaiming either interest or use. Nearly four-fifths (78%) of those who admit having tried marijuana say they only used it a few times—perhaps a dozen times or so on the average.

The poll, conducted August 18-20, also found that 12% of the people think the use of marijuana should be made legal, as compared with only 5% who thought so five years ago. About three-fourths of the people who favor making marijuana legal today did not favor its legalization five years ago.

If people said they didn't think the use of marijuana should be legalized, they were asked if they would approve of its legal use by people over 21 years of age. If there were a legal age limit, an additional 5% say "yes"—the use of marijuana should be made legal. Overall, then, one out of six people (17%) who are 18 years or older think that the use of marijuana should be made legal—at least if there is an age limit—as compared with 81% who say it should not be legal under any circumstances. About one-tenth (11%) of the people also think the sale of marijuana should be legal. These are, of course, almost without exception the same people favoring legalized use.

About seven-tenths of the public (71%) feel very strongly or fairly strongly that the use of marijuana is a "crime that should be punished." This is a larger number than thought five years ago that the use of marijuana was a crime (61%). Among those who say they changed their opinion during the past five years or so, there was a shift in a negative direction. That is, of the 32% of the sample who say they changed their minds during the past five years, about two-thirds

---

*These findings are based on a national random sample of 1,128 telephone interviews with respondents 18 and older, conducted on August 18, 19 and 20, 1970. There may be a sampling error of up to plus or minus three percentage points associated with each finding.

say they now feel using marijuana is a crime but didn't think it was five years ago.

The reasons for the change in a negative direction may be, as many people said, that five years ago they didn't know anything about marijuana. Now, with all the publicity—they say—there is a fear among many that was nonexistent before. The fear is reflected in the fact that an overwhelming majority of the public believes that the regular use of marijuana is dangerous to the user's mental and physical health. Today, 90% feel that marijuana is dangerous to mental health, as compared with 78% saying they thought it was dangerous five years ago; 85% feel it is dangerous to a person's physical health, as compared with 75% saying they felt the same way five years ago.

Most of the people who consider marijuana dangerous report they felt the same way five years ago. Among those who changed their opinion, most shifted in a negative direction. That is, of the 20% of the sample who changed their opinion about the danger to mental health, four-fifths changed negatively; and of the 26% of the sample who changed their opinion about the danger to physical health, two-thirds changed negatively. Four out of every five people say they believe that marijuana is an "addictive drug, that becomes habit-forming." More than one-half (55%) think that most or all of the people who use marijuana go on to using more serious drugs like heroin.

The majority of people sees the use of marijuana as less dangerous than the use of LSD or heroin, about equally or *more* dangerous than the use of "pep pills," alcohol, tranquilizers, or cigarettes. Reading across the following table shows the perceived danger of marijuana versus other substances:

Regularly Using Marijuana is:

Compared to using:	Less Dangerous	Equal/More Dangerous		
LSD	60%	33%	= 93%	(7% = no opinion)
Heroin	50	44	= 94	(6% = no opinion)
Pep Pills	22	67	= 89	(11% = no opinion)
Alcohol	14	82	= 96	(4% = no opinion)
Tranquilizers	16	78	= 94	(6% = no opinion)
Cigarettes	16	82	= 98	(2% = no opinion)

Nearly three-fifths (58%) feel that the legal penalties for using marijuana should be made more severe than they are now. This is about three times the number (18%) feeling that the penalties should be made more lenient. Nearly nine out of ten people (86%), however, feel that the penalties for selling marijuana should be more severe, as compared with only a handful (5%) who feel the penalties should be more lenient.

Compared with how they would treat teenagers, people are much harsher in recommending penalties for adults caught using marijuana. Including the 12% of the people who said that the use of marijuana should be legalized (thus, no penalties), about one-half (49%) of the public would not give a jail sentence to a teenager caught using marijuana, but a smaller number (38%) feel the same way about dealing with adult offenders.

While people make a distinction between teenagers and adults in terms of whether to give jail sentences, if they do think offenders should be jailed they do not greatly differentiate between teens and adults. Typically, people would sentence a teenager to jail for less than one year (19%) or from one to five years (14%). An adult typically would get about the same treatment—less than one year (21%) or from one to five years (22%).

Of the people who said they would sentence a teenager to jail for using marijuana, about one out of five changed their minds when asked if they would still give a sentence knowing that a teenager "could lose his right to vote, to hold public office, or to work for the government." Altogether, including these people who changed their minds, three-fifths (60%) of the total sample would not sentence a teenager to jail for using marijuana.

When it comes to punishment for the sale of marijuana, the public is much more severe in dealing with both teenagers and adults, although teenagers still are less likely to be given a jail term. Including the 11% of the sample that said the sale of marijuana should be legal (thus, no penalties), less than one-third (31%) would not sentence a youth to jail as compared with only 13% who would not sentence an adult caught selling marijuana.

Jail terms for both teens and adults are typically more severe for selling marijuana than for merely using it. About twice as many people would give a teenager one to five years in jail (29%) as would give him less than one year (15%). For adults, however, about four times as many people would sentence an adult to one to five years (35%) as would jail him for less than a year (9%). The following table shows how the public would deal with marijuana users and sellers.

Recommended Penalties	Adults Caught		Teenagers Caught	
	Using	Selling	Using	Selling
No penalty (should be legal)	12%	11%	12%	11%
No penalty: fines/probation/work	10	1	16	12
No penalty: treatment/help/lecture	16	1	24	9
Subtotal:	38%	13%	52%	32%
Less than one year in jail	21%	9%	19%	15%
One to five years	22	35	14	29
Six to 10 years	3	13	2	7
Eleven to 20 years	2	7	1	4
Twenty years to life in prison	2	11	1	4
Sentence to death	—	1	—	1
Subtotal:	50%	76%	37%	60%

As noted before, most people are opposed to the legalization of marijuana, think it is a crime that should be punished, and would make penalties for use and sale more severe. Some of the reasons for the opposition to marijuana are that: (1) about four out of every five people (82%) think that using marijuana "leads people to commit crimes and acts of violence"; (2) nine out of ten (89%) think that using marijuana over a long period of time "results in a change in the user's basic personality"; (3) a comparable number (88%) feels that using marijuana "weakens the user's will and self-discipline"; and (4) about three-fourths (74%) say that using marijuana has "harmful effects on the unborn babies of pregnant women."

There is less consensus on the question about the effects of marijuana on sexual enjoyment. About two-fifths (43%) of the public disagree that "using marijuana gives people greater sexual enjoyment than they have normally," as compared with about one-third (34%) feeling that marijuana adds to sexual enjoyment. Nearly one-fourth (23%), however, could not or would not answer the question. (Among those who use marijuana, nearly one-half [47%] say the use of marijuana heightens sexual enjoyment.)

In the public's mind, there seems to be a certain aura of immaturity and rebelliousness connected with the use of marijuana. Nearly three-fifths (58%) say that all or most of the marijuana users are teenagers and college students. A third (36%) say some or just a few are teens and college students. A majority (54%) feels that all or most of the people who use marijuana are "afraid to face reality," as opposed to 40% saying some or just a few. Close to a half (48%) say that all or most of the marijuana users are "showing their rebellion against society," as opposed to 44% who say some or just a few. Half (50%) say that all or most marijuana users do it "only because their friends do, and they don't want to be left out of the crowd."

Interestingly enough, while a substantial majority of people feel that using marijuana is a crime and that the penalties should be made more severe, people weakened when asked how they would treat one of their own employees if they found out he frequently used marijuana. On whether they would fire one of their better employees, about half of the people said "no" (47%) and half said "yes" (50%).

Following are profiles of the 71 people (6%) who admit to having used marijuana and the 77 people (6%) who say they would like to try marijuana. The two groups are quite similar in their demographic makeup.

Profile of People Who Have Used Marijuana

People who have used marijuana are more likely to be:

in the 18 to 24 age group (although those 25 to 29 are somewhat likely to be users);

males;

college graduates or at least with some college education;

in professional or managerial occupations or college students;

from families with yearly incomes of $15,000 or more;

independent in their political affiliation;

without a religious preference;

living in the Western region of the country (Easterners are also somewhat more likely to be users).

Profile of People Who Would Like to Use Marijuana

People who would like to use marijuana are more likely to be:

in the 18 to 29 age group;

males;

college students or graduates;

in professional or managerial occupations or college students;

independent in their political affiliation;

without a religious preference;

living in the Eastern and Southern regions of the country.

A comparison of the people who have used marijuana with those who say they have wanted to use marijuana, and those who neither use nor want to, shows great similarity in the attitudes of the users and the potential users, as the next section shows.

Attitudes of People Who Have Used Marijuana, Would Use It, and Those Who Neither Have nor Want To

	Have Used	Would Use	Won't Use
N =	(71)	(77)	(980)
Think it is not addictive	66%	46%	12%
It is less dangerous than heroin	90	73	46
It is less dangerous than LSD	84	83	56
It is less dangerous than pep pills	58	48	18
It is more dangerous than alcohol	19	31	52
It is more dangerous than tranquilizers	29	40	55
It is more dangerous than tobacco	43	51	68
Feel very strongly it is a crime to be punished	23	13	55
Felt that way five years ago	23	37	47
Feel it is very dangerous to physical health	22	24	64
Felt that way five years ago	34	36	54
Feel it is very dangerous to mental health	30	36	73
Felt that way five years ago	35	40	58
Would fire a good employee who used it frequently	22	22	54
Think penalties for use should be more severe	23	31	63
Think penalties for sale should be more severe	49	60	90
Think regular use weakens user's will and discipline	64	72	91
Think regular use results in change in personality	65	69	93
Think it has harmful effects on unborn babies	42	55	78
Think it leads people to commit crimes and violence	39	60	86
Think it increases sexual enjoyment	47	35	34
Think the use of marijuana should be legal	57	45	6
Thought its use should be legal five years ago	23	14	4
Think the sale of marijuana should be legal	56	42	6

	Have Used	Would Use	Won't Use
Think most users go on to using more serious drugs	25%	35%	59%
Think most users are showing rebellion against society	32	34	50
Think most users are afraid to face reality	31	39	57
Think most users are teenagers and college students	67	63	57
Think most users do it not to be left out of crowd	52	47	50
Have no one in their circle of friends who use it	30	63	82
If none who use it, friends who have tried it	61	44	19
Have used it less than twenty times	78	–	–

QUESTIONNAIRE AND RESULTS

The following are question-by-question responses to all questionnaire items in the August 18–20, 1970, national survey of public attitudes toward marijuana. The questions are shown exactly as they were worded in the questionnaire, with the percentages of people choosing each response. The percentages are rounded, and therefore may not always add up to 100%.

1. As you know, there's been a lot of talk about people using marijuana in this country. Do you think that marijuana is, or is not, an addictive drug that becomes habit-forming.

Is addictive	81%
Is not addictive	17
No response	2

2. In terms of its effects, do you think that the regular use of marijuana is more dangerous, less dangerous, or equally as dangerous:

	Using marijuana is:		
	More/Equal Dangerous	Less Dangerous	No. Response
a. as the regular use of heroin	44%	50%	6 (100%)
b. as the regular use of "pep" pills	67	22	11 (100)
c. as the regular use of alcohol	82	14	4 (100)
d. as the regular use of LSD	33	60	7 (100)
e. as the regular use of tobacco	82	16	2 (100)
f. as the regular use of tranquilizers	78	16	6 (100)

3. Do you feel very strongly, fairly strongly, or not too strongly that using marijuana is a crime that should be punished?

Very strongly	50%
Fairly strongly	21
Not too stronly	26
No response	3

4. Do you feel that using marijuana is very dangerous, fairly d ngerous, or not too dangerous to a person's physical health?

Very dangerous	59%
Fairly dangerous	26
Not too dangerous	14
No response	1

5. Do you feel that using marijuana is very dangerous, fairly dangerous, or not too dangerous to a person's mental health?

Very dangerous	68%
Fairly dangerous	22
Not too dangerous	7
No response	3

6. Now, let's look back to your feelings about five years ago. Five years ago, did you feel very strongly, fairly strongly, or not too strongly that using marijuana was a crime that should be punished?

Very stronly	45%
Fairly strongly	16
Not too strongly	28
No response	11

7. Five years ago, did you feel that using marijuana was very dangerous, fairly dangerous, or not too dangerous to a person's physical health?

Very dangerous	51%
Fairly dangerous	24
Not too dangerous	16
No response	9

8. And, five years ago, did you feel that using marijuana was very dangerous, fairly dangerous, or not too dangerous to a person's mental health?

Very dangerous	55%
Fairly dangerous	23
Not too dangerous	13
No response	9

9. If you owned a business, and found out that one of your better employees frequently used marijuana, would you fire him, or not?

Yes, would fire him	50%
No, would not fire him	47
No response	3

10. Just in general terms, do you think that the legal penalties for using marijuana should be made more lenient, be kept about the same, or be made more severe than they are now?

Should be made more lenient	18%
Should be kept about the same	21
Should be made more severe	58
No response	3

11. And, do you think that the legal penalties for selling marijuana should be made more lenient, be kept about the same, or be made more severe than they are now?

Should be made more lenient   5%
Should be kept about the same   7
Should be made more severe   86
No response   2

12A. Do you think that using marijuana over a long period of time weakens the user's will and self-discipline?

Yes   88%
No   8
No response   4

12B. Do you think that using marijuana over a long period of time results in a change in the user's basic personality?

Yes   89%
No   7
No response   3

12C. Do you think that using marijuana over a long period of time has harmful effects on the unborn babies of pregnant women?

Yes   77%
No   12
No response   14

13. Would you agree, or disagree, that using marijuana leads people to commit crimes and acts of violence?

Agree   82%
Disagree   15
No response   4

14. Would you agree, or disagree, that using marijuana gives people greater sexual enjoyment than they have normally?

Agree   34%
Disagree   43
No response   23

15. Looking back about five years ago, did you think then that the use of marijuana should be legal, or not?

Yes, should be legal (5 years ago)   5%
No, should not be legal   88
No response   6

16. As things stand today, do you think that the use of marijuana should be made legal, or not?

Yes, should be legal (today)   12%
No, should not be legal   86
No response   2

NOTE: Question 16, A–D, was asked only of the people who said marijuana should not be legal.
(Percentages are based on the total sample.)

A. What about an age limit, do you think the use of marijuana should be made legal for people over 21, or not?

Yes, should be made legal	12% (from Q. 16)
Yes, legal for people over 21	5
No, should not be legal	81
No response	2

B. What kind of a jail sentence, if any, would you give to an adult caught using marijuana? (RESPONSES BELOW)

C. What kind of a jail sentence, if any, would you give to a teen-ager caught using marijuana?

	Adults	Teenagers	
No penalty (should be legal)	12%	12%	(from Q. 16)
No penalty: fines/probation/work	10	16	
No penalty: treatment/help/lecture.	16	24	
Subtotal:	38%	52%	
Less than one year in jail	21%	19%	
One to five years	22	14	
Six to 10 years	3	2	
Eleven to 20 years	2	1	
Twenty years to life	2	1	
Sentence to death	—	—	
Subtotal:	50%	37%	

D. IF ANY SENTENCE FOR TEEN-AGERS: If you knew that a person could lose his right to vote, to hold public office, or to work for the government, would you still sentence a teen-ager to jail for using marijuana?

Yes, would still sentence	29% (of total sample)
No, would not sentence	7
No response	1
Not asked the question	63

17. What about selling marijuana, do you think the sale of marijuana should be made legal, or not?

Yes, should be made legal	11%
No, should not be legal	87
No response	2

NOTE: Question 17, A-B, was asked only of people who said marijuana sale should not be legal.

A. What kind of a jail sentence, if any, would you give to an adult caught selling marijuana? (RESPONSES BELOW)

B. And, what kind of a jail sentence, if any, would you give to a teenager caught selling marijuana?

	Adults	Teenagers	
No penalty (should be legal)	11%	11%	(from Q. 17)
No penalty: fines/probation/work	1	12	
No penalty: treatment/help/lecture	1	9	
Subtotal:	13%	32%	
Less than one year in jail	9%	15%	
One to five years	35	29	
Six to 10 years	13	7	
Eleven to 20 years	7	4	
Twenty years to life	11	4	
Sentence to death	1	1	
Subtotal:	76%	60%	

18. Do you think that almost all, most, some, or just a few of the people who use marijuana:

	All	Most	Some	Few	No Response
a. go on to using more serious drugs like heroin	20%	35%	28%	11%	6 (100%)
b. are showing their rebellion against society	18	30	30	14	8 (100)
c. are afraid to face reality	23	31	27	13	6 (100)
d. are teen-agers and college students	15	43	28	8	6 (100)
e. do it only because their friends do, and they don't want to be left out of the crowd	17	33	32	13	6 (101)

19. In your own circle of friends, would you say that most, some, just a few, or none of them use marijuana? (If "None" or "No response": Do you think that any of them have ever tried marijuana?)

Most friends use marijuana	2%
Some friends use marijuana	5
A few friends use marijuana	12
No friends use marijuana	77*
No response (to either question)	4*

20. Even if it was only once, and just an experiment, have you ever tried marijuana, just to see what it was like? (If "Yes": Roughly speaking, about how many times have you used marijuana?) (If "No": Have you ever wanted to try marijuana, just to see what it would be like?)

Yes, have used less than 20 times	5%
Yes, have used more than 20 times	1
No, haven't used but wanted to	6
No haven't used and don't want to	85
No response	3

*Of these two groups, 227 people — 17% of the sample—said "yes," they thought some of their friends had tried marijuana.

President Watching

Four years is a long time between Presidential elections, far too long for the public "pulse-takers"—the news media and the pollsters—to refrain from periodic attempts to measure the public's attitudes toward the occupant of the White House.

Even during periods of comparative tranquility, it is only natural for the media and the pollsters to ask themselves how the country feels about its President. During periods of turbulence, when Presidential policies may create or acerbate deep emotional divisions or bring demonstrators into the streets, the need to measure attitudes would appear to be imperative.

Desire and attainment are not necessarily one and the same, however, and the institution of President watching by public opinion poll warrants some careful examination. Since the late 1930s, public opinion research organizations have purported to reflect public attitudes toward the President, and their polls have achieved widespread acceptance as meaningful measures—but measures of what?

Generally, the authors of the polls have labelled them as measures of Presidential "popularity." By asking the public a generalized question about how the President is handling the responsibilities of his office, the pollsters have concluded that the response is indeed a measure of the President's popularity with the public. By extension, particularly as the Presidential election year approaches, they implicitly suggest that this measure is also a yardstick of the incumbent's chances for reelection.

Yet there is reason to believe that these so-called Presidential popularity polls are misleading, meaningless, or both. The problem is that for most Americans the President is, at any given time, the object of a host of mixed and sometimes contradictory emotions. There are elements of ideology, policy, personality, and party at play in any individual's attitude toward the President, and in any of these categories, attitudes may contradict each other. The Southern hawk who

126

approves of an aggressive foreign policy may disagree with equal emphasis on an aggressive integration policy, to use a simple example.

Even beyond the basic complexity of issues, there are other factors affecting the responses to questions about the President. There is the institutionalization of the Presidency itself, the difficulty for many Americans in differentiating their respect for the office from their view of its occupant in the context of a public opinion survey.

There is, too, particularly when personality is not a dominant factor, the "benefit-of-the-doubt" syndrome. When forced to a generalized decision, many Americans will base their response not on the substance of their beliefs, but upon their perception of the sincerity or the diligence of the subject. In surveys on President Nixon, for example, a frequent response is: "He's sincere and he's trying his best. Even though I don't approve of everything he's done, I guess I'd have to say he's doing a good job." In most surveys, this somewhat reluctant approval is usually accorded the same weight as that of enthusiastic support.

What it all comes down to is the difficulty of trying to measure public reaction to the President in the context of a single question. Obviously the desirable objective of a survey on the President is to end up with a single summary measure of his standing in the country. The problem stems from the fact that most polls attempt to achieve this objective through a single summary-type question.

Gallup, for example, asks: "Do you approve or disapprove of the way Richard Nixon is handling his job as President?" The respondent is simply asked to respond "yes" or "no."

The Harris Poll attempts more gradation, asking the following question: "How would you rate the job Richard Nixon is doing as President—excellent, good, only fair or poor?" Harris then aggregates "excellent" and "good" into a "positive" category and "only fair" and "poor" into a "negative" response group.

In both surveys, and others like them, the objective is to "force" a response in one of the categories, despite the fact that the respondent may have mixed feelings about the different aspects of the man and his record. The trouble with this approach is that it ignores all the elements that go into an individual's reaction to the President, while promoting the institutionalization and "benefit-of-the-doubt" factors that push a response toward the favorable side.

The answer to the problem—and in the end, to a more meaningful measurement—may lie in reversing the procedure. Instead of attempting to summarize attitudes toward the President through the responses to a single summary question, it might prove more accurate and meaningful to attempt to break down the attitudes into their individual elements and to attempt from these results to build a scale of Presidential popularity.

BACKGROUND AND METHODOLOGY

The CBS News Poll experimented with this approach. Although we did not reach the point where we could begin to assemble all of the elements into a single popularity scale, we did attempt to break them into their individual categories and to make individual measurements. These attempts yielded some insights into the problem.

One experiment was to contrast the results of the summary-type question with a series of more specific issue-oriented questions. In general, we found that the positive rating for the President in the summary-type question was almost twice as high as the average positive ratings on the issues questions. For example, the March 10–12, 1970 CBS News Poll asked the summary question, "All things considered, are you very satisfied, fairly satisfied, fairly dissatisfied or very dissatisfied with Mr. Nixon as President?" The responses: "very satisfied," 22%; "fairly satisfied," 50%; "fairly dissatisfied," 13%; "very dissatisfied," 12%. In short, 72% of the public claimed to be satisfied, 25% dissatisfied.

However, we also asked the public to rate, in terms of "excellent," "good," "fair," "poor," or "very poor," the President's handling of specific problems. By collapsing the responses to "good/excellent," "fair," and "poor/very poor," we got the following results. On Nixon's handling of Vietnam, his best showing, 45% rated him good/excellent, 33% fair, and 18% poor/very poor. On all other issues—his handling of inflation, race relations, law enforcement, and problems of the cities—his good/excellent rating was in the 30s percentile, and his poor/very poor rating in the 20s. (See Survey.)

The point is, of course, that 45% approval on Vietnam, 32% on inflation, 31% on race relations, 38% on law enforcement, and 30% on urban problems, all are far cries from the overall 72% satisfaction response to the summary question. They are far more revealing of real public feeling than the summary question alone.

If one wanted to give the President the benefit of the doubt on the specific issues by the device of adding the "fair" responses to the good/excellent ones, then the totals begin to approximate the findings of the summary question. That is precisely the problem, though to intermix at best lukewarm approval with intensive approval in a single percentage figure indicative of "popularity" or satisfaction with a President is to be misleading, or, to repeat, to produce a measure without meaning. To reverse the process, to lump lukewarm dissatisfaction with intense dissatisfaction would be an equal disservice.

Although Harris and Gallup do poll the public on the President's handling of specific problems, their summary questions tend to dominate the headlines and news stories, and the public rarely gets below the surface into a comparison of the headline with the specific issue. Our own attempt was to combine the two types of results into a single report, stressing both—the overall "satisfaction" rating contrasted with the far lower level of the ratings on specific issues, with appropriate analysis of the differences.

One of the weaknesses, however, of this approach is that we had to make a priori decisions about which issues were most important to the public. We therefore attempted to rectify the problem by asking respondents to rank the problems facing the country in order of importance. Although we utilized this ranking in order subsequently to list the specific issues we wished to measure, the ranking could have been used in other ways.

For example, one could assign issues weights in relation to their importance, and then utilize these weights as part of a statistical summarization of responses from the public on the President's handling of a series of specific issues. If, for example, the Vietnam war ranked highest in importance, then the responses on the President's handling of the war could have been weighted more heavily than those on his handling of, say, aid to the cities.

This type of weighting scheme, along with an expanded set of questions dealing more specifically with personality, ideology, and party loyalty, might have been developed into a sophisticated summary formula which in the end could have provided a more accurate and meaningful measure than now exists of the President's standing with the public. Such a formula would take time to develop—it requires experimentation with new kinds of questions, constant evaluation and testing, and continual flexibility to remain current with new issues and problems. Still, it is an experiment well worth undertaking, and it is a source of regret among those of us who began it that we were unable to bring it to a successful conclusion.

FALL 1969: SUMMARY OF FINDINGS*

At the time of this survey, President Nixon is riding a crest of wide popular support for his general performance as President, with 81% of the adult public expressing themselves "satisfied" as against only 18% stating they were "dissatisfied" with Mr. Nixon as President.

However, when the questions are turned from the general to the specific, the degree of enthusiasm for Mr. Nixon's performance diminishes, although it remains considerably more favorable than unfavorable. The public was asked about Mr. Nixon's handling of five specific problems—the war in Vietnam, inflation, race relations, law enforcement, and urban problems—and the average ratings for his handling of these problems were 41% "good" or "excellent," 37% "fair," and 18% "poor" or "very poor." The averages were weighted by the relative importance placed on each problem by the public, which ranked them in the order indicated above.

The so-called "Southern Strategy" of the Administration appears to be working, the findings indicate. Mr. Nixon enjoys more support in the South than in any other region—86% of Southerners are satisfied and only 13% dissatisfied—and even on his handling of specific problems the South gives him his highest marks, with 46% rating him as good/excellent, 37% as fair, and only 12% as poor.

National support for and approval of the President, though widespread, is not particularly intense. For example, a breakdown of the 81% expressing satisfaction with Mr. Nixon as President shows 27% "very satisfied" and 54% "fairly satisfied." In addition, the fact that his "good/excellent" average on the five issues is only half that of the overall satisfaction rating would appear to indicate only moderate enthusiasm for the Administration.

The overall level of satisfaction is very high, though. Among the specific is-

*The findings are based on a national random telephone sample of 1,154 adults, conducted on November 23, 24, and 25, 1969, with an associated sampling error of up to plus or minus three percentage points.

sues, his handling of Vietnam ranks best—60% of the public feel he is doing a good or excellent job, 28% say he is doing a fair job and 10% believe he is doing a poor job. His lowest rating is in his handling of problems of the cities—31% good or excellent, 42% fair, and 18% poor.

Overall response can be broken down as shown.

| | General Satisfaction | | Specific Performance Average | | |
	Satisfied	Dissatisfied	Good	Fair	Poor
National	*81%*	*18%*	*41%*	*37%*	*18%*
Men	82	16	42	32	17
Women	79	20	39	34	19
East	78	20	35	37	22
Midwest	80	19	40	37	18
South	86	13	46	37	12
West	77	22	42	35	19
Republicans	90	9	52	31	12
Democrats	73	26	32	41	22
Other	83	12	39	33	19

The national ratings on Mr. Nixon's performance on specific problems are as follows:

	Good	Fair	Poor
Vietnam	60%	28%	10%
Inflation	36	37	22
Race relations	37	37	22
Law enforcement	40	37	17
Cities	31	42	18

SPRING 1970: SUMMARY OF FINDINGS*

President Nixon's popularity, which rose to a peak last November after his Vietnam speech, has begun to slip, according to a nationwide CBS News Poll of 1,136 adults conducted by telephone this week. Seventy-two percent of the public is generally satisfied with Mr. Nixon as President—an extremely high level, but still down substantially from the 81% who registered satisfaction with him in November's CBS News Poll.

The rating the public gives him on his handling of specific problems is down uniformly too. In November, Mr. Nixon's performance was rated good or excellent on his handling of Vietnam, inflation, race relations, law and order and city problems by an average of 41% of the public. In March, this approval rating average is down to 35%.

The largest drop came on his handling of the war in Vietnam, down to 45% good in March from 60% in November. Vietnam was also considered the most important of the problems by the public. The responses on specific problems are listed in order of importance.

*The findings are based on a national random telephone sample of 1,136 adults, conducted on March 10–12, 1970, with an associated sampling error of up to plus or minus 3 percentage points.

	March 1970			November 1969		
	Good/ Excellent	Fair	Poor/ Very Poor	Good/ Excellent	Fair	Poor/ Very Poor
Vietnam	45%	33%	18%	60%	28%	10%
Inflation	32	35	28	36	37	22
Race relations	31	36	27	37	37	22
Law enforcement	38	34	22	40	37	17
Cities	30	38	23	31	42	18

Approval of his performance on inflation dropped slightly from 36% in November to 32% in March. On race relations problems, approval dropped to 31%, from 37% in November.

There was no real change in people's ratings of the President's handling of law and order or city problems; 38% approve of his handling of law enforcement, as compared with 40% in November, and 30% approve of his handling of city problems, as compared with 31% in November.

Mr. Nixon has slipped in all regions of the country, including the South, where he remains more popular than in any other region. Most of his slippage has occurred among Democrats and Independent voters, with Republicans virtually unchanged. Satisfaction has dropped among both whites and nonwhites.

	General Satisfaction March 1970		General Satisfaction November 1969	
	Satisfied	Dissatisfied	Satisfied	Dissatisfied
National	*72%*	*25%*	*81%*	*18%*
Men	73	25	82	16
Women	71	26	79	20
East	70	25	78	20
Midwest	71	27	80	19
South	75	22	86	13
West	68	29	77	22
Republicans	90	8	90	9
Democrats	59	39	73	26
Independents	68	20	83	12
White	73	24	83	16
Nonwhite	56	37	61	34

SUMMER 1970: SUMMARY OF FINDINGS

This measure of Presidential performance was conducted as part of a survey on reactions to the scheduled withdrawal of American troops from Cambodia at the end of June 1970. The portion of the study dealing with reactions to the Cambodian campaign showed great skepticism about America's future in Indochina.

Despite all this, President Nixon's performance rating on how well he handles the war in Vietnam has improved slightly over early May. His performance on the war is rated as good or excellent by 49% of the public.

His handling of other problems like inflation, campus unrest and race relations is given a considerably lower rating. Overall satisfaction with Mr. Nixon as President is down from the last measure by the CBS News Poll in March.

Women tend to oppose the Administration policies and to be more firm in opposition to future military action than men. The President finds his strong support principally among Republicans and Independents; Democrats are likely to split nearly evenly on approval of his policies and future action in Indochina.

By region, the East and Midwest tend to be most dovish, the South the most hawkish, with the West falling between the extremes. By race, the extreme opposition to Administration policy and future moves in Indochina comes from the nonwhites.

The responses on both general satisfaction or dissatisfaction, and on specific issues, are summarized in the results of the following questions.

Taking everything into account, do you approve or disapprove of the way Mr. Nixon is handling his job as President?

Approve	65%
Disapprove	26
No response	7

Would you say President Nixon is doing an excellent, good, fair, poor, or very poor job in handling:

	Ex	Gd	Fr	Pr	V/P	NR
Inflation in this country	7%	24%	36%	17%	10%	6%
Campus unrest	5	21	34	22	10	8
Problems between the races	6	27	38	17	8	5
The war in Vietnam	11	38	29	11	7	4

Excellent/Good Trend Scores

	June	May	March	Nov. '69
Inflation	31%	—%	32%	36%
Campus unrest	26	—	—	—
Problems between	33	—	31	37
War in Vietnam	49	46	45	60

Summing up then, would you say you are generally satisfied or dissatisfied with Mr. Nixon as President?

	June	March	Nov. '69
Satisfied	65%	72%	81%
Dissatisfied	29	25	18
No response	6	3	1

Political Polling

Of all the varieties of public opinion polling, political polling is far and away the most controversial. Ever since Harry Truman's 1948 victory over Thomas E. Dewey in the face of confident predictions to the contrary by the pollsters, political polling has been viewed with skepticism, suspicion, and often hostility.

Serious critics charge it with undermining the electoral process by keeping potential candidates out of the race for office, and by creating self-fulfilling prophecies. Others, more concerned with methodology, challenge the credibility, accuracy, and above all, significance of the results. The polling organizations and their supporters claim they cast an accurate reflection of the electorate that is useful to public and politicians alike, and that they furnish needed data which is otherwise unavailable upon which decisions can be made. The truth, as in so many areas of controversy, lies somewhere between the extremes.

Political polling basically divides into four types. Public polling is undertaken for publication and dissemination to the public, either by the syndicated pollsters such as Gallup and Harris, by single newspaper-sponsored polls (the *Minneapolis Tribune*-sponsored Minnesota Poll, the *Boston Globe's* Becker polls), television network or station-sponsored polls (NBC's Quayle surveys), or combinations of both (Mervyn Fields' California Poll, underwritten by television stations and newspapers throughout California).

There is private polling, undertaken for political parties and candidates, utilized for a variety of purposes—a clarification of how the public may stand on particular issues; a picture of the candidate's image and standing with the public; the basis for an analysis of the strengths and weaknesses of a given campaign; an indicator of areas where more intensive campaign work is required; even a campaign propaganda tool to be leaked to the press in order to bolster one candidate and undermine another. Favorable private poll results can be used to raise campaign funds, to enlist key workers, to prop up sagging morale. Unfavorable results can lead to a shift in strategy or policies, in organization, and sometimes, a decision that the cause is hopeless.

Each of these two varieties—public and private—breaks down into two classes. One is the "predictive poll," an attempt to measure quantitatively the candidates' standings at a particular point in time. The other type of poll confines itself to issues and attitudes without attempting to measure specific candidate standings relative to each other, or attempting to "predict" the outcome of an election. Although public polls tend to emphasize the quantitative, predictive elements, they also study issues and attitudes. The public poll devoted solely to issues and attitudes without the predictive elements has been a comparative rarity. There have, however, been a number of recent examples of such polls, such as the Daniel Yankelovich studies of the New York gubernatiorial race in 1970 and the Presidential race of 1972 as published in the *New York Times.*

In the private area, emphasis on issues polling is much greater, particularly in the earliest stages of a campaign. Politicians find it useful in order to sort out specific campaign issues and positions, to establish a broad strategy on both issues and image. The findings may lead to basic decisions on policy and on advertising strategies.

This latter use of polling has drawn some critical fire. Its critics claim that the use of such data makes followers instead of leaders of political candidates; that the candidates tend to conform their own positions to public opinion instead of campaigning to mold public opinion to more enlightened positions. The critics charge that the use of this kind of polling inhibits political courage and integrity, encourages conformity, and at its worst makes the politician pander to the worst instincts of the electorate.

Up to a point these charges are undoubtedly true. There are politicians who prefer to be followers of public opinion rather than leaders, if this seems the safe way to election. There are issues hot enough for a candidate to duck if he thinks they could endanger his chances. In either of these cases, however, the candidate would have probably acted the same way in the absence of a poll. After all, a poll is merely a systematized way of collecting the information that every candidate must gather prior to a campaign in some manner. It may offer more conclusive evidence, more insights and more precise information, but any politician worth his salt (and some not worth it) will collect similar information through some means, and act upon it.

From the opposite perspective, such polling makes a considerable amount of sense, even for the politician who wishes to lead rather than follow public opinion. A sensitive, imaginative poll can probe beyond the mere measure of pro or anti sentiment on a specific issue, and uncover the factors that have caused this sentiment. A wise candidate, with an understanding of why the public has arrived at a position, can tackle an unpopular issue at its underpinnings, can chip away at the fears or rumors or myths that caused public sentiment to solidify in the first place. If information is power, then polling may give the candidate the weapons with which to lead public opinion as well as the excuses for following it.

There has been far more criticism of "predictive" polling. Some political scientists have claimed that it erodes the democratic process by discouraging support for worthy potential candidates. The argument goes that when the polls show a worthy candidate trailing badly, possible political support in the form of endorsements and organizational manpower is discouraged, and financial support is difficult to come by. Without this support, the candidate's effort is doomed, and he decides to drop out of the race, if he is already in it, or to forego it if he has not yet declared himself.

Again, there is considerable truth in this point of view, but does that necessarily make it evil? Furthermore, is the poll itself the message, or merely the messenger? There comes a point for any potential candidate when he must decide whether he wishes to continue to expend other people's money, time, and effort, as well as his own energies, on what may be a losing cause. He must ask himself if anyone out there knows who he is, and whether anyone is listening to him. If the answer to both questions is yes, then he must attempt to find out how strong his support actually is. If there is enough support to give him a reasonable chance, he may go on. If there is not, he must ask himself whether he has enough time and money and organization to rally support and give him a reasonable chance at victory. If the answer is no, he must decide whether to quit.

This kind of political agonizing predates polling, and for many candidates who can't afford polls or who are not the subject of polls, it goes on in the absence of polls. Polls or not, though, it is a normal, natural part of the political process. When George Romney decided to call it quits on the eve of the 1968 New Hampshire Republican primary, he did so on the basis of his poor showing in the polls, but it took no magic to recognize that the polls had merely confirmed what any experienced political observer could already see. Romney had already lost, having failed to build the organization, support, and enthusiasm for his campaign that could win in New Hampshire, or in any other primary. The polls simply confirmed what everyone, including Romney, already knew.

On the other hand, the McCarthy campaign that same year began in discouraging fashion, insofar as the early poll results went. But the McCarthy people used the early results as a goad to strengthen their efforts, as the basis for bringing to New Hampshire the "Children's Crusade" and engaging in a statewide doorbell-ringing campaign. Instead of persuading the McCarthy staff that the situation was hopeless, the polls showed them what had to be done.

Of course, the question of whether polls tend to eliminate worthy candidates relates to that stage of the political process that precedes a primary, whether a Presidential primary, or one to choose candidates for statewide or local office. Nobody has asserted that once a candidate has been chosen by his party as its nominee, poor showings in the polls have caused him to drop out of the race.

What critics have asserted is that the polls exercise the effect of a self-fulfilling prophecy, that if they continue to show a candidate trailing badly, they begin to exert a causal effect. The public, they say, believes that the candidate will lose and therefore tends to abandon him either through indifference or a shift to the winner.

It probably could be argued with equal effect that the polls cause an "underdog" movement that gathers support for the trailing candidate, but it's not really necessary to argue either case. The history of polling and the Humphrey campaign in 1968 tells its own story. After the unsettling events of the Democratic convention, the polls showed Humphrey trailing Nixon badly. As the campaign passed through September and into early October, Humphrey showed no discernible improvement. If the self-fulfilling prophecy theory were true, then no change should have occurred for the better; at best, Humphrey's standing should have dropped further. Then, after nearly two months of hopeless disorganization and confusion, Humphrey pulled his staff together and began to address the issues forcefully. His standings in the polls began to move up and the noncampaign became, in the end, a cliff-hanger.

Part of the argument is that poor showings in the polls dry up financial support, and the same critics say that money started to come in only after Humphrey's showings in the polls improved. Again, this seems a reversal of cause and effect. Financial support started after Humphrey took a new position on the war, and it was this and the new aggressiveness in his campaign that brought in money and at the same time lifted his standings in the polls.

All of the arguments over the influence of polls on elections tend to ignore the key questions—not merely the status and relative effectiveness of the candidate and the candidacy, but also the basic matters of what motivates people to vote as they do. The influences of party loyalty, economic, social, and cultural conditioning, of personalities and issues, are disregarded by the self-fulfilling prophecy theorists. These forces are far more powerful than a mere survey in influencing people to vote as they do.

Not that the polls are without their faults. For all their usefulness, they can often be misleading or meaningless. One common practice, for example, is for pollsters to disregard their own statistical caution flags in order to make some definitive-sounding conclusion. When a headline reads "Nixon Leads Muskie in Poll," and the copy shows 45% for Nixon and 43% for Muskie, the pollster is misleading the public. The sampling errors indigenous to most polls of the size of Gallup or Harris are usually about plus or minus three percentage points around the candidate's percentage. What the headline should say is that they are about even, and so should the copy. For the truth of the matter is that the results mean that Nixon is running at 42 to 48%, and Muskie between 40 and 46%. In other words, due to sampling error, it is conceivable that the true measure could be Muskie 46%, Nixon 42%—not likely, but a statistical possibility.

Another common problem in political polling is the size and disposition of the "undecided." When the public is asked to choose among candidates and a sizeable portion remain undecided, the pollster has a problem. If the size of the undecided group is larger than the spread between the candidates, the poll is rendered meaningless. Pollsters have tried to counter the problem in a number of ways, none particularly satisfactory. One is through the use of follow-up questions—in polling jargon, "probes." If the respondent won't say whom he favors, the interviewer asks to which candidate he "leans." Another method is simply to pair candidates in order to limit the freedom of the respondent to say he's undecided. When all else is done and a considerable number of "undecideds" remain, the pollster will often "allocate" the undecided voters to the candidates. Sometimes, they will simply prorate them, proportionate to the survey results.

Others involve more complicated techniques, such as comparing party registration, vote in a previous election, and demographic factors, thus emerging with a formula to place a specific respondent with a specific candidate. Whatever the technique, there is nothing to warrant the assumptions the pollsters make in allocating undecided responses to candidates. Nevertheless, in order to avoid the publication of an inconclusive poll, they continue to do so.

Finally, the traditional premise on which the political poll is based is the "if the election were held today" technique. It entails asking the public for their choice "if the election were held today," no matter how far off in time the election actually is, and basing the conclusions on this statement. In recent years, the leading pollsters have pointed with considerable pride to how closely their results have matched the outcome of the election. Of course, in each case they point to their final survey, usually taken the weekend before the election.

They ignore their earlier studies, and with good reason. They are neither very reliable or very meaningful. The earlier studies tend to confuse, rather than to clarify, the picture, for several reasons. For one thing, the election is not held "today" at the time a poll is taken, and events themselves can change the outcome. For another, the polls attempt to screen out nonvoters, but the farther from an election the poll occurs, the more difficult this process becomes. One yardstick—whether the voter is registered or not—may not work because there is still ample time before registration closes. Another, intent to vote, is often inadequate because a respondent is likely to say he intends to vote whether he really does so or not. It is not until quite close to an election that a nonvoter may admit he will not vote, and even then many nonvoters will continue to insist until the end that they have every intention of voting.

The abuse is particularly deceptive in the Presidential election years prior to the conventions. A poll that compares the standing of a Presidential incumbent with the frontrunner for the other party's nomination is simply unrealistic; it ignores the fact that the incumbent does not yet have an opponent, or a unified party behind him. It ignores the element of a one-to-one campaign for the Presidency, reflecting instead the comparative monolithic status of the incumbent as opposed to the scattered opposition of a half-dozen or more contenders for the other side. In short, it does precisely the opposite of what a public opinion poll is supposed to do. Instead of reflecting reality, it is simply a contrivance.

The problems addressed above are particularly reflective of a Presidential election year. The survey which follows, of course, was taken in 1970, a non-Presidential election year, and presented another set of problems and objectives. The off-year election is a battle for legislative control, and the 1970 election involved some 35 Senate seats and the 435 seats in the House of Representatives. The outcome serves as a base for evaluating the relative popularity of the Administration and its policies, as well as determining the future of its legislative programs.

In framing the study, CBS News decided to eschew attempts to predict the outcome. Instead, we looked at the issues which might play a role in the election, at the role that the Administration was attempting to play, and at the influences that motivate voters. Thus, we cannot look back with pride at having predicted a particular outcome, with the exception that our conclusion that the intervention of Messrs. Nixon and Agnew appeared to have hurt their candidates, rather than helped, was borne out in the results. Still, that portion of the study dealing with voter motivation seems to us a useful and revealing application of public opinion polling that is more meaningful than the customary predictive poll.

BACKGROUND AND METHODOLOGY*

This report is divided into four sections:

1. White House Campaigning in the '70 Elections
2. Issues in the '70 Elections
3. Regional Differences in Public Opinion
4. Candidates, Congress, and Constituents

The CBS News Poll uses a stratified random sample comprised of 105 geographic locations throughout the country. Telephone households within each area are chosen proportionate to the size of the area. Respondents within each household are chosen by a random procedure based on the number of adult residents, their sex, and relative ages.

Just about 90% of all housing units in the country have telephones. Homes without phones are thought to have a disproportionately high number of minority group members, people of low educational attainment, and people of low socioeconomic status. To compensate for underrepresentation of these groups, we statistically weight the sample within subgroups of respondents defined on the basis of sex and education. Education, or the lack of it, is highly correlated with race and income. Thus, by giving additional weight to the number of less-educated respondents, the sample in effect accounts for the proper representation of such persons in the final results. In addition, among low-income groups there are disproportionately more female heads of households, so respondents' sex is a factor in weighting.

The sample also includes households with unlisted telephone numbers in the same proportion that they exist in the population. First, using directories, numbers are randomly selected within each sample area. Each number is put into a computer program which uses the first five digits to create another number randomly. Having 50% of the sample numbers created by computer randomization, we are able to obtain unlisted numbers in about the same proportion they are in the population. To improve the representation of unlisted numbers, we also reweight the sex-by-education categories by the proportion of listed and unlisted numbers in the population.

To summarize: the sample uses probability selection of areas, households, and respondents, and the sample is weighted by matching it against known population characteristics.

*This is a report of findings from a national telephone survey of 1,289 people, 21 years or older, conducted Sunday to Tuesday, October 25, 26, and 27, 1970. There may be a sampling error of up to plus or minus three percentage points associated with any given findings.

SUMMARY OF FINDINGS

White House Campaigning in the '70 Elections

In a personal effort to marshal support for Republican candidates, Richard Nixon has thrown himself and the prestige of his office into off-year elections, hoping to change the composition of the 92nd Congress.

In terms of his influence on the American people, it appears that the President's aggressive involvement in state and Congressional elections as well as Vice President Agnew's activities are having limited, if not negative, impact on the general public. Although not appreciably different, Mr. Nixon's personal campaigning seems, however, to be carrying slightly more weight among those people who are likely to vote on November 3 than among people who are not likely to vote.

These are some of the findings of a national CBS News Poll conducted by telephone from Sunday to Tuesday, October 25, 26, and 27, with 1,289 people selected at random to represent a cross section of the country's voting population.

Despite the limited personal impact of the White House on the campaign, other findings in the survey indicate that the Republican party in general is emerging in the public's eye as slightly more effective than the Democrats in coping with some of the major problems facing the country—Vietnam, drugs, and law enforcement. The general effectiveness of the GOP, however, does not appear to be a decisive factor in the election.

The public is rather evenly divided in its feelings about the propriety of Mr. Nixon's involvement in elections around the country during a non-Presidential election year. Just about one-half (47%) said that they feel it is proper for the President "to personally campaign in state elections," and a comparable number (46%) say they feel the President's personal electioneering is improper—as the following table shows.

Question. President Nixon has been campaigning for Republican candidates in several states. Since it is not a Presidential election year, do you feel it is proper or improper for the President to personally campaign for candidates in state elections?

Response:	Percent of People
Proper	47%
Improper	46
No Response	7

The people most likely to have no objection to the President's off-year electioneering are Republicans, and are whites usually among the better educated and higher income groups and in white collar occupations. Also, as compared with people who probably won't vote on November 3, probable voters are less likely to be offended by the President's incursion into state campaigns.

In terms of the President's personal influence on their voting decisions, the largest number of people say that Mr. Nixon's support for a candidate in their state would have no effect on their voting preference. Most of those for whom

Mr. Nixon's endorsement of a candidate would make a difference would react negatively.

Specifically, somewhat less than one-half (45%) of the people said that the President's endorsement of a state candidate could make no difference to them and would not affect their voting. While one-fifth (20%) said they would be more likely to vote for a candidate supported by the President, a larger number (30%) said they would be less likely to vote for a Nixon-supported candidate.

In short, then, Mr. Nixon's greatest effect to date has been no effect, while among those for whom a Presidential endorsement would make a difference in their voting, three-fifths would be affected negatively—saying Nixon's support would make them less likely to vote for a candidate. Altogether, fully three out of four people say that the President's support for a candidate would make no difference or would have a negative effect on their voting.

Naturally, people who say they are Republicans are more likely than Democrats or Independents to be influenced favorably by Mr. Nixon's support for a candidate.

The people most likely to say that Presidential support would make no difference to their voting also are Republicans and Independents (as opposed to Democrats). Too, these people are more likely to be probable voters, in high income and education groups, in white collar occupations, and living in the suburbs. People in the western part of the country are more likely than those in other regions to say Nixon's endorsement would have no influence on their voting.

The people who would react negatively to a Nixon endorsement are most likely to be Democrats, in lower income and education groups, and in blue collar occupations. Interestingly enough, people in the South are more likely to be adversely affected by Nixon's support for a candidate than are people in other regions.

Mr. Agnew's support for state and Congressional candidates has about the same positive impact and somewhat greater negative impact than the President's, with 35% less likely and 17% more likely to vote for a candidate known to be supported by the Vice President. For two-fifths of the people (40%), Mr. Agnew's endorsement would have no influence on their voting.

Like the President, Mr. Agnew's endorsement would do more harm than good at this time—about two-thirds of those who feel that the Vice President's endorsement would make a difference would react negatively. Altogether, three out of every four people say either that the Vice President's support for a candidate would make no difference or would affect their voting intentions negatively.

Across different subgroups in the population, reactions to the Vice President's support for a candidate are fairly similar to reactions to Mr. Nixon's support. Republicans, of course, are more likely than Democrats or Independents to be favorably impressed by an Agnew endorsement.

Those people most likely to say that the Vice President's support would have no effect on their voting are whites, Republicans and Independents, people in higher income and education groups, white collar workers, probable voters, and people living in the Southern and Western states.

The people most likely to be negatively influenced by Agnew's endorsement are Democrats, nonwhites, residents of large cities, people in lower income and education groups, blue collar workers, unlikely voters, and people living in the Eastern states.

The following table compares the findings for the total sample regarding the effects of candidate support by either Mr. Nixon or Mr. Agnew.

Question. If you knew that (Mr. Nixon) (Mr. Agnew) supported a candidate for election in your state, would you be more likely or less likely to vote for that candidate?

	Candidates Supported by	
Percent saying:	Mr. Nixon	Mr. Agnew
More likely to vote	20%	17%
Less likely to vote	30	35
No difference/No effect	45	40
No Response	5	8

As the most visible spokesman for Administration policies, the Vice President has been actively involved in state electioneering for months. However, not only does Mr. Agnew have somewhat more negative impact on people's voting intentions than does the President, but just about one-half (46%) of the people feel that Mr. Agnew is not representing their views when he speaks out "against people who criticize our society." Only a slightly smaller number (42%) feel, on the other hand, that the Vice President is speaking for them.

Question. Vice President Spiro Agnew has been speaking out against people who criticize our society. When Mr. Agnew speaks, do you feel he is representing your own views or not?

Response:	Percent of People
Yes, represents my views	42%
No, does not represent my views	46
No Response	11

There are not many differences across segments of the population in terms of whether people feel Mr. Agnew does or does not represent their views. Those most likely to say he does not speak for them are Democrats, blacks, and people in the higher educational groups.

More people feel that the Vice President is his own man than feel that he is really speaking for Mr. Nixon. That is, one-half (51%) say that Mr. Agnew is "just giving his own personal opinions" in his speeches. By contrast, one-fourth (23%) say he is "really speaking for Mr. Nixon," and another 14% say he is speaking partly his own mind and partly that of the President too. Altogether, then, two-fifths (37%) feel that the Vice President is not expressing just his own ideas.

Question. In his speeches, do you think that Mr. Agnew is just giving his own personal opinion, or is he really speaking for Mr. Nixon?

Response:	Percent of People
Speaks for himself	51%
Speaks for Mr. Nixon	23
Speaks for both	14
No Response	12

The people most likely to say that Mr. Agnew is speaking for himself, and not the President, are women, Republicans, high school graduates, Midwesterners, and people in middle income groups.

Issues in the '70 Elections

Vietnam, crime, and student disorders remain the most important concerns of the American people in the final week of the 1970 state and Congressional election campaign. It appears unlikely, however, that people's feelings about these issues will translate into voting decisions.

Although viewing the "Social Issues" (crime, drugs, campus disorders) from a position of the Right, most people do not distinguish between the Republicans or the Democrats as more effective in coping with such problems. Moreover, although the public concern focuses on Vietnam and crime as the prominent issues of the campaign, there is little evidence that people will choose among candidates on the basis of the candidates' positions on these or other issues.

The so-called shift to the right among the U.S. electorate is evident in the findings that a substantial majority of people feel that college student protests have "gone too far and should be stopped" (81%); tougher laws and stronger police forces will "put an end to violence and disorder" in the country (62%); and the students were "more to blame" than the National Guard in the deaths of four Kent State University students last May (63%).

A climate of uncertainty is seen in the findings that two out of every five adult Americans believe that our government is "in danger of being overthrown by the radical beliefs of the younger generation" (43%); a comparable number say that it is not safe "to walk the streets alone at night" in their neighborhoods (41%); and one out of six people—three times higher than the unemployment rate—is worried today about losing his or her job "because of the business recession and rising unemployment" (16%).

Nonetheless, people almost routinely do not cite these problems as reasons for voting for one candidate or another. Although over one-half (54%) of the people claim that the candidates' stand on the issues is "most important" to them in choosing among candidates, less than one-fourth (22%) of them could name one issue that has been "really important" in helping them to decide who they would like to see elected in state or Congressional races.

If issues are salient to voters' decisions, it is significant to note that the Administration has not established the Republican party in general as the "best party" equipped to deal with many major issues. Since the Nixon Administration is generally thought to have preempted the Democrats on the issue of Vietnam, a rather surprising finding is that the Democratic party and the Republican party are virtually tied in terms of people's perceptions of which party can do "the best job of handling the war in Vietnam"—32% say the Republicans and 29% say the Democrats.

Equally significant is the public's feeling that the Democratic party is just as likely to do the best job of "reducing crime in the streets"—25% say the Democrats and 22% say the Republicans. The same is true for "dealing with student disorders" (Democrats, 28%; Republicans, 25%) and for "stopping the sale and use of narcotic drugs" (Democrats, 22%; Republicans, 24%).

Whereas the Republican party has no clear margin over the Democratic party in terms of perceived capability to deal with a number of problems, the Democrats get noticeably higher marks as the best party to halt "inflation and the high cost of living" (Democrats, 39%; Republicans, 30%) and as the party more likely to be able "to resolve the differences between young people and our system of government (Democrats, 32%; Republicans, 24%). Too, the Democratic party is viewed as somewhat more likely to do the best job "controlling air and water pollution" (Democrats, 30%; Republicans, 24%).

Only in one area, and a significant one, does the Republican party hold a substantial edge over the Democrats: in that three-fifths of the public believes that tougher law enforcement will be an effective deterrent to violence, it is notable that 37% of the people feel that the Republicans are more likely "to make tougher laws and strengthen the police" as compared with 26% saying the same about the Democrats.

The Most Important Problems in the Country

When asked what they considered to be the "greatest problem in our country," 15% of the people said that the Vietnam war concerned them most. While Vietnam was mentioned first more often than any other problem, it does not rank much higher than people's concern about crime and violence (13%), racial problems (10%), the sale and use of drugs, (10%), campus disorders and student protests (10%), and the generation gap—the hippie movement and lack of communication with young people (10%).

Other problems such as inflation, unemployment, high taxes, and pollution received comparatively few mentions. In this latter group of issues, it is mildly surprising that inflation and the high cost of living was mentioned by only 5% of the people as the "greatest problem." Inflation is, of course, the major issue that Democratic candidates around the country are trying to use to their advantage in linking the economic ills of the nation with the Nixon administration.

While people were asked to volunteer what they considered the country's "greatest problem," their answers were probed for additional mentions of problems. Given three opportunities to mention an issue, about one-third of the people mentioned Vietnam (32%); one-fourth mentioned crime (25%); and one-fifth mentioned each of these issues: racial conflict, drug abuse, the generation gap, and student disorders (all 19%).

The following table shows the problems people mentioned, ranked by frequency of mentions, when asked what they considered the single greatest problem facing the country.

Question. In this election year, there's been a lot of talk about problems in this country. What do you personally feel is the greatest problem in our country?

Rank	Problem Mentioned	Percent of People
1.	Vietnam/Indochina	15%
2.	Crime/Violence/Law and Order	13
3.	Racial Conflict/Problems/Tension	10
4.	Youth/Hippies/Generation Gap	10
5.	Drug Sale and Use	10
6.	Student Protests/Campus Disorders	10
7.	Inflation/High Cost of Living	5
8.	Unemployment/Poverty/Low Social Security	4
9.	Pollution/Environment	3
10.	Declining Religion/Moral Decay	2
11.	High Taxes/Government Spending	1
12.	Declining Quality of Education/Schools	1

Only a handful of people said that there are no real problems in the country, but one out of every 12 people (8%) could not answer the question—saying they did not know what the greatest problem is in the country.

Underlying specific issues, there is a kind of moody feeling of general malaise. That is, 6% of the people (more than the number mentioning inflation) felt that the country is in general trouble because the contemporary way of life is too impersonal and too disrespectful, plus the feeling of others that our political system is unfair or rife with dishonesty and lack of responsiveness to the people.

As for the overall significance of the "Social Issues," if we combine mentions of crime, racial conflict, drug abuse, and campus disorders, we find that two-fifths of the public (43%) mention these problems as the greatest in the country.

There are few clear-cut differences in the problems mentioned by various subgroups in the population. For example, whether a person seems likely to vote or which region of the country he lives in typically has no real relationship to his feeling about the single greatest problem in the country.

Vietnam is most likely to be mentioned by younger people, Democrats (as opposed to Republicans, but not Independents), and whites. There are no significant differences in people's answers when they are compared by sex, level of education, place of residence, region of the country, likelihood of voting, and so on.

As for the "Social Issues," there are only occasional differences among subgroups. Men are more likely than women to mention crime and violence, but there are no differences when people are compared in terms of living in a city, a suburb, or a small town or rural area.

Women and Caucasians are more likely to mention drugs than are men and nonwhites. Blacks are more likely than whites to mention racial problems, and whites are more likely to mention campus disorders. Younger people are more likely than their elders to see racial conflict as the great problem in the country.

Inflation and the high cost of living received comparatively few mentions as the greatest problem in the country. Yet, although only 5% of the people cite inflation as the singularly greatest problem confronting them, three times that number (16%)—and three times the rate of unemployment—said that someone in their family was "worried right now about losing his or her job," as opposed to 81% saying "no."

Question. Is anyone in your family worried right now about losing his or her job because of the business recession and rising unemployment?

Response:	Percent of People
Yes, worried now	16%
No, not worried	81
No Response	3

The kinds of people most likely to say that someone in the family is presently worried about losing employment are Democrats and Independents, Midwesterners, blue collar workers, and blacks. There were no real differences when people were compared by income, education, place of residence, and so forth. One difference we did find was that people who could name a specific issue as the reason for favoring one candidate or another are somewhat more likely to be concerned about loss of employment in the family, than are people who could not link an issue with their candidate preference.

Relevance of Issues for Voting

Most people (54%) claim that the candidates' "stand on the issues" is the most important factor in their choice among state or Congressional candidates. Less than one-half that number (22%), however, could actually name a specific issue as a basis for preferring one candidate over another.

Thus, for four out of five people (78%) issues may be relatively unimportant for their voting decisions. Moreover, the issues cited as reasons for voting are not always the "great problems" of the day.

First, people were asked if they knew whether there was an election for Senator in their state this year. One out of every 14 people (7%) did not know whether a Senatorial election was being held. Of these people, about one-fourth also did not know whether a Gubernatorial race was being held.

Although the differences sometimes are not statistically large, the people least likely to know whether there currently is a Senatorial election in their state are women, Independents, people in lower income and educational groups, and rural residents.

Next, depending on whether the person interviewed was talking about a Senatorial, Gubernatorial, or House candidate, people were asked which candidate they favored for election. Answers across the three types of races were combined simply to get a general feeling of Republican/Democratic partisanship and to set up responses for following questions.

Although the responses are not predictive of November 3 outcomes, more than two-fifths (44%) of the voting public said they favored Democratic candidates and one-third (32%) favored Republican candidates. What is important here is that people say that a candidate's issue positions are most important and his party affiliation least important to their voting decision. Yet, much political science research indicates that party affiliation is a highly significant determinant of voting, as the following table suggests:

Question. Whether or not you're planning to vote, which man . . . the Democrat, the Republican, or another candidate . . . do you favor in the election for (Senator) (Governor) (U.S. Congressman)?

Response:	Total Sample	People Who Say They Are:		
		Republicans	Democrats	Independents
Democrat	44%	12%	71%	27%
Republican	32	68	10	26
Other Candidate	3	5	2	5
Undecided/No Response	20	15	17	42

As the above table shows, Republican voters prefer Republican candidates, Democrats prefer Democrats, and Independents split evenly between the parties and are most likely to be undecided about how they would vote. Although people claim it is relatively unimportant, party affiliation does appear to be a strong factor in voting preferences in state and Congressional elections.

As opposed to Republican candidates, Democratic candidates are strongest among the lower education and income groups, among people living in the South and the West, among blue collar workers and blacks, as well as among those people who name a specific issue as a reason for favoring one candidate over another. There is no difference in the type of candidate preferred between people who are likely to vote on November 3 and those who are not.

Next, we asked people which was the most important factor in their preference for a candidate—his personal attributes, his position on the issues, or his party affiliation. Over one-half (54%) said the candidate's "stand on the issues" was most important for them. About one in five (22%) said his personal qualities and only 14% said party affiliation:

Question. In thinking about which candidate you'd like to see elected, what has been most important for you . . . his own personal qualities, his stand on the issues, or his political party affiliation?

Response:	Percent of People
His stand on the issues	54%
His personal qualities	22
His party affiliation	14
No Response	9

The old, poor, black, and uneducated are least likely to say issues are important. Those most likely live in suburbs, are probable voters, and are people who could name a specific issue as a reason for favoring a candidate. There are no real differences by people's party affiliation, sex, or type of occupation.

Finally, people were asked if there was any particular issue that had been important in helping them decide among candidates. As opposed to the majority who claimed issues were important, only 22% named an issue and 78% could not. This follows what many political scientists maintain: issues per se—particularly as they are more remote from the voter's personal life—typically are less relevant to voting in Congressional elections than are, first, the voter's party affiliation and, second, the personal image of the candidate.

Since only one-fifth of the people could name an issue, the percentage for any issue is just a fraction of the total sample. The percentages below are based on the 22% of the people who gave an issue.

Compared with what they felt were the "greatest problems" of the day, there is a considerable shifting of people's emphasis when they think of issues in connection with voting. Vietnam, mentioned by 17% of the people, still ranks high, but crime and violence now ranks first, with 18% mentions, as a campaign-related issue.

The youth issues—campus disorders and the generation gap—which ranked third and fourth as the country's greatest problem, drop substantially in the ratings by frequency of mention. Of those naming an issue, only 4% said campus disorders (now ranked 10th) and only 1% mentioned the younger generation (now ranked 11th).

Whereas high taxes ranked 11th as a great problem, it now ranks third as a campaign-related issue—mentioned by 15% of the people who could name an issue. Pollution is another topic that ranked low (9th) as a national problem but now ranks relatively high (4th).

The following table compares the ranking of issues when mentioned as our "greatest problem" (old rank) and when mentioned as issues relevant to voting (new rank). The first column of percentages shows what percent of the total sample mentioned each issue, and the second column converts that percentage figure to a proportion of those who mentioned issues.

Question. In the election for (Senator) (Governor) (Congressman), is there any particular issue that has been really important in helping you choose between the candidates?

Old Rank	New Rank		Total Sample	% of People Who Named as Issue
2.	1.	Crime/Violence/Law and Order	4%	18%
1.	2.	Vietnam/Indochina	3	17
11.	3.	High Taxes/Government Spending	3	15
9.	4.	Pollution/Environment	2	11
12.	5.	Declining Quality of Education/Schools	2	9
7.	6.	Inflation/High Cost of Living	2	8
8.	7.	Unemployment/Poverty/Low Social Security	2	7
3.	8.	Racial Conflict/Problems/Tension	2	7
5.	9.	Drug Sale and Use	1	5
6.	10.	Student Protests/Campus Disorders	1	4
4.	11.	Youth/Hippies/Generation Gap	–	1
10.	12.	Declining Religion/Moral Decay	–	–

An analysis of people's comments shows that their concern for campaign issues tends to be specific to their personal or community situation, rather than abstract or global. For example, while 10% of all people mentioned economic issues (inflation, taxes, unemployment) as great national problems, 30% of those naming campaign-related issues talk about economics—particularly as related to themselves or their locale. Conversely, while 43% of all people cited the "Social Issues" (crime, drugs, race, campus disorders) as national problems, a smaller proportion (34%) of those naming issues mention these problems in connection with voting.

Because the number of people in the total sample mentioning a given issue is so small, no reliable conclusions can be drawn for the kinds of people selecting one issue or another.

The people most likely to mention any issue in connection with candidate preference are men, people in higher income and educational groups, residents of large cities or in suburbs, people living in the Eastern states, and people who will probably vote on November 3.

The Mood of the Electorate

Findings from this national survey support the impression that much of the country's adult population is—apparently from frustration, anger, and worry—at a position on the "right," particularly in its appraisal of student disorders and crime.

A substantial majority of people (63%) feel the students were more to blame than the National Guard for the deaths at Kent State University; four out of five (81%) believe that student protests should be stopped; and three-fifths (62%) think that stronger law enforcement will curb crime and violence.

Although not a majority, a sizable group of people (43%) feel that the structure of our society is in danger of being overthrown by the "radical beliefs" of the younger generation, and a comparable number (41%) say they are afraid to walk the streets at night in their neighborhoods.

The questions asked, and the responses, were:

Question. A few months ago, four students were killed by National Guard troops during a demonstration at Kent State University in Ohio. Who do you think was more to blame for those deaths, the students or the National Guard?

Responses:	Percent of People
The students	63%
The National Guard	12
Both equally to blame	9
Miscellaneous/No Response	15

Those most inclined to blame the students for precipitating the Kent State deaths are older people, Republicans, whites, people in lower educational categories, middle-income people, residents of small cities and in rural areas, and people in all regions of the country except the East.

Question. Do you agree, or disagree, that college student protests and demonstrations in general have gone too far, and should be stopped?

Responses:	Percent of People
Agree, should be stopped	81%
Disagree, should not be stopped	12
No Response	6

Across the various subgroupings in the population, those most likely to want to put a halt to student demonstrations are people in the lower educational groups, people in the middle income groups, rural residents, whites, Republicans, (and Democrats more than Independents), all age groups except people in their twenties, all regions except people in the East, and those who are probably going to vote on Election Day.

Question. Do you think that tougher laws and stronger police forces will be able to put an end to violence and disorder in the country, or not?

Response:	Percent of People
Yes, will end violence	62%
No, will not end violence	29
No Response	9

On this question, a few groups stand out prominently as least likely to believe that stronger laws and police forces will deter violence and disorder: people in their twenties, people with incomes over $15,000, and residents of large cities.

Those most likely to think stronger law enforcement will be effective are whites, people in low educational groups, Republicans (and Democrats more so than Independents), and people living in the South—and to some extent in the East.

Question. Do you believe that the structure of our society, and the government as we know it today, are in danger of being overthrown by the radical beliefs of the younger generation?

Responses:	Percent of People
Yes, in danger	43%
No, not in danger	48
No Response	9

Note in the table that a majority of people (52%) either feel that our social structure is in danger of being overthrown or are not sure (No Response). Given whatever time perspective the individual chooses, it is startling nonetheless that at least two out of five American adults feel that our society is endangered by the beliefs of the young.

Those most likely to feel that our social system is endangered by the successive generations are people over 40 years of age, people in lower educational and income groups, blue collar workers, Midwesterners and Southerners, and Republicans and Democrats, but not Independents.

Probably for reasons not motivated by fear, but rather by disenchantment with the existing order, blacks, as well as big city residents and young people in their twenties, are frequently likely to say that the sociopolitical structure of society is in danger of being overthrown by the radical beliefs of the younger generation.

Question. Do you feel it is safe to walk the streets alone at night in your neighborhood?

Responses:	Percent of People
Yes, it is safe	55%
No, it is not safe	41
No Response	4

People most likely to feel that their streets are unsafe at night are women, older people, people in large cities, in lower education and economic groups, Democrats, blue collar workers, blacks, and people in Eastern states—and to some extent in the South.

Comparisons of different subgroups in the population show that men and women share about equal concern in all of the areas mentioned above. Nor are there differences between people who could or could not cite a specific issue as an important factor in choosing among candidates. With the exception of stopping student protests, none of the issues differentiated probable voters from nonvoters.

The Best Party to Handle Problems

We have seen that while people say they are concerned with issues, there is little evidence that they will vote on the issues. The real determinant of voting intentions appears to be the individual's political party affiliation. As seen earlier, Democrats prefer Democratic candidates and Republicans prefer Republicans.

What weighs favorably in the balance for the Democratic party nationally is that while people see no clear-cut distinction between the parties with respect to dealing with Vietnam, crime, drugs, and student disorders, the Democrats have an edge as the "best party" to handle inflation, to cope with the disaffection of young people, and to control air and water pollution. Two of these three issues are relatively prominent among the issues linked to candidate preference. Possibly offsetting the Democrats' advantage is the fact that people are more likely to feel that the Republicans will initiate stronger laws and strengthen the police, which are measures considered by most people to be effective against violence and disorder.

The table below shows the paraphrased questions and answers regarding the "best party" to handle problems in the country. The "Both/Equal" column shows the percentages of people saying there is no difference between the parties' abilities to cope with problems. The "Neither" column shows the percentage of people saying the problem is insoluble—thus transcending party or any other considerations.

Which is the best party:	Demo-crats	Repub-licans	Both/Equal	Neither	No Response
		Percent of People Saying:			
a. to handle the war in Vietnam	29%	32%	15%	10%	(13%)
b. to reduce crime in the streets	25	22	25	14	(14)
c. to stop the sale and use of drugs	22	24	24	12	(18)
d. to halt inflation	39	30	10	8	(13)
e. to control air and water pollution	30	24	20	9	(14)
f. to deal with student disorders	28	25	19	12	(15)
g. to resolve differences between young people and our system of government	32	24	17	12	(16)

The results show that anywhere from about one-tenth to one-fourth of the public sees no distinctions between the Republicans and the Democrats on any of the issues studied, and roughly one-tenth pessimistically feels that the problems cannot be solved.

To reinforce the notion that party affiliation is the key to the 1970 campaigns, we found that the people selecting the Democrats (conversely, Republicans) as the best to handle any problem are preponderantly Democrats (conversely, Republicans).

Those who choose the Democrats are Democrats; they are most likely to live in large cities, to be blue collar workers, to be in lower educational and income groups, to be younger, and to be nonwhite. The reverse profile typifies the people who choose the Republicans.

With only a few exceptions, the following characteristics typically have little or nothing to do with which party a person chooses as the best party: sex, region of country, likelihood to vote, and whether the person named an issue as important to his or her candidate preference.

Independents feel that the Republicans can do the best job of dealing with Vietnam, drug abuse, and crime, and that the Democrats can do best with inflation. People who named campaign-related issues feel that the Democrats can do best in handling crime and reconciling youth and our system of government.

Whereas the better-educated people are more likely to favor the Republicans on most issues, people with at least some college education see the Democrats as the better party for dealing with student disorders and for resolving problems between youth and the political system.

A final question in the survey asked:

Question. Which party, the Democrats or the Republicans, do you feel is more likely to make tougher laws and strengthen the police?

Response:	Percent of People
Republicans	37%
Democrats	26
Equal/Both/No Difference	19
No Response	18

The people most likely to choose the Republicans are Republicans, better educated, younger, living in the East and the West, in higher income brackets, living in the suburbs, white collar workers, whites, and people for whom issues are relevant to their voting preferences.

Regional Differences in Public Opinion

Following are regional breakdowns of responses to each question asked in the national public opinion survey conducted by CBS News. Some of the highlights are:

Easterners and Westerners are more likely to accept a President's campaigning in off years (50%). In the South and Midwest, almost half think it is improper for a President to campaign in state elections, while only two of five Westerners believe this.

Proportionately more Southerners (33%) would be inclined away from a Nixon-endorsed candidate than Westerners (27%). More Easterners would be negative toward an Agnew endorsee (40%) than Westerners (31%). More Westerners (44%) wouldn't be affected one way or the other.

Opposition to Mr. Agnew's views is somewhat stronger in the East and West, where one-half of the people feel he does not represent their thinking. Midwesterners are more likely to think he speaks for them (46%). About one in six Southerners, a larger proportion than in other sections, reserves judgement on Agnew.

Midwesterners (57%) are substantially more likely to believe Agnew is his own man; Easterners are more likely to think he speaks for the President (29%), and more Westerners (21%) think he shares Mr. Nixon's views. All sections are reasonably uniform in their judgement of Agnew as a President, although proportionately more Easterners (22%) than people elsewhere think he would be very poor. On issues, Easterners are more likely to be bothered by the war (19%) and drugs (16%) than people in other sections.

Westerners are much more likely than Easterners to say they will vote for a Democrat in the principal race in their state. Inclination to vote Democratic in the West is as strong as in the South (49%), although this is perhaps because fewer Westerners (13%) are undecided—in the Midwest almost a quarter are still making up their minds a week before election. Third party strength is significant only in the East (9%). Slightly fewer Southerners, although still a majority (51%), see issues as the major reason for their vote choice.

Although a strong majority of Easterners (57%) blame the students for the Kent State killings, they are still less likely to do so than people in other regions, while people on both coasts (19% East, 16% West) are more likely to assign the blame to the Guardsmen. In the West, substantially more people (63%) are afraid of street crime than those in other sections, while Easterners (47%) are least afraid.

The East is much less likely (34%) to believe there is a danger of revolution in this country than the South (48%) or the Midwest (46%). Easterners (75%) are also less likely to think college protests have gone too far. More people in the West (53%) are skeptical of tougher laws as a deterrent to violence and disorder.

Two of five people in the East and West see the Republicans as a law and order party compared to one in three in other sections.

There is little difference among the sections of the country as to which party will do the best job of handling Vietnam, although Westerners favor Republicans most (36%) and Midwesterners least (29%). Easterners (36%) are most skeptical of the Democrats' handling of inflation, while Southerners (26%) are least likely to mention Republicans in this context (26%). Little difference is seen between the parties on pollution control among regions.

In the East Democrats inspire less confidence on stopping drug sale than in the South, and Midwesterners are slightly less confident in the Republicans on this issue than people in other sections. In the Midwest Republicans also rate lower on reducing crime than elsewhere, partly because more people in this part of the country think the parties are equal in their capacity to stop crime.

Westerners are more likely to have greater confidence in Democrats' ability to reconcile young people's differences with their system of government, while Midwesterners have least confidence in the Democrats. The four sections do not differ in their view of the parties' relative competence to handle student disorders.

The South has more hawks on Vietnam than other sections (25%), but also more doves (29%). Southerners are not likely to choose a gradual withdrawal in Vietnam, and are less likely than residents of other sections to want to reduce weapons programs.

Easterners (29%) are much less opposed to wage and price freezes than Westerners (39%). Only in the East does a majority favor guaranteed minimum income. More than half in the Midwest and South are opposed. The South is twice as likely to believe too much has been done for the blacks, with 25% saying this, compared to only 11% in the West. There is no major regional difference in views on Supreme Court action on criminal rights.

Candidates, Congress, and Constituents

In preparation for Election Night coverage, CBS News conducted a national public opinion poll of 1,289 people, 21 years or older. Findings from that survey, conducted by telephone on October 25, 26, and 27, 1970, are presented here for 1,112 people abstracted from the larger sample.

These 1,112 people are those who self-reported their political party affiliation as being Republican or Democrat. In the following pages, these people are often called the "partisan public"—those who willingly label themselves politically. The purpose of excluding people who call themselves Independent voters (10% of the sample) and members of other parties is so that we can make direct comparisons between Democrats and Republicans in the general population and in the two-party Congress.

Also in connection with its Election Night coverage, CBS News conducted a survey of all incumbents in both houses of Congress as well as of all nonincumbents running for election. Over a four-week period using mailed questionnaires or, if necessary, personal and telephone interviews, we got answers to six basic questions for all members (530) in both houses of the present Congress as

well as for 442 (98%) of the 452 major party nonincumbents running for seats
in the 92nd Congress.

This survey, the Congressional Issues Poll, consisted of questions dealing with
Vietnam, military defense, inflation, income maintenance, assistance to blacks,
and criminal rights. The same questions were asked in the national public
opinion survey. Three of the questions in both surveys were identically worded,
and three were modified slightly for telephone use with the general population,
but they are comparable to the questions asked in the Congressional Issues Poll.

The questions shown on the following pages as well as the responses to them
are paraphrased for ease of presentation. A copy of the questionnaire used for
the Congressional Issues Survey is attached for reference. Because we were able
to code answers for all members of the House and the Senate, the percentages
for the responses of the Republicans and Democrats in the general population
have been recomputed on the basis of those who answered each question.

In the comparisons below of the answers to the six issue questions by members of Congress and by the partisan public, the term "constituents" is sometimes used. By constituents, we do not mean just the state or district electorate
for a given Congressman; rather, constituents are politically like-minded people
throughout the country.

Vietnam

Question. In Vietnam, do you think (1) we should maintain our troops there as
long as necessary; (2) withdraw gradually at a rate geared to the ability of the
South Vietnamese forces; or (3) speed up our withdrawal independent of the
progress of the South Vietnamese forces?

Responses:	PUBLIC			HOUSE			SENATE		
	Total	Reps.	Dems.	Total	Reps.	Dems.	Total	Reps.	Dems.
Maintain troops or withdrawal gradually	73%	76%	70%	70%	88%	56%	55%	72%	42%
Speed up our rate of withdrawal	27	24	30	30	12	44	45	28	58

Among the public, Democrats are somewhat more "dovish" than Republicans.
That is, 30% of the Democrats as opposed to 24% of the Republicans would
speed up our troop withdrawals from Vietnam, irrespective of the rate of improvement of the South Vietnamese armed forces.

Senate Republicans look pretty much like their constituents, but House Republicans are considerably more likely to want to stay in Vietnam or withdraw
gradually. Both Senate and House Democrats are more likely to want to pull
troops out of Vietnam more rapidly than are Democrats in the general public.

Thus, looking at the totals for all groups, the House of Representatives as a
whole closely reflects the partisan public's views on Vietnam, but the total Senate is much more likely than the public to accelerate our withdrawal from
Vietnam.

Within the Congress, four times as many House Democrats (46%) as Republicans (12%) are doves. In the Senate, twice as many Democrats (58%) as Republicans (28%) are doves. Republican Senators are more than twice as likely to be "dovish" than are Republicans in the House, and Democrats in the Senate are substantially more likely to be doves than are their counterparts in the House.

In the general population, the people most likely to want to speed up troop withdrawals are young people, blacks, and the better educated.

The two groups most inclined to keep our troops in Vietnam to prevent a Communist takeover are blue collar workers and people in the $10,000 to $15,000 income bracket.

The following characteristics have no relationship to people's feelings about Vietnam: the region of the country in which they live, the type of community they live in, their sex, whether they are likely to vote on election day, or whether they could name an issue related to their candidate preference.

Military Defense

Question. Which comes closer to your view of strategic weapons programs: (1) we should maintain our preparedness by supporting such programs at least to the extent proposed by the Nixon administration; or (2) in view of other important needs of the country, we should place less emphasis on such programs than we have in recent years?

Responses:	PUBLIC			HOUSE			SENATE		
	Total	Reps.	Dems.	Total	Reps.	Dems.	Total	Reps.	Dems.
Support weapons programs	70%	79%	63%	63%	83%	48%	55%	77%	39%
Deemphasize programs	30	21	37	37	17	52	45	23	61

About one out of every three Democrats (37%) as compared with one out of five Republicans (21%) is ready to spend less on strategic weapons programs for military defense.

Republicans in both houses of Congress come quite close to representing the views of their Republican constituents, but House Democrats and Senate Democrats are far more willing to cut defense spending than are their partisan counterparts in the general population.

As a totality, the House is more likely to want to place less emphasis on strategic weapons programs than are people in the country generally, and the Senate as a whole is more willing than the House to feel there should be less emphasis on military defense programs.

In the House, one-half of the Democrats (52%) would reduce military defense programs, as compared with less than one-fifth of the Republicans (17%). In the Senate, three out of every five Democrats (61%) as compared to one out of four Republicans (23%) favors less emphasis on military defense.

While there is not much difference in the feelings of Republicans in the two houses, Democratic Senators are more likely than their colleagues in the House to want to cut back on military defense—although a majority in each case favors reduction.

Among people in the partisan public, those most likely to favor putting less emphasis on strategic weapons programs are younger, better educated, residents in small cities, residents in the Eastern and Midwestern states, as well as people who named an issue as a basis for voting.

Inflation

Question. If inflation continues unabated by the time the new Congress convenes in January, which comes closer to your view: (1) continue the Administration's monetary and fiscal restraints; or (2) impose new restraints including wage and price controls?

	PUBLIC			HOUSE			SENATE		
Responses:	Total	Reps.	Dems.	Total	Reps.	Dems.	Total	Reps.	Dems.
Impose wage and price controls	66%	62%	68%	48%	17%	72%	48%	12%	75%
Continue administration policies	34	38	32	52	83	28	52	88	25

Both Republicans and Democrats among the general population favor stronger controls over the forces of inflation. Just about two-thirds of the partisan public favors imposing wage and price controls, with Democrats (68%) somewhat more likely to select this alternative than Republicans (62%).

Both Senate and House Democrats closely reflect the views of their constituents, although Democratic Senators are somewhat more likely than their Democratic constituents to favor wage and price controls. On the other hand, Republicans in both houses are far removed from the views—albeit superficial—of their constituents.

The fact that Republicans in both houses are so uniformly against a wage-price freeze results in less than a majority in support of the proposal in either house (48% in each case). Overall, then, both houses have considerably fewer advocates for these strong fiscal measures when compared proportionately with the public.

Within the Congress, members of the House of Representatives for both parties look very much like members of the Senate. Within the House, Democrats (72%) are four times more likely than Republicans (17%) to favor a wage-price freeze. And, in the Senate, Democrats (75%) are six times more likely than their Republican counterparts (12%) to support a wage-price freeze.

In the general public, the people most likely to favor stronger fiscal restraints— even to the extent of imposing mandatory wage and price controls—are blue collar workers, people in lower education and income groups, big city residents, blacks, older people, people who live in all regions of the country except the West, and people who could name an issue as a reason for favoring one candidate over another.

Income Maintenance

Question. President Nixon proposed a federal program of income maintenance based on a minimum of $1,600 a year for a family of four. Which comes closest to your view: (1) the federal government should not sponsor a program of this kind; (2) I favor the program pretty much as the President presented it; or (3) the program does not go far enough to meet the needs of the poor?

Responses:	PUBLIC			HOUSE			SENATE		
	Total	Reps.	Dems.	Total	Reps.	Dems.	Total	Reps.	Dems.
Government should not have such a program	52%	63%	45%	35%	39%	32%	24%	19%	28%
At least favor the program in principle	48	37	55	65	61	68	76	81	72

The partisan public is fairly evenly divided in its feelings about the President's program proposed for income maintenance—48% favor the plan and 52% oppose it. But Democrats (55%) are much more likely than Republicans (37%) to favor the program.

Congress appears far more ready than the general public to adopt some form of an income maintenance program, at least in terms of the markedly higher degree of support in both houses than among the citizenry.

With two-thirds of the House and three-fourths of the Senate favoring Mr. Nixon's proposal, neither house reflects the views of the public very closely. Democrats in both houses, although somewhat more so in the House, are closer to their constituents than are Republican Congressmen.

Within Congress, Senate and House Democrats (72% and 68%, respectively) have comparable feelings about the guaranteed income program. Senate Republicans (81%), however, are much more likely than House Republicans (61%) to support the President's proposal.

In the House, Democrats (68%) are somewhat more inclined than Republicans (61%) to back the plan. But the situation reverses in the Senate where Republicans (81%) are more likely than Democrats (72%) to favor the proposal.

The profile of the general public subgroups that favor the income maintenance program holds no surprises. Those most likely to support the idea are people in low income and low education groups, blacks, residents of cities, blue collar workers, women, people in their twenties, people living in the Eastern and Western states, and people who are not likely to vote on election day.

Black People

Question. Which comes closer to your view of what has been done in recent years by the federal government to improve the social and economic conditions of black people in America: (1) we have gone too far; (2) we have gone far enough; or (3) we have much further to go?

Responses:	PUBLIC			HOUSE			SENATE		
	Total	Reps.	Dems.	Total	Reps.	Dems.	Total	Reps.	Dems.
Gone too far or gone far enough	47%	54%	43%	42%	46%	39%	24%	23%	25%
Have much further to go	53	46	57	58	54	61	76	77	75

Just over one-half of the partisan public (53%) believes that the federal government has much further to go in aiding black people. Nearly three-fifths of the Democrats (57%) as opposed to less than one-half of the Republicans (46%) in the general population feel that more government programs should be undertaken.

The House overall is closer to the views of the partisan public than is the Senate. While there is little difference between House Democrats and Democrats generally, House Republicans are more likely than Republicans generally to say the federal government has much further to go to improve the social and economic conditions of blacks.

Members of both parties in the Senate are much more likely than their constituents to say the government has much more to do, with the greatest discrepancy existing between Republicans in the Senate and in the general population.

Within Congress, proportionately more Senators in both parties—Republicans, 77%, and Democrats, 75%—think the government has a long way to go in helping blacks than do members of the House of Representatives.

In the House, Democrats (61%) are only somewhat more likely than Republicans (54%) to call for more government effort on behalf of blacks, but the difference between the parties in the Senate is virtually nil—as was seen above.

People in the South are least likely to favor additional government programs for aiding blacks. Although the difference is not great, people in small cities are more often opposed to expanded government efforts than are residents of other types of communities.

Of course, blacks are most likely to look for more government effort, as are younger people, people in the higher educational groups, people in the lowest income bracket, and people who cite a specific issue as a reason for favoring one candidate or another.

Criminal Rights

Question. Do you feel that the Supreme Court rulings of recent years have on the whole given too much consideration to the rights of persons suspected of crimes: (1) yes; or (2) no?

	PUBLIC			HOUSE			SENATE		
Responses:	Total	Reps.	Dems.	Total	Reps.	Dems.	Total	Reps.	Dems.
Yes	71%	80%	64%	64%	82%	51%	44%	56%	35%
No	29	20	36	36	18	49	56	44	65

Republicans in the general population are much more likely than Democrats to say that the Supreme Court rulings of recent years have given too much consideration to the rights of criminal suspects. Four out of five Republicans (80%) feel this way, as compared with two out of three Democrats (64%)—sizeable majorities in either case.

Both the House and the Senate are more concerned for the constitutional rights of the criminal suspect than are their constituents in the partisan public. The House Republicans are very close to the views of the public's Republicans, but this is the only similarity among the various groups.

Democrats in both Houses are considerably less likely than their Republican colleagues to feel that the Supreme Court has overemphasized the rights of suspects. A much larger proportion of Senators than Representatives in both parties expresses disagreement with the question. Looking at the groups as a whole, well over one-half of the entire Senate (56%) disagrees that the Supreme Court has overreached itself, compared with just about one-third of the House members (36%).

In the House of Representatives, Democrats (49%) are far more likely than Republicans (18%) to disagree with the question. The same is true in the Senate, where about two-thirds of the Democrats (65%) disagree, as compared with roughly two-fifths of the Republicans (44%).

Those people who disagree that the Supreme Court has given too much consideration to the rights of criminal suspects are most likely to be females, young people, residents of big cities and suburbs, blacks, people with higher educational attainment, and people who are not likely to vote on election day.

1970 ELECTION SURVEY

1. President Nixon has been campaigning for Republican candidates in several states. Since it is not a Presidential election year, do you think it is proper—or improper—for the President to personally campaign for candidates in state elections?

	Percent of People				
	Total Sample	East	Midwest	South	West
Proper	47%	50%	46%	45%	50%
Improper	46	44	48	48	42
Don't Know/No Answer	7	6	7	7	8

2. If you knew that Mr. Nixon supported a candidate for election in your state, would you be more likely or less likely to vote for that candidate?

More	20%	21%	18%	22%	20%
Less	30	28	28	33	27
No Difference	45	47	47	39	48
DK/NA	5	4	6	5	4

3. If you knew that Mr. Agnew supported a candidate for election in your state, would you be more likely or less likely to vote for that candidate?

More	17%	16%	20%	17%	16%
Less	35	40	34	33	31
No Difference	40	39	38	41	44
DK/NA	8	6	8	9	9

4. Vice President Spiro Agnew has been speaking out against people who criticize our society. When Mr. Agnew speaks, do you feel he is representing your own views or not?

Yes	42%	39%	46%	43%	39%
No	46	50	46	42	50
DK/NA	11	10	8	16	11

5. In his speeches, do you think that Mr. Agnew is just giving his own personal opinion, or is he really speaking for Mr. Nixon?

| | Percent of People | | | | |
	Total Sample	East	Midwest	South	West
Himself	51%	47%	57%	49%	48%
Nixon	23	29	21	22	22
Both	14	14	11	15	21
DK/NA	12	11	11	15	9

6. Do you think that Mr. Agnew, himself, would make an excellent, good, fair, poor, or very poor President?

Excellent	4%	4%	4%	4%	5%
Good	22	21	21	22	22
Fair	25	22	26	26	27
Poor	19	19	20	17	19
Very poor	18	22	15	16	19
DK/NA	12	11	12	15	9

7. In this election year, there's been a lot of talk about problems in this country. What do you personally feel is the greatest problem in our country?

Rank:					
1. Vietnam/Indochina	15%	19%	15%	13%	14%
2. Crime/Violence/Law and Order	13	13	14	12	13
3. Racial Conflict/Problems/Tension	10	10	10	12	9
4. Youth/Generation Gap/Hippies	10	9	12	9	10
5. Drugs	10	16	7	8	10
6. Student Protest/Campus Disorder	10	7	11	12	9
7. Inflation/Living Costs	5	4	5	7	3
8. Unemployment/Poverty	4	3	4	2	6
9. Pollution/Environment	3	3	3	3	6
10. Declining Religion/Morality	2	1	2	4	1
11. Taxes/Government Spending	1	1	2	1	2
12. Declining Quality of Education/Schools	1	—	—	—	1

8. Whether or not you're planning to vote, which man—the Democrat, the Republican, or another candidate—do you favor in the election for (Senator/Governor/U.S. Congressman)?

Democrat	44%	38%	42%	49%	49%
Republican	32	35	33	26	37
Other	3	9	1	3	1
DK/NA	20	19	23	22	13

9. In thinking about which candidate you'd like to see elected, what has been most important for you—his own personal qualities, his stand on the issues, or his political party affiliation?

	Percent of People				
	Total Sample	East	Midwest	South	West
Personal	22%	24%	24%	22%	17%
Issues	54	57	54	51	57
Party	14	14	13	13	18
DK/NA	9	5	8	15	8

10. In the election for (Senator/Governor/Congressman)—is there any particular issue that has been really important in helping you choose between the candidates? (IF YES: What is the issue?)

	Total Sample	East	Midwest	South	West
Could mention an issue	22%				
Could not mention an issue	78				
Rank: 1. Crime/Violence/Law and Order	4%	4%	4%	3%	4%
2. Vietnam/Indochina	3	6	4	1	3
3. High Taxes/Government Spending	3	4	4	2	3
4. Pollution/Environment	2	4	2	1	2
5. Declining Quality of Education/Schools	2	1	2	3	2
6. Inflation/High Cost of Living	2	3	1	1	1
7. Unemployment/Poverty/ Low Social Security	2	2	1	2	2
8. Racial Conflict/Problems/ Tension	2	–	1	3	1
9. Drug Sale and Use	1	1	1	1	1
10. Student Protests/Campus Disorders	1	1	1	1	–
11. Youth/Hippies/Generation Gap	–	–	–	–	–
12. Declining Religion/ Moral Decay	–	–	–	–	–

11. Is anyone in your family worried *right now* about losing his or her job—because of the business recession and rising unemployment?

	Total Sample	East	Midwest	South	West
Yes	16%	16%	20%	12%	15%
No	81	81	78	85	81
DK/NA	3	3	3	3	4

12. A few months ago, four students were killed by National Guard troops during a demonstration at Kent State University in Ohio. Who do you think was more to blame for those deaths—the students or the National Guard?

	Total Sample	East	Midwest	South	West
Students	63%	57%	67%	65%	62%
Guardsmen	12	19	8	9	16
Both/Equal	9	10	10	7	9
DK/NA	15	14	14	17	12

13. Do you feel it is safe to walk in the streets *alone at night* in your neighborhood?

| | Percent of People | | | | |
	Total Sample	East	Midwest	South	West
Yes	55%	47%	58%	53%	63%
No	41	48	37	42	32
DK/NA	4	4	5	4	4

14. Do you believe that the structure of our society, and the government as we know it today, are in danger of being overthrown—by the radical beliefs of the younger generation?

Yes	43%	34%	46%	48%	39%
No	48	57	46	42	52
DK/NA	9	8	8	11	9

15. Do you agree—or disagree—that college student protests and demonstrations *in general* have gone too far, and should be stopped?

Agree	81%	75%	86%	83%	81%
Disagree	12	19	9	11	12
DK/NA	6	6	5	6	7

16. Do you think that tougher laws and stronger police forces will be able to put an end to violence and disorder in the country?

Yes	62%	65%	57%	68%	53%
No	29	28	32	23	39
DK/NA	9	7	12	9	7

17. And, which party . . . the Democrats or the Republicans . . . do you feel is more likely to make tougher laws and strengthen the police?

Republicans	37%	40%	34%	35%	42%
Democrats	26	25	26	26	28
Equal	13	14	14	12	12
Neither	6	6	7	5	5
NA	18	16	19	21	12

18. In trying to solve the problems of this country, which party—the Democrats or the Republicans—do you feel can do the best job of handling the war in Vietnam?

Democrats	29%	30%	30%	28%	31%
Republicans	32	33	29	33	36
Equal	15	17	18	13	11
None	10	9	11	11	8
NA	13	11	13	15	13

19. In trying to solve the problems of this country, which party—the Democrats or the Republicans—do you feel can do the best job of halting inflation and the high cost of living?

Democrats	39%	36%	40%	42%	41%
Republicans	30	30	32	26	34

cont.

	Percent of People				
	Total Sample	East	Midwest	South	West
Equal	10%	12%	11%	7%	8%
None	8	9	6	9	6
NA	13	13	11	17	11

20. In trying to solve the problems of this country, which party—the Democrats or the Republicans—do you feel can do the best job of controlling air and water pollution?

Democrats	30%	33%	28%	28%	31%
Republicans	24	23	21	26	26
Equal	20	19	24	16	19
None	9	8	11	9	7
NA	19	17	17	22	18

21. In trying to solve the problems of this country, which party—the Democrats or the Republicans—do you feel can do the best job of stopping the sale and use of narcotic drugs?

Democrats	22%	19%	21%	25%	22%
Republicans	24	26	21	24	26
Equal	24	25	27	20	23
None	12	12	12	12	13
NA	18	18	19	20	15

22. Which party—the Republicans or the Democrats—do you feel can do the best job of reducing crime in the streets?

Republicans	22%	24%	18%	23%	26%
Democrats	25	26	25	26	21
Equal	25	23	29	22	26
Neither	14	16	14	14	14
NA	14	11	15	15	13

23. Which party—the Democrats or the Republicans—do you feel is most likely to be able to resolve the differences between young people and our system of government?

Republicans	24%	25%	21%	25%	24%
Democrats	32	33	29	31	37
Equal	17	18	20	15	17
Neither	12	13	13	11	11
NA	16	12	17	19	12

24. Which party—the Republicans or the Democrats—do you feel can do the best job of dealing with student disorders?

Republicans	25%	24%	23%	26%	28%
Democrats	28	30	28	28	28
Equal	19	19	21	17	21
Neither	12	12	13	12	11
NA	15	15	16	17	13

25. Vietnam has been a campaign issue. Which of the following statements *comes closest* to your feelings about what we should do in Vietnam:

	Percent of People				
	Total Sample	East	Midwest	South	West
Keep combat troops there	21%	18%	22%	25%	19%
Gradually withdraw	48	53	50	40	50
Speed up our withdrawal	27	27	24	29	26
DK/NA	5	2	4	7	6

26. And which statement *comes closest* to your feelings about weapons programs for military defense:

Maintain our preparedness	61%	59%	60%	62%	64%
Place less emphasis on such programs	28	34	31	21	24
DK/NA	12	7	10	17	11

27. If inflation continues unchecked for the rest of the year, would you favor or oppose putting government controls on wages and prices—by *freezing* them at a certain level?

Favor	60%	62%	62%	58%	51%
Oppose	32	29	31	33	39
DK/NA	8	9	7	8	9

28. It's been proposed that all families in America be guaranteed a *minimum income*. For example, a family of four would be guaranteed $1600 a year. If the family couldn't earn $1600, the government would make up the difference. Would you favor or oppose a program for guaranteed income?

Favor	45%	51%	42%	41%	49%
Oppose	50	45	54	53	43
DK/NA	5	5	4	7	7

29. In trying to improve the social and economic conditions of black people in America, do you think the federal government has done too much—has done enough for now—or has much more to do?

Too much	18%	16%	15%	25%	11%
Done enough	26	25	24	27	30
More to do	50	55	54	42	53
DK/NA	6	4	7	6	6

30. On the whole, do you feel that the *rulings* of the Supreme Court in recent years have given *too much* consideration to the rights of people suspected of crimes?

Yes	63%	63%	65%	62%	63%
No	26	26	26	26	26
DK/NA	11	11	9	12	12

The War in Vietnam

Few events in modern American history have so divided and confused public opinion as the U.S. involvement in Vietnam. The changing nature of this involvement itself was a factor in confusing the public, starting with military aid, stepping up to the use of more and more "advisers," and escalating to full-scale combat and aerial warfare in response to attacks on American personnel and the threat of a Vietcong and North Vietnamese victory in the South.

As American participation escalated during the Johnson Administration, so did charges of a "credibility gap," of a deliberate effort by the Administration to mislead the public, to withhold bad news and to exaggerate talk of military successes. The frequent optimistic reports by members of the Administration—promises of military victory, of bringing troops back home, of seeing "the light at the end of the tunnel" within a year—contributed to the volatility of the issue.

Serious doubts about the American role in Indochina began to surface in 1965 among a handful of Senators and a scattering of foreign policy experts. Dissent slowly grew through 1966 as Administration promises of a quick military victory failed to materialize. In 1967, while American bombers pounded away at North Vietnam with little apparent effect and the number of troops in Vietnam kept rising, dissatisfaction spread to the point where the war promised to become a major issue in the 1968 campaign. Late in the year Senator Eugene McCarthy agreed to challenge the President, using the war as his issue.

Although the McCarthy challenge at the end of 1967 was regarded lightly, the events of February and March of 1968 produced the first significant change in public opinion on the war. In February, the Vietcong launched their Tet offensive, penetrating key American positions, occupying such major cities as Hue, and sending a shock wave of incredulity through the American public. Although President Johnson insisted the Vietcong had suffered severe losses and the final effect of the offensive had been to hurt the enemy, the American public's latent skepticism began to harden into disbelief.

165

Early in March, Senator McCarthy, with the aid of dedicated amateurs and college students, stunned the nation by nearly upsetting the President in the New Hampshire primary. Although Johnson won the primary with about 49% of the vote to McCarthy's 41%, and although public opinion polls at the time pointed to dissatisfaction with Johnson among New Hampshire Democrats for reasons other than the war, the effect was nonetheless devastating. On April 30, President Johnson announced he would not run for reelection, and the primary campaign became a battle between two critics of the war, Senator McCarthy and Senator Robert Kennedy, with Vice-President Humphrey in the background, awaiting the Democratic convention in August.

Meanwhile, on the Republican side, Richard Nixon, mindful of President Eisenhower's highly successful 1952 campaign promise to end the war in Korea once elected, announced that he had a secret plan to end the war. As the summer progressed, the war issue continued to divide the Democrats, who first voted down the peace forces' platform amendments, then nominated Humphrey amid violent demonstrations in Chicago, and finally saw Humphrey go down to defeat as many Democrats on the Left, unhappy with his stand on Vietnam, refused to vote for him in November.

When President Nixon took office in 1969, the Paris peace talks had begun, along with a suspension of the bombing of the North. Little else had changed, though, and as the year progressed, the peace groups began to organize for massive demonstrations in the fall to underscore their unhappiness with the situation. In the fall of 1969, they organized two Moratorium Marches on Washington, one in October and a second in November.

With the establishment of the CBS News Poll during the summer of 1969 and the war issue once again escalating, we scheduled the first of several polls on the war for October, during the Moratorium. During the next several months of the CBS News Poll's existence, we would poll in depth on the Vietnam issue in November, in May of 1970 (immediately following President Nixon's announcement of the Cambodian invasion) and in late June (on the eve of the completion of the American combat role in Cambodia).

These four surveys, read in context with the events of the period, illustrate a dramatic change in public opinion on the war within the short period of nine months between October 1969 and June 1970. During that period, the number of people favoring an immediate withdrawal doubled, from about one-fourth of the public to nearly half, and for the first time a majority of the public expressed skepticism and doubt about our ability to extricate ourselves from Southeast Asia.

At this writing, President Nixon's Vietnamization program had reduced the American troop level below 100,000, and he had appeared successfully to defuse the war as a campaign issue, despite the failure to negotiate a peace settlement. However, early in April of 1972, North Vietnam began a massive invasion of the South, bombings of the North were resumed, and the possibility that once again Vietnam might become a major issue in the Presidential campaign became evident.

The changes in opinion during the nine-month period covered by the CBS News Poll should be read in the context of the events of the period. The

October poll occurred midway during the October Moratorium, an impressive
and peaceful outpouring of people opposed to the war. The success of the
October demonstrations impelled Mr. Nixon to take to television on November
3 with his famous "silent majority" speech, in which he revealed specific
aspects of the Vietnamization program and withdrawal plan and in which he
attacked his critics by appealing to the "silent majority" which he claimed
supported American policy.

The speech was immensely successful in rallying support to the Administration, but as time went by, its effects began to wear off. In November, for
example, the CBS News Poll rating of his performance in handling the Vietnam
war had risen to a 60% affirmative level, largely in response to his speech. By
the following March, it had dropped to 45% affirmative. (See the chapter on
President Watching.)

On April 30, in the face of sagging public approval, President Nixon again took
to television to announce that American and South Vietnamese forces had
invaded Cambodia to wipe out Vietcong supply depots and command posts,
and that the purpose of the eight-week operation was to speed up both the
Vietnamization and the American withdrawal program. This speech was far less
successful than the "silent majority" address of November; it raised substantial
doubts about our presence in Southeast Asia, it enhanced fears about expansion
of the war, and it increased support for immediate withdrawal of American
troops from Indochina.

In late June, on the eve of the American withdrawal from Cambodia back
into South Vietnam, this skepticism and dissatisfaction had hardened further.
Although accompanied by relief that American troops were being withdrawn on
schedule, the American attitude toward our entire role in Southeast Asia had
taken a dramatic turn in favor of getting out. Only a small group thought we
should stick it out and fight on for a military victory, and even many among
those who had supported a gradual withdrawal had shifted to the view that we
should get out right away. The following tables trace the shifts in sentiment.

	October	November	May	June
Favor immediate withdrawal	28%	25%	36%	47%
Oppose immediate withdrawal	60	67	58	49
No opinion	12	8	6	4
Favor immediate withdrawal	28%	25%	36%	47%
Favor gradual withdrawal	44	47	N.A.	34
Oppose withdrawal	18	24	N.A.	15

The second chart breaks down the views of those against immediate withdrawal into those favoring gradual withdrawal and those opposing any kind of
withdrawal at all. What is noteworthy is that both Presidential addresses

served to reduce the number of people without a firm opinion, in November toward his views, in May away from them. Also noteworthy is that those favoring gradual withdrawal, at a peak following his silent majority speech, decreased in number by the following June from nearly half to only a third of the public.

Most striking of all, those favoring immediate withdrawal, only a handful of people in early 1969 (to judge by other surveys), had increased by October to more than a quarter and by the following June to nearly a half of the public.

It is unfortunate that external circumstances forced the suspension of polling operations at CBS News in November, 1970. The continuation of surveys, utilizing many of the same questions and covering the events of 1971 and 1972, would have provided a fascinating continuum on attitudes toward the war—the revelations of My Lai, the court-martial of Lieutenant Calley, the unopposed reelection of President Thieu, the retaliatory bombing of the North, the revelation of secret peace negotiations, the Presidential visit to China, the April offensive and the resumption of bombing. But we were happy to have been able, at the least, to record a major turning point in attitudes on the war.

SUMMARY OF FINDINGS

Withdrawal From Vietnam—October 1969*

As of this survey, public discontent with the war in Vietnam has grown to the point where seven out of every ten Americans want to withdraw our troops from South Vietnam either on an immediate or gradual basis. Only two out of ten Americans now want us to "stick it out and do whatever is necessary to win."

The largest segment of opinion, more than four out of ten, favors gradual withdrawal of troops, accompanied by "Vietnamization" of the war—letting South Vietnam take on more of the fighting. But three people out of ten favor an immediate pullout of all of our troops, although nearly half of these would change their minds if they thought immediate withdrawal would result in a Communist takeover.

Therefore, the hardliners at either end of the hawk–dove scale remain a minority. Some 15% of the public would pull out immediately, even if it meant a Communist takeover. And at the other end, 18% wants to stay and do whatever is necessary to achieve victory.

In between is the majority of the public, committed to some kind of gradual withdrawal and assurance that the Communists won't overrun South Vietnam.

Profile of the Public

Favor unconditional immediate withdrawal	15%
Favor conditional immediate withdrawal	13
Favor gradual withdrawal and Vietnamization	44
Favor staying and doing whatever necessary to win	18
Don't know	10

*Based on a national random telephone sample of 1,225 adults, conducted on the evenings of October 14, 15 and 16, 1969, with an associated sampling error of up to plus or minus 3 percentage points.

Interviewing took place the night of the moratorium as well as the night before and the night after. The survey attempted to get at a key issue involved in the moratorium—the rate of withdrawal from the war.

We arrived at our profile of public opinion on Vietnam by first asking whether the public favors or opposes immediate withdrawal. These were the results:

Favor immediate withdrawal	30%
Oppose immediate withdrawal	60
Don't know	10

Of those who favored immediate withdrawal, we then asked if they would still favor it if they knew it would result in a Communist takeover as soon as our troops left. Faced with this alternative, about one-half of those who at first favored withdrawing immediately, now would oppose a withdrawal or could not offer an opinion.

	% of Public	% Favor
Favor immediate withdrawal	30%	100%
Still favor even if it means Communist takeover	15	49
Oppose if it means Communist takeover	13	42
Don't know	2	9

Of those opposed to and unsure about immediate withdrawal, we asked whether they would favor a gradual withdrawal of our troops—letting South Vietnam take on more of the fighting—or would they favor sticking it out and doing whatever is necessary to win. By a margin of two to one, these people would prefer to phase out gradually.

	% of Public	% Opposed
Oppose or unsure about immediate withdrawal	70%	100%
Favor gradual withdrawal and Vietnamization	44	65
Favor sticking it out and doing whatever is necessary to win	18	26
Don't know	7	9

Looking at various groups in the national population, there are some interesting differences in their feelings about an immediate withdrawal from Vietnam.

In particular, the persons most likely to want to withdraw from Vietnam immediately are Democrats, people under 30 years of age, members of minority groups—especially Negroes, people in lower income groups, and people who never attended college.

Probably the only surprising finding is that college-trained people are more likely to oppose withdrawing from Vietnam right now than are people in the lower education groups. College-educated people are most likely to favor a gradual withdrawal, rather than getting out immediately regardless of the consequences.

Other groups most likely to favor a gradual withdrawal are Republicans, Protestants, people over 30, whites and people with incomes over $10,000 a year.

American Opinion on Vietnam—November 1969*

The Administration has apparently had some success in rallying public opinion to its policy of gradual withdrawal of American troops from Vietnam and Vietnamization of the war. A comparison of findings in surveys in November and in mid-October 1969 with both President Nixon's November 3, 1969 speech and the November Moratorium occurring between the two surveys, shows that fewer people—one in four—now insist on immediate withdrawal than in October, and a larger number—nearly half the public—now favor the gradual withdrawal/Vietnamization policies outlined by the President on November 3.

Moreover, his identification of his supporters as a "silent majority" has evoked a strong response, with nearly three-quarters of the public identifying itself as closer to the "silent majority" which supports his policies than to the "vocal minority"—one in five—which opposes them. More than 60% of the public takes the position that the public protest against the President's Vietnam policies have hurt our chances of achieving a peaceful settlement of the war.

Along with increasing his support for gradual withdrawal, the President apparently has encouraged the all-out hawks as well. The number of those who want to stick it out in Vietnam and do whatever is necessary to win has also increased to nearly one in four. In fact, numbered among the "vocal minority" who oppose Mr. Nixon's policies are some hardline hawks who oppose his policies as not tough enough.

It is important to note that the survey was restricted to adults (21 and above). Since much of the opposition to the President's policies comes from youth, it is reasonable to assume that a general population survey (18 and over, for example) would have resulted in less support for Administration policies.

Yet despite the overall strength displayed for Administration policies, the survey also indicated strong areas of doubt and apparent contradiction over U.S. policies. While 60% of the public interprets the President's meaning of "gradual withdrawal" as occurring within three years (one in four sees him meaning more than three years), when people are asked for their own estimate of a realistic timetable, only 48% see us actually out of Vietnam within three years, while 43% see it taking longer than three years.

Moreover, fully half the public does not believe the South Vietnamese are capable of holding their own in the war once we have turned the fighting over to them and have withdrawn our troops. Interestingly enough, among both

*The findings in this study are based on a national random telephone sample of 1,154 adults, conducted on November 23, 24 and 25, 1969, with an associated sampling error of up to plus or minus 3 percentage points.

those who favor and oppose immediate withdrawal, a majority feel the South Vietnamese are incapable of holding out on their own.

Most Americans—55%—believe the government of South Vietnam is more of a dictatorship than a democracy; this is true of the President's supporters as well as his detractors.

A measure of dissatisfaction with the way the war is going is indicated by the apparent contradiction between support for the "domino theory" on the one hand and the desire to get out on the other. Seven out of ten Americans say they would be willing to keep our troops in Vietnam for several more years if they knew it would prevent Communist takeovers in other countries of Southeast Asia. But only one in four Americans feels we should stick it out in Vietnam and do anything that is necessary to win.

An overriding factor in public opinion is the desire to end our involvement in any way possible. Asked if they would favor an all-out attack on North Vietnam if they knew it would end the war immediately, seven out of ten Americans said they would favor such an attack. Remarkably, among those who favor immediate withdrawal, six out of ten said they would favor such an attack if they knew it would end the war immediately. In other words, even among this group, the desire to get out overrides the method.

Following are some of the findings.

Withdrawal

Question. Do you favor—or oppose—withdrawing all of our troops from Vietnam immediately?

	November poll	October poll	Diff.	% Diff.
Favor	25%	28%	−3	−11%
Oppose	67	60	+8	+12

Proportionately more men than women, more Southerners than from any other region, and more Republicans than Democrats or Independents oppose immediate withdrawal. This is also true for older and wealthier people and whites.

Those who opposed immediate withdrawal or who could not answer were also asked this question:

Question. Which would you rather see us do, gradually withdraw our troops and let South Vietnam take on more of the fighting . . . or stick it out in Vietnam and do whatever is necessary to win?

	November	October	Diff.	% Diff.
Gradually withdraw	47%	44%	+3	+ 7%
Stick it out	24	18	+6	+33
Don't know	4	10	−6	−60

(Note: November and October results are percent of total public.)

Those who favored immediate withdrawal were asked:

Question. If you knew that the Communists would gain control of South Vietnam as soon as the Americans left, would you still favor or oppose withdrawing our troops?

	November	October	Diff.	% Diff.
Still favor	12%	15%	−3	−20%
Oppose	12	13	−1	− 8

(Note: November and October figures represent percent of total public.)

It is therefore possible to draw a comparative public profile ranging from those favoring unconditional immediate withdrawal to those who favor sticking it out in Vietnam.

Profile of the Public

	November	October	Diff.	% Diff.
Unconditional immediate withdrawal	12%	15%	−3	−20%
Conditional immediate withdrawal	12	13	−1	− 8
Gradual withdrawal/ Vietnamization	47	44	+4	+ 7
Stick it out/Do what is necessary to win	24	18	+6	+33
Don't know	4	10	−6	−60

Peace Protests

On the question of the silent majority and vocal minority and peace protests, the public was asked the following questions:

Question. President Nixon says a silent majority of the American people support his Vietnam policies and a vocal minority oppose them. Do you see yourself as being closer to the silent majority or the vocal minority?

Question. Different groups around the country have been holding public protests against the United States involvement in Vietnam. Generally, do you approve, or disapprove of these public protests?

Question. Do you think such public protests help, hurt, or have no effect on our chances of reaching a peace settlement with North Vietnam?

	Silent Majority	Vocal Minority	Protests Approve	Protests Disapprove	Help	Hurt	No effect
National	74%	21%	19%	77%	13%	62%	19%
Men	75	21	19	77	12	66	18
Women	72	21	19	77	15	58	20
East	72	24	26	70	17	53	24

cont.

| | Silent Majority | Vocal Majority | Protests | | Protests | | |
			Approve	Dis-approve	Help	Hurt	No effect
Midwest	72%	22%	18%	76%	13%	60%	20%
South	79	14	14	83	11	69	15
West	69	30	16	81	13	69	14
Democrats	66	27	22	75	16	58	21
Republicans	84	12	15	82	8	69	17
Age 21–29	66	32	37	61	22	48	26
30–44	74	20	17	79	13	60	24
45–64	77	20	16	81	11	70	14
65+	74	15	7	83	10	64	14
White	75	20	18	78	12	64	19
Nonwhite	58	35	31	66	28	42	17
Protestant	76	18	15	81	12	65	18
Catholic	75	21	21	74	15	59	21
Jewish	37	63	49	51	32	42	19
Income							
under $5M	76	16	13	80	15	60	14
$ 5–10M	75	21	17	80	12	68	21
$10–15M	74	23	20	77	14	64	20
Over $15M	68	29	35	65	17	61	20

Rate of Withdrawal

Question. President Nixon says he is going to gradually withdraw all of our troops from Vietnam. What do you think Mr. Nixon means by a gradual withdrawal, that we will be out of Vietnam within six months, within one year, two years, three years or longer than three years?

Question. In your own mind, do you think all of our troops will be out of Vietnam within six months, within one year, two years, three years or longer than three years?

	Nixon meaning	Own belief
Within six months	2%	1%
Within one year	16	11
Within two years	27	19
Within three years	15	17
Longer than three years	25	43
Don't know	15	9

Men, people from the West and Midwest, Democrats and Independents, and those who favor immediate withdrawal tend to be more pessimistic than their counterparts about the rate of withdrawal, both in terms of their interpretation of Mr. Nixon's meaning and in terms of their own belief as to how long it will actually take.

Opinion on South Vietnam

Question. Once we turn all of the fighting over to South Vietnam and withdraw our troops, do you think South Vietnam will or will not be able to hold its
own in the war?

Question. In your opinion, is the government of South Vietnam more of a
democracy or more of a dictatorship?

	Will Be Able	Will Not Be Able	More Democracy	More Dictatorship
National	38%	51%	33%	55%
Men	38	52	36	56
Women	38	50	30	55
East	39	49	30	57
Midwest	36	52	35	55
South	39	51	35	52
West	39	53	31	60
Democrats	37	55	33	56
Republicans	41	47	33	54
Those favoring immediate withdrawal	31	58	23	65
Those opposing immediate withdrawal	41	51	37	54
Age 21–29	41	56	28	69
30–44	42	50	30	58
45–64	35	54	37	51
65+	35	42	36	43
Protestant	40	50	37	53
Catholic	36	55	38	54
Jewish	36	49	17	74
Some high school	38	51	37	48
High school graduates	41	50	35	53
Some college or more	37	53	27	65

The Domino Theory

Question. Suppose you really knew that our presence in Vietnam for several
more years would prevent Communist takeovers in other countries of Southeast
Asia. Would you be willing, or not willing, to keep our troops there?

	Willing	Not willing
National	71%	23%
Men	73	23
Women	69	23
East	68	26
Midwest	67	24
South	79	16
West	70	29

cont.

	Willing	Not willing
Democrats	73%	22%
Republicans	71	22
Those favoring immediate withdrawal	56	38
Those opposing immediate withdrawal	79	17

Public Impatience

Question. Suppose you really knew, right now, that an all-out attack on North Vietnam would end the war immediately. Would you favor, or oppose such an attack?

	Favor	Oppose	Don't Know
National	69%	24%	7%
Those favoring immediate withdrawal	16	7	2
Those opposing immediate withdrawal	48	16	3
Those unable to answer on immediate withdrawal	5	1	2

By taking the cross-categories, we can produce a profile of public attitudes:

"Doves": Those favoring immediate withdrawal and opposed to all-out war-ending attack	7%
"Frustrated": Those favoring immediate withdrawal *and* favoring all-out attack—anything to end our involvement	16
"Bewildered": Oppose immediate withdrawal and oppose all-out attack	16
"Hawks": Those opposing immediate withdrawal and favoring all-out attack	48
Indecisive	13

The President's Cambodian Speech—May 1970*

As of the date of this survey (May 3, 1970), the public is giving President Nixon wide support—by a margin of nearly two to one—on his decision to send troops into Cambodia. Unfortunately, it is support strongly laced with pessimism, skepticism, and frustration about the outcome of the war and implications of the Cambodian campaign. The poll was conducted Friday and Saturday, after the President's speech but before the news of the bombing of North Vietnam.

*The findings in this section are based on a national random sample of 1,022 telephone interviews with respondents 18 and older, conducted on Friday night, May 1, and Saturday, May 2, 1970. There may be a sampling error of up to plus or minus three percentage points associated with each finding.

Some 59% approve of his decision, with 32% disapproving, but a majority of the public—51%—now feels we are caught in a war in Asia we can't get out of. Only 38% believe we can extricate ourselves.

The public is evenly split—42% to 41%—on the question of whether the move into Cambodia will expand the war to include many other countries in Southeast Asia. Despite the President's statement that the Cambodian action is designed to shorten the Vietnam war, the public is evenly split on whether it will shorten or prolong it. Forty-four percent feel the action will prolong the war, 41% believe it will shorten it.

A plurality believes the Cambodian action will slow the rate of the troop withdrawal program. Only 18% feel troop withdrawals will be speeded; 42% believe they will be slowed; 28% feel the action will have no effect on the withdrawal rate.

In spite of support for the Cambodian action, the number of Americans who favor immediate withdrawal from Vietnam is now 36%, up dramatically from the 25% who felt that way following the President's Vietnamization speech last November. In fact, more people favor immediate withdrawal than oppose the Cambodian action, a fact explained by some people who feel "we ought to get out altogether, but if we're not going to withdraw right now we ought to try something to get it over with."

There is even skepticism over the duration of the attack on Cambodia. Only 9% feel it will take a few weeks, while 22% see us in Cambodia for a few months and a majority, 54%, feel we won't be out of Cambodia for a year or more.

The rating by the public of the job the President has been doing in handling the Vietnam war has stayed about the same as it was in March, with about 46% of the public rating it as good or excellent. It is still down dramatically from its peak in November, when it was 60%.

The public also has some misgivings about the lack of consultation by the President with Congress in advance of his Cambodian announcement. Forty-seven percent feel he should have consulted Congress first; 45% feel it was all-right to act without doing so.

An examination of the findings indicates the President is getting strong backing from Republicans and Independents, but a bare majority of support from Democrats. Men are more likely than women to approve his action, and by region he has his strongest support in the South.

Those most likely to disapprove of the President's action are Jewish, people under 30, and those in the middle income groups.

*Total Sample Responses (N=1022 People)**

1. President Nixon spoke on television (last night) (the night before last) explaining why he sent American troops into Cambodia, a country next to Vietnam. Have you heard or read anything about that speech?

Yes	70%
No	30

*Percentages may not add to 100% due to rounding.

2A. IF KNEW OF SPEECH: The President said that the purpose of going into Cambodia is to drive enemy troops out of their hiding places and destroy their supplies. Do you approve or disapprove of the President's decision to send combat troops into Cambodia?

Approve	62%	(43% of total sample)
Disapprove	31	(22% of total sample)
No response	6	(4% of total sample)

2B. IF DIDN'T KNOW OF SPEECH: North Vietnam troops have been operating in Cambodia. They cross the border, attack our troops, and go back safely into Cambodia. Now, the President has sent troops into Cambodia to drive enemy troops out of their hiding places and destroy their supplies. Do you approve or disapprove of the President's decision to send combat troops into Cambodia?

Approve	50%	(16% of total sample)
Disapprove	33	(10% of total sample)
No response	15	(6% of total sample)

2A+B PERCENTAGES OF TOTAL SAMPLE:

Total approve	59%
Total disapprove	32
Total no response	10

3. Our attack on enemy hiding places in Cambodia is only supposed to last six to eight weeks. Do you believe we'll be out of Cambodia within a few weeks . . . or will it take a few months, maybe a year, or even longer than a year?

A few weeks	9%
A few months	22
A year	14
Longer than a year	40
No response	15

4. Do you think that the President's action in Cambodia will shorten the Vietnam war, or make it last longer?

Shorten the war	41%
Prolong the war	44
No response	15

5. About ten days ago the President said he would withdraw 150,000 more troops from Vietnam. Do you think that going into Cambodia will speed up, slow down, or have no effect on our plans for withdrawing troops?

Speed up	18%
Slow down	42
Have no effect	28
No response	12

6. What about right now, do you favor or oppose withdrawing all of our troops from Vietnam immediately?

Favor withdrawal	36%
Oppose withdrawal	58
No response	6

7. President Nixon acted without asking Congress to approve his decision. Do you think he should or should not have acted without consulting Congress first?

Should have acted	47%
Should not have acted	45
No response	8

8. Taking everything into account, do you feel President Nixon is doing an excellent, good, fair, poor, or very poor job in handling the war in Vietnam?

Excellent	13%
Good	33
Fair	32
Poor	10
Very poor	7
No response	8

9. Do you feel that going into Cambodia will or will not expand the war to include many countries throughout Southeast Asia?

Will expand	42%
Will not expand	41
No response	17

10. When you come right down to it, do you feel we are or are not caught in a war in Asia that we can't get out of?

We are caught	51%
We are not caught	38
No response	11

The War in Indochina—June 1970*

While the public continues to support President Nixon's decision to send American troops into Cambodia, it tends to draw the line on further large-scale combat operations outside Vietnam. It also emphatically feels any further action in Cambodia should require Congressional approval.

The "draw-the-line" attitudes prevail despite the fact that the public strongly approves of the President's original decision on Cambodia and also considers it to have been a military success. By a margin of 57% to 38%, the public approves of the April 30 decision to attack enemy sanctuaries in Cambodia. As of May 2, on the same question, the public favored the decision by a 59% to 32% margin. Purely in military terms, people believe the Cambodian operation has been a success, by a margin of 60% to 24%.

By 58% to 36%, the public would oppose sending American troops to attack

*The findings below are based on a national random sample of 1,120 telephone interviews with respondents 18 and older, conducted on June 24, 25 and 29, 1970. There may be a sampling error of up to plus or minus three percentage points associated with each finding.

enemy sanctuaries in Laos and Thailand, even if the President thought it was necessary.

By nearly two to one—62% to 33%—the public feels the President should be required to get Congressional approval in order to send American troops back into Cambodia.

A majority, 54% to 41%, would favor sending American troops back into Cambodia to attack enemy sanctuaries again if the President thought it necessary. A majority favors sending American troops into Cambodia in order to "prevent a Communist takeover" there, 51% in favor and 40% against.

Balancing the military gains against the controversy the Cambodian decision evoked at home, the public is more divided. Asked whether they agreed or disagreed with the statement, "Some people claim that the bitter controversy here at home . . . was too high a price to pay for the military gains . . . achieved," 42% agreed and 51% disagreed.

In the eight weeks since the President announced the Cambodian action, sentiment for immediate withdrawal from Vietnam has jumped significantly. Almost half the American public—47%—now favors immediate withdrawal, with 49% opposed. At the beginning of May, only 36% favored immediate withdrawal, and in November, after the President's Vietnamization speech, only 28% were in favor of immediate withdrawal.

The public does tend to favor limited American support actions in Cambodia. Some 56% would approve of the continuance of American air strikes into Cambodia after our troops withdraw; 38% are opposed. With the likelihood that South Vietnamese troops will remain in Cambodia after June 30, 60% favor supporting the South Vietnamese with military advisers and 65% favor supporting them with equipment and supplies. Less in the way of public enthusiasm is evident for air support for the South Vietnamese in Cambodia, 51% in favor and 43% against. The public is vehemently opposed to support by American combat troops, 69% against and 26% in favor.

Pessimism over the course of the war continues to prevail. Asked if they feel we are "caught in a war in Asia that we can't get out of," 53% replied yes, 40% no. At the beginning of May, 51% responded yes and 38% no to the same question.

By a margin of 46% to 43%, the public believes it very likely that American troops will be sent back into Cambodia. Despite their opposition to sending troops to Laos and Thailand, 45% feel that American troops will be sent to those countries in any event, 44% feel they won't. A plurality feels that the South Vietnamese will remain in Cambodia for a long time: 39% believe they'll remain for a long time, 34% a short time, and 13% believe they will get out when the Americans leave. On the effect of our Cambodian action on the rate of troop withdrawal from Vietnam, 38% feel the Cambodian action will speed up withdrawal, 33% sees no effect on the withdrawal rate and 19% feel it will slow down our withdrawal rate. On this one item, the public is more optimistic than it was in May.

Despite all this, President Nixon's performance rating on how well he handles the war in Vietnam has improved slightly over early May. His performance on the war is rated as good or excellent by 49% of the public. But his handling of other problems like inflation, campus unrest, and race relations is given a considerably lower rating. Overall satisfaction with Mr. Nixon as President is down from the last measure by the CBS News Poll in March.

Women tend to oppose the Administration policies and to be more firm in opposition to future military action than men. The President finds his strong support principally among Republicans and Independents; Democrats are likely to split nearly evenly on approval of his policies and future action in Indochina.

By region, the East and Midwest tend to be most dovish, the South the most hawkish, with the West falling between the extremes. By race, the extreme opposition to Administration policy and future moves in Indochina comes from the nonwhites.

Total Sample Responses (N=1120 People)

1. About eight weeks ago, President Nixon sent American combat troops into Cambodia to attack enemy sanctuaries. As things stand today, do you now approve or disapprove of the decision to send American troops into Cambodia?

	June	May
Approve	57%	59%
Disapprove	38	32
No response	5	9

2. Purely in military terms, would you say the Cambodia operation was successful or unsuccessful?

Successful	60%
Unsuccessful	24
No response	17

3. If the President decides it is necessary to attack enemy sanctuaries again, would you approve or disapprove of sending American troops back into Cambodia?

Approve	54%
Disapprove	41
No response	5

4. Should the President be required to get the approval of Congress before sending troops back into Cambodia?

Should be required	62%
Should not be required	33
No response	5

5. Looking ahead a bit, do you think it is very likely or very unlikely that American troops will be sent back into Cambodia?

Very likely	46%
Very unlikely	43
No response	11

6. Although our troops are scheduled to leave Cambodia by June 30, there is a possibility that we will continue to send bombing missions into Cambodia. Do you approve or disapprove of continuing air raids into Cambodia?

Approve	56%
Disapprove	38
No response	6

7. The South Vietnamese say their troops will remain in Cambodia after the U. S. troops leave. Do you think they will stay there for just a short time . . . for a long time . . . or leave when we do?

Stay a short time	34%
Stay a long time	39
Leave when we do	13
No response	13

8. Suppose the South Vietnamese do stay in Cambodia when we withdraw our troops, should we continue to support their troops in Cambodia:

	Yes	No	No Response
With equipment and supplies	65%	31%	4%
With military advisers	60	34	6
With bombing raids	51	43	6
With combat troops	26	69	5

9. If the President thought it necessary to send American troops to attack enemy sanctuaries in other parts of Indochina such as Laos or Thailand, would you approve or disapprove?

Approve	36%
Disapprove	58
No response	6

10. Looking ahead again, do you think it is very likely or very unlikely that American troops will be sent into countries like Laos or Thailand?

Very likely	45%
Very unlikely	44
No response	11

11. Some people claim that the bitter controversy here at home over the decision to send American troops into Cambodia was too high a price to pay for the military gains it achieved. Do you agree or disagree?

Agree	42%
Disagree	51
No response	7

12. Do you think the Cambodia action will speed up . . . slow down . . . or have no effect on the rate of withdrawing troops from Vietnam?

	June	May
Speed up withdrawal	38%	18%
Slow down withdrawal	19	42
No effect on withdrawal	33	28
No response	10	12

13. Would you favor or oppose sending American troops back into Cambodia in order to prevent a Communist takeover of that country?

Favor	51%
Oppose	40
No response	8

14. As of today, do you favor or oppose immediate withdrawal of all American troops from Vietnam?

	June	May	Nov. '69
Favor immediate withdrawal	47%	36%	25%
Oppose immediate withdrawal	49	58	67
No response	5	6	8

15A. (If Favor Withdrawal): If you knew that the Communists would gain control of South Vietnam as soon as the American troops left, would you still favor or oppose withdrawing our troops?

Still favor	54%	(25% of total sample)
Still oppose	41	(19% of total sample)
No response	5	(3% of total sample)

15B. (If Oppose Withdrawal): Which would you rather see us do: gradually withdraw our troops, and let South Vietnam take on more of the fighting . . . or stick it out in Vietnam, and do whatever is necessary to win?

Gradually withdraw	64%	(34% of total sample)
Stick it out	29	(15% of total sample)
No response	7	(5% of total sample)

16, When you come right down to it, do you feel we are caught in a war in Asia that we can't get out of?

	June	May
We are caught	53%	51%
We are not caught	40	38
No response	7	11

17. Taking everything into account, do you approve or disapprove of the way Mr. Nixon is handling his job as President?

Approve	65%
Disapprove	26
No response	7

18. Would you say President Nixon is doing an excellent, good, fair, poor or very poor job in handling:

	Ex	Gd	Fr	Pr	V/P	NR
Inflation in this country	7%	24%	36%	17%	10%	6%
Campus unrest	5	21	34	22	10	8
Problems between the races	6	27	38	17	8	5
The war in Vietnam	11	38	29	11	7	4

Excellent/Good Trend Scores

	June	May	March	Nov. '69
Inflation	31%	—%	32%	36%
Campus unrest	26	—	—	—
Problems between races	33	—	31	37
War in Vietnam	49	46	45	60

19. Summing up then, would you say you are generally satisfied or dissatisfied with Mr. Nixon as President?

	June	March	Nov. '69
Satisfied	65%	72%	81%
Dissatisfied	29	25	18
No response	6	3	1

The Environment

All of the studies in this volume, up to this point, test public attitudes toward
social, economic, and political issues. The survey on the environment which
follows, unlike the others, is basically a test of factual knowledge of the subject.

This departure from the norm was prompted by a number of interrelated
factors. The basic one was a decision at CBS News, which had done a number
of documentaries on ecology, as well as news and special coverage of the
environmental movement, to produce "The National Environment Test." The
test format had been successfully applied in the past as a means of obtaining
information on driving, citizenship, current affairs, smoking, and income taxes.
The application of the test format to the subject of environment in the spring of
1970 was a "natural."

There was more to it than that. The ecology issue had been so passionately
embraced by its adherents that despite its underlying gravity, the movement
took on aspects of missionary zeal on the one hand, and faddism on the other.
For the documentarian, this posed the danger of giving the limelight to the
loudest but not necessarily the sanest voices. For the survey researcher, a
different problem presented itself: to be against ecology was akin to being
against virtue and motherhood, and an attempt at a meaningful survey of
public attitudes could easily produce instead a list of public platitudes.

In a way, the decision to document environmental problems in the test
format resolved both problems. The use of factual questions as the basis of
the broadcast presented the opportunity to sort out fact from fiction in the
barrage of ecological information and theory with which the public was being
bombarded.

Not that there wasn't a good deal of solid evidence for concern. Air pollution had reached dangerous levels in many areas of the country. Water pollution
had not merely wreaked havoc with the natural beauty and resources of the
countryside, but was actually threatening drinking water sources. Solid waste,
from garbage to junked automobiles, was despoiling the landscape. By its

very nature, however, much of the outcry about ecology was simply unprov-
able, inasmuch as it concerned itself with fears for the future. One popular
theory was that by the 21st century the earth would no longer be able to
support life.

A more striking example of the nature of the ecological alarms was the
conflict between two theories on the long-term effect of air pollution. One
school of scientists held that the increase in pollutants in the atmosphere would
have the effect of filtering out sunlight and eventually causing climate to grow
colder. Another equally persuasive school argued that increased carbon
dioxide levels would trap sunlight, resulting in a "greenhouse effect" that would
heat the earth, cause the polar icecaps to melt and deluge coastal cities of the
earth with massive floods.

The kind of information available to the public, then, was a mix of actual
experience on the one hand, and informed theory and projection—some of it
contradictory—on the other. Complicating matters further were two additional
factors. One was the fact that vested interests, as in the case of the pesticide
industry, were bringing counterarguments to bear against the conservationists
(the most famous case being that of the controversies over Rachel Carson's
The Silent Spring theories of the upsetting of natural cycles). The other lay in
the enthusiasm of the amateur environmentalists, who had a propensity for
exaggeration which could, at times, be self-defeating. An example was a widely
circulated "finding," accepted as fact, that concentrations of DDT in mothers'
milk had reached unacceptable levels. Some research uncovered the facts: a
small group of mothers had been tested in an uncontrolled experiment at one
university in Southern California, and apart from the presence of high DDT
levels in the breast milk of about 20 young mothers, no other data existed to
support the contention. Yet most books and articles dealing with ecology had
adopted the findings as proven fact.

Given this rather curious situation of an overenthusiastic reaction to a significant public problem, the preparations for the "National Environment Test"
involved an intensive research effort to check and doublecheck original sources
of many of the prevailing claims.

The objectives of the broadcast were to give the viewer a basic factual course
in ecology, to provide some insights and perspectives on the scope and per-
vasiveness of the problem, and yet to test him with questions which were not
impossible for the reasonably informed to answer. The questions themselves
therefore were primarily factual and dealt wherever possible with everyday
experience, or with problems affecting the widest number of people.

The survey, in which the same questions were administered in advance by
telephone to a nationwide sample, was used basically as a device by which the
audience could compare its own test scores against some national standard, both
in individual questions and in an overall pass/fail context. Except for three
"opinion" questions used on the broadcast and in the survey, all the questions
are factual in nature.

The value of the survey lies essentially in indicating the level of public
knowledge in an area of high public interest and acceptance. No doubt some

sort of attitudinal study could have been developed, had we been able to anticipate some of the difficult choices facing the public as new ecological standards began to be enforced.

In retrospect, for example, it would have been interesting to put to New Yorkers the question of whether they were willing to accept an increase in air pollution (or the risk of thermal pollution) which would result from additional power facilities as the price of eliminating the summer brownouts caused by the shortage of electrical power that persisted during the summer of 1971. Or, in 1971 and 1972, to ask new automobile owners whether the frequent difficulties in cold-starts and engine stalling caused by new engine design was an appropriate price to pay for lowering exhaust emissions. Unfortunately, it is only recently that the public has begun to learn that ecology, too, has its price, not merely in public funding, but in private convenience.

BACKGROUND AND METHODOLOGY

The survey* described in this report was conducted in preparation for a CBS News Special, "The National Environment Test," which was broadcast over the CBS Television Network on Tuesday, May 19, 1970, 10:00–11:00 P.M., EDT.

The survey consisted of 27 questions about various specific causes of air, water, and land pollution, as well as three opinion questions on pollution problems. Each knowledge question had a score of four points. The attitude questions were not scored as part of the test.

Two shortened versions of the test were used in the telephone interview. Each respondent was asked only fourteen of the 27 information questions. Both versions started with the same test question and ended with the same three attitude items. Half of the remaining 26 questions were assigned randomly to each version. While no further precautions were taken to insure that Version A and Version B were equally difficult, the sub-samples given for each version had a similar distribution in test scores.

The test versions were randomly assigned to the respondents in the sample. Of the 900 completed interviews with people 16 and older, 460 respondents were given Version A and 440, Version B. The two groups had the same composition with respect to age, sex, level of education, geographic region, and community size and type. For the purpose of the broadcast, the two samples were treated as one, and the sample size was referred to as 450.

The findings discussed in the text of this report are based on the full sample of 900 people. They include the distribution of test scores and the three attitude items.

SUMMARY OF FINDINGS
Ecology and Other National Problems

About a week after "Earth Day" (April 22, 1970), one-fifth of the American public considered pollution the most important problem facing us. Roughly

*The findings are based on a national random sample of 900 telephone interviews with respondents 16 and older. The survey was conducted on Tuesday night, April 28, and Wednesday night, April 29, 1970. There may be a sampling error of up to plus or minus three percentage points associated with each finding.

the same proportion said either crime (19%) or poverty (17%) was the most important problem. Vietnam was ranked first by about three out of every ten people, while race relations was seen as the most important problem by one out of ten.

The Environment as a Political Issue

It can no longer be assumed that rapid industrial development, unlimited population growth, and a better life through technology are possible without revenge from the environment. Now that the problems of ecological balance have attracted nationwide concern, it has become evident that, at least in the short run, different groups have more or less to gain from the various legislative proposals being considered for controlling the abuse of the environment. The ecological dilemma is a subject for political controversy as well.

Support for environmental controls was measured in the interview by one generalized question which pitted progress against conservation, and by one specific question regarding the limitation of population growth. While the majority (56%) of the public identifies with the cause of conservation, there is little support (29%) for a measure that would eliminate tax deductions based on the number of children in a family as a way of discouraging population growth.

Report Card: Subject—Ecology

The grading scheme and test results are as follows:

# Correct	% Correct	Evaluation	%
12–14	86–100	Excellent	3
10–11	71– 79	Good	15
8– 9	57– 64	Fair	28
0– 7	0– 50	Poor	54
			(900)

In the discussion that follows, the "Good" and "Excellent" categories will be combined and the top 18% will be considered "high scorers."

Age

Young people are the most likely to be concerned about environmental hazards. This greater involvement with the issue of ecology is reflected in each of the three attitude questions.

The younger the respondent, the more likely he was to consider pollution the most important problem facing us today. As age increases, the proportion of people who consider pollution most important decreases:

Age:	16–20	21–29	30–44	45–64	65–plus
% ranking pollution "most important"	42%	31%	18%	15%	6%

Most of the young people (68%) in the 16-20 age group see themselves on the side of conservation as compared with only 46% of the people 65 or older.

The youngest group seems to be the only segment of the public willing to translate its conservationist attitude into the specific proposal regarding the elimination of income tax deductions based on the number of children in a family. Roughly one-half (46%) was in favor of such a proposal. Support for the proposal in each of the other age groups was roughly 30%. The 30–44 year-old group, presumably the group with the greatest proportion of dependent children, was least likely to support the tax measure.

The concern and involvement of the respondents in their late teens is not reflected in a greater amount of knowledge on the subject of ecology. Test scores seem to peak in the middle years and to drop off considerably in the 65-plus group:

Age:	16–20	21–29	30–44	45–64	65–plus
% scoring Good and Excellent	14%	20%	24%	17%	10%

Sex

While males were more likely to get high scores on the test than females (23% vs. 15%), there were no differences between them with respect to the attitude items.

Education

Attitudes toward pollution do not seem to be related to amount of schooling, but since the test questions were on specific points of information, it is not surprising that respondents who completed more years of schooling were more likely to score high on the test:

Education:	Grade School	Some H. S.	H.S. Grad.	Some Coll.	Coll. Grad.
% scoring Good and Excellent	7%	12%	16%	24%	36%

Geographic Region

People from the South and West were less likely than those from the East and Midwest to see themselves on the side of conservation. Where people live has no relationship to their answers to the other two attitude items, but it is related to their test scores. Westerners did considerably better than those from any of the other regions.

Community Size and Type

Community size and type was related only to the conservation versus progress issue. There is a considerable difference between suburbanites and large city residents, with 62% of the former and only 48% of the latter favoring conservation. The proportion supporting conservation among residents of small cities and small towns or rural areas was more like that of the suburbanites—around 58% identifying themselves with conservation.

TEST SCORE RESULTS

Evaluation:	Poor	Fair	Good	Excellent
No. Correct:	0–7	8–9	10–11	12–14
% Correct:	0–50%	57–64%	71–79%	86–100%
TOTAL SAMPLE (N = 900):	54%	28%	15%	3%
Sex:				
Male	47	30	19	4
Female	58	27	13	2
Age:				
16–20	58	28	11	3
21–29	49	31	16	4
30–44	45	32	19	5
45–64	56	27	15	2
65+	71	20	9	1
Education:				
Grade school	76	17	6	1
Some high school	65	23	11	1
High school grad.	52	32	14	2
Some college	42	34	20	4
College grad.	34	31	26	10
Region:				
East	55	29	11	4
Midwest	52	28	17	3
South	62	25	11	2
West	43	30	24	3
Residence:				
City: Over 100,000	57	27	14	2
City: Under 100,000	55	24	18	3
Suburb	50	28	18	5
Small town/Rural area	54	30	13	2

FACTUAL QUESTIONS

1. As you know, air pollution and water pollution are major problems in this
country. First, I'd like to ask your opinion about air pollution. Which one,
factories, automobiles, or incinerators, is the major cause of air pollution in this
country?

Sub-SampleA:	Automobiles	55% (Correct answer)
(N=460)	Factories	37
	Incinerators	5
	No response	3
Sub-Sample B:	Automobiles	55
(N=440)	Factories	32
	Incinerators	7
	No response	6

2. "DDT" is a chemical for killing insects, and traces of it have been found in

people. Would you say that most of the "DDT" in our bodies does or does not come from the air we breathe?

Sub-Sample:	Does not	47% (Correct answer)
(N=460)	Does	44
	No response	9

3. Do you believe that *continuous* exposure to loud noise will or will not result in a loss of hearing?

Sub-Sample:	Will	81% (Correct answer)
(N=460)	Will not	14
	No response	5

4. Now, just guessing, about how many motor vehicles do you think people will *abandon* on American roads this year? Would you say two hundred and fifty thousand, one million, or three million?

Sub-Sample:	One million	40% (Correct answer)
(N=460)	250,000	36
	Three million	18
	No response	6

5. Do you think it is or is not true that *many* communities dump their sewage into sources of drinking water?

Sub-Sample:	Is true	72% (Correct answer)
(N=460)	Is not	23
	No response	5

6. In washing clothes, which cleanser *produces* the least water pollution—non-sudsing detergents or soap flakes?

Sub-Sample:	Soap flakes	47% (Correct answer)
(N=460)	Nonsudsing	
	detergent	44
	No response	9

7. As you know, salmon is a type of fish. Do you think salmon will or will not lay their eggs in other areas of the river if they can't get back to their original nesting place?

Sub-Sample:	Will not	60% (Correct answer)
(N=460)	Will	32
	No response	8

8. In this country, would you guess that most cow manure is or is not *reprocessed* for use as fertilizer?

Sub-Sample:	Is not reprocessed	36% (Correct answer)
(N=460)	Is	55
	No response	9

9. Nuclear power plants are built near bodies of water. Do you think that's

because the water is used as another source of power, is used for cooling
purposes, or as a disposal place for waste?

Sub-Sample:	Cooling	32% (Correct answer)
(N=460)	Power	23
	Waste disposal	35
	No response	10

10. In South America, do you think that the waters of the Atlantic and Pacific
oceans do or do not mix freely in the Panama Canal?

Sub-Sample:	Do not mix freely	41% (Correct answer)
(N=460)	Do mix	37
	No response	22

11. You may have heard several times about oil being spilled into the sea
around our coastlines. Do you think that *most* of the oil spilled is or is not
a result of off-shore drilling operations?

Sub-Sample:	Is not	21% (Correct answer)
(N=460)	Is	71
	No response	8

12. How many children, two, three, or four, would each family have to limit
itself to if we wanted to keep the United States' population from increasing
beyond its present size?

Sub-Sample:	2	72% (Correct answer)
(N=460)	3	13
	4	8
	No response	7

13. Do you believe that federal law does or does not require that all land in
national parks is to remain undeveloped?

Sub-Sample:	Does not	37% (Correct answer)
(N=460)	Does	50
	No response	13

14. One way of mining coal is to tunnel beneath the ground. Another way is to
strip off large areas of land, and mine the coal near the surface. Which do you
think costs *less*—underground mining or strip mining?

Sub-Sample:	Strip mining	69% (Correct answer)
(N=460)	Underground	25
	No response	6

15. Air pollution has caused many deaths. Do you think that the deadliest
periods of air pollution have or have not been during the summer months?

Sub-Sample:	Have not	27% (Correct answer)
(N=440)	Have been	57
	No response	16

16. Which one, burning fuel or cutting down the forests, has *most* to do with increasing carbon dioxide in the air?

Sub-Sample:	Burning fuel	69% (Correct answer)
(N=440)	Cutting down forest	22
	No response	9

17. In a year's time, do you think that individual people in America do or do not create as much garbage and waste as manufacturers do?

Sub-Sample:	Do	77% (Correct answer)
(N=440)	Do not	19
	No response	4

18. Which soft-drink container, the returnable bottle, the no-deposit bottle, or the aluminum can, causes the *least* problem for garbage disposal?

Sub-Sample:	Returnable bottle	59% (Correct answer)
(N=440)	No-deposit bottle	8
	Aluminum can	31
	No response	2

19. Would you say that most communities do or do not treat their sewage before dumping it into nearby sources of water?

Sub-Sample:	Do	30% (Correct answer)
(N=440)	Do not	59
	No response	11

20. When a series of dams is built along a river, do you think the average water temperature goes up, or down, or remains the same?

Sub-Sample:	Up	48% (Correct answer)
(N=440)	Down	15
	Same	21
	No response	16

21. Would you say that lack of oxygen is or is not *the major* reason for fish dying or disappearing from some of the large lakes in this country?

Sub-Sample:	Is	67% (Correct answer)
(N=440)	Is not	25
	No response	8

22. The San Francisco bay has shrunk to two-thirds its original size. Would you guess the bay shrank because the water was taken for industrial use, because of land slides, or because the bay was filled for land development?

Sub-Sample:	Bay filled	56% (Correct answer)
(N=440)	Water taken	17
	Land slides	15
	No response	12

23. Rain often washes fertilizer off the farm lands and into the river. Do you think this fertilizer does or does not promote plant growth in the river?

Sub-Sample:	Does	58%	(Correct answer)
(N=440)	Does not	35	
	No response	7	

24. Would you say it is or is not true that chemicals used to protect food crops kill only those insects and animals that are harmful to food crops?

Sub-Sample:	Is not true	75%	(Correct answer)
(N=440)	Is	19	
	No response	6	

25. Would you guess that one-fourth, one-half, or three-fourths of all the electrical power produced in America each year is consumed in our homes?

Sub-Sample:	One-fourth	25%	(Correct answer)
(N=440)	One-half	48	
	Three-fourths	21	
	No response	6	

26. We are using *nuclear* explosions to open up underground deposits of natural gas. Do you think that the nuclear radioactivity caused by the explosions is or is not removed from the gas before it is brought to the surface?

Sub-Sample:	Not removed	53%	(Correct answer)
(N=440)	Is	27	
	No response	20	

27. In Alaska do you think that corrosion, stress due to freeze and thaw, or earthquakes would be most likely to cause a break in a cross-country oil pipeline?

Sub-Sample:	Earthquake	43%	(Correct answer)
	Corrosion	13'	
	Stress	32	
	No response	12	

OPINION QUESTIONS

A. Despite all we've talked about, which do you think is the *most important* problem facing us today—Vietnam . . . crime . . . pollution . . . race relations . . . or poverty?

Total Sample:	Vietnam	28%
(N=900)	Pollution	20
	Crime	19
	Poverty	17
	Race relations	11
	No response	5

B. Those who argue for *progress* say that new dams, buildings, bridges, and highways help industries grow, create new jobs, and strengthen the economy. Those who argue for *conservation* say that such projects destroy animal feeding

grounds, cause pollution, and ruin our scenic areas. Where do you see youself—
on the side of progress or on the side of conservation?

Total Sample:	Conservation	56%
(N=900)	Progress	34
	No response	10

C. Do you think *income tax* deductions, based on the number of children in a
family, should or should not be eliminated as one way to discourage population
population growth?

Total Sample:	Should	29%
(N=900)	Should not	60
	No response	11

Suggested Reading

Almond, G. A. *The American People and Foreign Policy.* New York: Praeger, 1961.

Berelson, Bernard, and Janowitz, M., eds. *Reader in Public Opinion and Communication,* 2nd ed. New York: Free Press, 1966.

Cantril, H. *The Human Dimension.* New Brunswick, N.J.: Rutgers University Press, 1967.

Childs, H. L. *A Reference Guide to the Study of Public Opinion.* Ann Arbor, Mich.: Gryphon Books, 1971.

de Grazia, Alfred, et al., comps. *Public Opinion, Mass Behavior, and Political Psychology: an annotated and indexed compilation of significant books, pamphlets, and articles.* Elmsford, N.Y.: Pergamon, 1969.

Hennessey, B. C. *Public Opinion.* 2nd ed. Belmont, Calif.: Wadsworth, 1970.

Key, Vladimer O. *Public Opinion and American Democracy.* New York: Alfred A. Knopf, 1961.

Lane, R. E., and Sears, D. O. *Public Opinion.* New York: Prentice-Hall, 1964.

Lippman, Walter. *Public Opinion.* New York: Free Press, 1965.

Lipset, Seymour M., and Schaflander, Gerald M. *They'd Rather Be Left.* Boston: Little Brown, 1971.

Lubell, Samuel. *Hidden Crisis in American Politics.* New York: W. W. Norton, 1971.

Parten, M. B. *Surveys, Polls, and Samples.* New York: Cooper Square, 1966.

Public Opinion Quarterly, W. Phillips Davison, ed. Columbia University, New York.

Steele, A. T. *The American People and China.* New York: McGraw-Hill, 1966.

Stouffer, S. A. *Communism, Conformity, and Civil Liberties.* Worcester, Mass.: Peter Smith, 1964.

Note. The Suggested Reading list was compiled by the publisher.